ANNA HOWARD SHAW

Dr. Shaw, late in life, as chair of the Woman's Committee of the Council of National Defense. The Schlesinger Library, Radcliffe College.

ANNA HOWARD SHAW

Suffrage Orator and Social Reformer

**Wil A. Linkugel
and
Martha Solomon**

Great American Orators, Number 10
Bernard K. Duffy and
Halford R. Ryan, Series Advisers

Greenwood Press
New York • Westport, Connecticut • London

Library of Congress Cataloging-in-Publication Data

Linkugel, Wil A.
  Anna Howard Shaw : suffrage orator and social reformer / Wil A.
Linkugel and Martha Solomon.
    p. cm.—(Great American orators, ISSN 0898-8277 ; no. 10)
  Includes bibliographical references and index.
  ISBN 0-313-26345-0 (lib. bdg. : alk. paper)
    1. Shaw, Anna Howard, 1847-1919. 2. Suffragettes—United States—
Biography. 3. Feminists—United States—Biography. 4. Women—
Suffrage—United States—History—Sources. 5. Feminism—United
States—History—Sources. I. Solomon, Martha. II. Title.
III. Series.
JK1899.S6L56   1991
324.6′23′092—dc20
[B]   90-38414

British Library Cataloguing in Publication Data is available.

JK
1899
S6
L56
1991

Library of Congress Catalog Card Number: 90-38414
ISBN: 0-313-26345-0
ISSN: 0898-8277

First published in 1991

Greenwood Press, 88 Post Road West, Westport, CT   06881
An imprint of Greenwood Publishing Group, Inc.

Printed in the United States of America

∞™

The paper used in this book complies with the
Permanent Paper Standard issued by the National
Information Standards Organization (Z39.48-1984).

10 9 8 7 6 5 4 3 2 1

Copyright Acknowledgments

The authors and publisher gratefully acknowledge the following sources
for granting permission to use copyrighted material:

Anna Howard Shaw letter to Caroline Bartlett Crane, August 18, 1917,
other written material from the Shaw Papers, and the photographs are
courtesy of Schlesinger Library, Radcliff College.

Excerpts from *The Story of a Pioneer* by Anna Howard Shaw. Copyright
© 1915 by Harper & Row, Publishers, Inc. Reprinted by permission of the
publisher.

Contents

Series Foreword
by Bernard K. Duffy and Halford R. Ryan   vii

Foreword
by Halford R. Ryan   xi

Preface   xiii

Acknowledgments   xv

Part I: Anna Howard Shaw   1

Introduction: The Career of a Life-Long Reformer   3

1. A "Gal Preacher": Shaw as Pastor   23

2. On the Lecture Circuit: "My Real Work Had Begun"   35

3. Campaigning for Suffrage: From "Bonnet Holder" to "Queen of the Suffrage Platform"   49

4. President of the National: Eleven Eventful Years   61

5. Helping Win the War: Recipient of the Distinguished Service Medal   77

6. The Last Campaign: Advocate for the League of Nations   91

Conclusion: A Rhetorical Portrait   97

Part II: Collected Speeches 113

    The Heavenly Vision 115

    The New Man 127

    God's Women 131

    The Fate of Republics 139

    The Fundamental Principle of a Republic 147

    The Other Half of Humanity 165

    Select Your Principle of Life 185

    What the War Meant to Women 193

Notes 205

Bibliography 219

Index 235

Series Foreword

The idea for a series of books on great American orators grew out of the recognition that there is a paucity of book-length studies on individual orators and their speeches. Apart from a few notable exceptions, the study of American public address has been pursued in scores of articles published in professional journals. As helpful as these studies have been, none has or can provide a complete analysis of a speaker's rhetoric. Book-length studies, such as those in this series, will help fill the void that has existed in the study of American public address and its related disciplines of politics and history, theology and sociology, communication and law. In books, the critic can explicate a broader range of a speaker's persuasive discourse than reasonably could be treated in articles. The comprehensive research and sustained reflection that books require will undoubtedly yield many original and enduring insights concerning the nation's most important voices.

Public address has been a fertile ground for scholarly investigation. No matter how insightful their intellectual forebears, each generation of scholars must reexamine its universe of discourse, while expanding the compass of its researches and redefining its purpose and methods. To avoid intellectual torpor new scholars cannot be content simply to see through the eyes of those who have come before them. We hope that this series of books will stimulate important new understandings of the nature of persuasive discourse and provide additional opportunities for scholarship in the history and criticism of American public address.

This series examines the role of rhetoric in the United States. American speakers shaped the destiny of the colonies, the young republic, and the mature nation. During each stage of the intellectual, political, and religious development of the United States, great orators, standing at the rostrum, on the stump, and in the pulpit, used words and gestures to influence their audiences. Usually striving for the noble, sometimes achieving the base, they urged their fellow citizens toward a more perfect Union. The books in this series chronicle and explain the accomplishments of representative American leaders as orators.

A series of book-length studies on American persuaders honors the role men and women have played in U.S. history. Previously, if one desired to assess the impact of a speaker or a speech upon history, the path was, at best, not well marked and, at worst, littered with obstacles. To be sure, one might turn to biographies and general histories to learn about an orator, but for the public address scholar these sources often prove unhelpful. Rhetorical topics, such as speech invention, style, delivery, organizational strategies, and persuasive effect, are often treated in passing, if mentioned at all. Authoritative speech texts are often difficult to locate and the problem of textual accuracy is frequently encountered. This is especially true for those figures who spoke one or two hundred years ago, or for those who persuasive role, though significant, was secondary to other leading lights of the age.

Each book in this series is organized to meet the needs of scholars and students of the history and criticism of American public address. Part I is a critical analysis of the orator and his or her speeches. Within the format of a case study, one may expect considerable latitude. For instance, in a given chapter an author might explicate a single speech or a group of related speeches, or examine orations that comprise a genre of rhetoric such as forensic speaking. But the critic's focus remains on the rhetorical considerations of speaker, speech, occasion, and effect. Part II contains the texts of the important addresses that are discussed in the critical analysis that precedes it. To the extent possible, each author has endeavored to collect authoritative speech texts, which have often been found through original research in collections of primary source material. In a few instances, because of the extreme length of a speech, texts have been edited, but the authors have been careful to delete material that is least important to the speech, and these deletions have been held to a minimum.

In each book there is a chronology of major speeches that serves more purposes than may be apparent at first. Pragmatically, it lists all of the orator's known speeches and addresses. Places and dates of the speeches are also listed, although this is information that is sometimes difficult to determine precisely. But in a wider sense, the chronology attests to the scope of rhetoric in the United States. Certainly in quantity, if not always in quality, Americans are historically talkers and listeners.

Because of the disparate nature of the speakers examined in the series, there is some latitude in the nature of the bibliographical materials that have been included in each book. But in every instance, authors have carefully described original historical materials and collections and gathered critical studies, biographies and autobiographies, and a variety of secondary sources that bear on the speaker and the oratory. By combining in each book bibliographical materials, speech texts, and critical chapters, this series notes that text and research sources are interwoven in the act of rhetorical criticism.

May the books in this series serve to memorialize the nation's greatest orators.

Bernard K. Duffy
Halford R. Ryan

Foreword

The Reverend Anna Howard Shaw assumes herein her rightful place in the pantheon of the Great American Orators Series. Called to the Christian pulpit, where her preaching was pedestrian but nonetheless a precursor of her later persuasive practices, she was inexorably summoned to secular platforms to proclaim women's rights. The conversion from pulpit to podium was fortunate, for hers was a voice crying in the political wilderness. Like the ancient prophets, Shaw beseeched women to seek their rightful legal status in the nineteenth-century American democratic experiment where, as in George Orwell's *Animal Farm*, all humans were equal but men were more equal than women. She implored men, who held the power, to grant women their just places in the republic.

This book is the collaborative effort of two distinguished scholars in communication. Professor Wil Linkugel, chairman of the department of communication studies at the University of Kansas, and Professor Martha Solomon, editor of the *Quarterly Journal of Speech*, bring to this analysis of Shaw's oratory a consistency of style and a concentration of substance that belies its joint authorship. Combining sensitivity to the moral, political, and sexist exigencies that Shaw faced with a close criticism of the reverend's civil rhetoric, Linkugel and Solomon detail why, unlike the biblical prophet who was without honor in his own country, Shaw was esteemed by her countrymen, males as well as females. Shaw's is a story of how her dogged determination to be heard and her wit and grandmotherly charm prevailed over ignorance and ill will.

Halford R. Ryan

Preface

"Early woman's rights activists were constrained to be particularly creative because they faced barriers unknown to men. They were a group virtually unique in rhetorical history because a central element in woman's oppression was the denial of her right to speak." With these words, Karlyn Kohrs Campbell in her book, *Man Cannot Speak for Her* (New York: Praeger, 1989, vol. 1, p. 9), clearly delineated the central problem nineteenth century women faced when they sought to achieve social and political equity. Her insightful analysis of key rhetorical texts from that movement helps to alleviate another obstacle faced by women today: ignorance about their heritage as women because the works of their predecessors have been excluded from the rhetorical canon. This volume, like that of Kohrs Campbell's, is an attempt to flesh out rhetorical history as it relates to women.

A woman rhetor in the nineteenth century had the task of creating a "new woman" in the minds of people: a woman who was capable of doing things, such as public speaking; a woman who was not too emotional to vote meaningfully; a woman who could stand on her own without a man protecting her from the "slings and arrows" of the hard, cruel world; and, perhaps even, a woman who had a sense of humor.

Anna Howard Shaw was an advocate for social reform all her life. She came from humble birth and lowly heritage, but kings and queens, presidents and governmental dignitaries, as well as innumerable popular audiences came to be moved by her rhetorical force and her personal fervor. Dr. Shaw embodied the "new woman." The rhetorical concept of *enactment* explains her effectiveness as a public speaker and social reformer. Quite simply, enactment occurs when the speaker herself is the proof of her argument and incarnates her message. Kohrs Campbell in *The Rhetorical Act* (Belmont, Calif.: Wadsworth, 1982, p. 273) stated that "enactment is powerful evidence because members of the audience see and hear the evidence for themselves, directly. The proof is particularly vivid--it is alive in front of them!" Our goal in this book is to demonstrate that the life and rhetoric of Dr. Shaw, who in her day was labeled "Queen of the Suffrage Platform," enacted the new woman who was equally qualified with males to be a citizen-voter.

Acknowledgments

The authors of this volume are indebted to many persons for their support and encouragement in the project. We are first of all indebted to Ed Pappas, who, over our annual Greek meal, suggested our co-authorship. Our special thanks are also extended to Robin Holladay, Jeanne Torneden, and Terri Rubio, not only for their splendid work but also for their patience and support.

Professor Solomon wishes to acknowledge the financial support of the vice-president for research at Auburn University and The Auburn Humanities Foundation for funds to acquire materials and to travel for research.

Professor Linkugel wishes to thank the University of Kansas for a sabbatical leave that greatly abetted the completion of the volume. He also wishes to acknowledge: Frederick W. Haberman of the University of Wisconsin, who first suggested the study of Dr. Shaw; Barbara M. Solomon, director of Radcliffe Women's Archives, and Mary E. Howard, librarian, who were extraordinarily helpful in his original dissertation research; Susan Von Salis of the Schlesinger Library, Radcliffe College, for research assistance; and Howard Sypher for arranging the photocopying of the Laura Clay Papers at the University of Kentucky.

Finally, both authors wish to dedicate this volume to Helen Linkugel. Not only was she an invaluable assistant in the early stages of research (only her notes were legible to Professor Solomon!), but she was also a staunch supporter, devoted helpmeet, and wonderful friend. To her we dedicate whatever virtues this volume possesses; the faults and flaws we claim as our own.

I

ANNA HOWARD SHAW

Introduction:
The Career of a
Life-Long Reformer

I was born on a cold, dreary morning in February, and it is said
that my protests against existing conditions began immediately
and that they have continued without cessation ever since.

Partial Autobiography, Shaw papers, box 19, folder 436

For the last two decades of the nineteenth century and the first
two decades of the twentieth, the voice of Anna Howard Shaw
was one of the strongest that American audiences heard
protesting social and political injustices, especially women's lack
of suffrage. Her adult life was given to reform efforts and she
ultimately was acknowledged as the best protest orator the
woman's movement had produced. Carrie Chapman Catt, herself
an accomplished speaker, wrote that Shaw "stood unchallenged
throughout her career as the greatest orator among women the
world has ever known."[1]

The career of this able speaker who unrelentingly protested
injustices moved from a "gal preacher" on Cape Cod to a highly
popular lecturer for temperance and suffrage, from "Bonnet
Holder" for Susan B. Anthony to "Queen of the Suffrage Platform"
as national lecturer for the National American Woman Suffrage
Association, from the eleven-year president of the national
suffrage association to the most admired campaign speaker for
woman suffrage, and from chairwoman for the Woman's
Committee of the Council of Nationalf Defense during World War
I to advocate for the League of Nations. The New York *Sun*
called her "the strongest force for the advancement of women
that the age has known"; Mary Earhart Dillon labeled her "a
worthy successor to Susan B. Anthony"; and the *Wisconsin State
Journal* quite simply called her the "the foremost American
woman." Carrie Chapman Catt eulogized Shaw by saying: "She
was of the suffrage struggle its greatest orator, its wit, its humor,
its deathless spirit. She staked her whole life on the cause, she

conquered for it and with it, and death cannot rob her nor us of the victory that was so largely her work."(2)

Anna Howard Shaw's life began in Newcastle-on-Tyne, England, on Valentine's Day, 1847. She was the sixth child born to Thomas and Nicolas Shaw (three boys and two girls preceded her, and a sister and brother were to follow). Thomas Shaw, like many young men of the day, dreamt of a new and better life in the United States. Thus, in 1851 he moved his family to Lawrence, Massachusetts, a hotbed of progressive thinking. Life there proved intellectually stimulating for young Annie on several counts (she was not known as Anna until 1892, when Susan Anthony convinced her that it looked more dignified on her lecture brochures). At the impressionable age of nine, she learned about the abolition movement from many who were directly involved, including her family. One day, for example, Annie discovered a Negro woman her father was hiding until she could escape. She also read the highly fermentative book of the day, *Uncle Tom's Cabin*, which she reported she "freely moistened with my tears" in repeated perusals. Additionally, the Unitarian community the Shaws joined included many of the town's more prominent intellectual citizens. Her concern for social and political injustices was already beginning to take shape.(3)

After seven years in Lawrence, Thomas Shaw became obsessed with another dream. He and a group of Englishmen planned to take up tracts of land in the northern forests of Michigan to establish a colony. Taking his oldest son, James, with him, Thomas left the family behind and traveled to Michigan, where he staked a claim to 360 acres of land, located one hundred miles from a railroad, forty miles from the nearest post office, and half a dozen miles from any neighbor, save Indians, wolves, and wildcats. Here, the two men erected the walls of a rudimentary cabin with no floor and only rough openings for windows and doors. Thomas returned to Massachusetts, and he packed his family off with a few essentials for a trip west to Michigan; he himself remained in Lawrence working and sending financial support as he was able.

The journey west was difficult. The Shaws traveled to the end of the train line in Grand Rapids, Michigan, and from there rented a wagon for the remaining 100 miles of their journey through dense forest. The day after they arrived at the cabin the family assigned responsibilities to everyone to assure their survival. Annie, feeling uncomfortable with the confinement of the house, was assigned to work outside with James and eight-year-old Henry. The three set to work finding food and water as best as they could and finished the cabin. After a few months, James, who had done much of the work in building the cabin and constructing the furniture, took ill and was forced to return East for an operation. For a full year, until Thomas's arrival,

Annie at age twelve assumed primary responsibility for outdoor work. Thus, for example, in the spring, to provide a ready supply of water, Annie, with the help of an eighteen-year-old neighbor, dug what proved to be a practical, thoroughly serviceable well. As a result of these experiences, Annie became a totally self-reliant, resourceful young person.(4)

Despite criticizing her father for his lack of practicality, Annie respected his curiosity and lively mind. From him she got a love of reading; and the papers he sent from Massachusetts, in addition to a small supply of books on hand, afforded one of the few diversions available in the wilderness. Annie especially liked the speeches the New York papers published. "They were mostly political speeches," she later recalled, "great thundering orations, such as they made in those troubled days before the war--chock full of history." When he arrived from Lawrence, Thomas brought a stack of new books that Annie fell upon "as a starving man falls upon food."(5)

Not long after her father's arrival, fourteen-year-old Annie rebelled mildly against him. One day she went to the woods with a book to avoid some unpleasant duty in the house and stayed all day. Upon returning home her father chided her for remaining too long in the woods daydreaming while her mother labored, and he concluded with the admonition that she would make nothing of herself if she followed such tendencies. Annie, who had shouldered unusual responsibilities during his absence, resented his comment and responded that she fully intended to go to college. "Father," she declared, "before I die I shall be worth ten thousand dollars," the largest sum she could easily imagine.(6)

This newly articulated ambition was accompanied by a new sense of mission. "For some reason, I wanted to preach--to talk to people, to tell them things," she wrote in her autobiography. "Just why, just what, I did not yet know--but I had begun to preach in the silent woods, to stand up on stumps and address the unresponsive trees, to feel the stir of aspiration within me." Shortly thereafter, despite the fact that most of her education in Michigan had been at home, she took her first step toward achieving that ambition when she accepted a job as a schoolteacher in the county of Mecosta. For two dollars a week plus board, Annie taught fourteen pupils with few books except those she herself provided.(7)

She saved as much from her meager earnings as she could for her own education. But the money accumulated slowly. Youth, she felt, was passing. On a sudden impulse, she moved to Big Rapids in 1870 to live with her sister Mary, who had moved there after her marriage. At the advanced age of twenty-three Shaw entered high school. The preceptress of the school, Lucy Foot, encouraged Shaw in her ambitions and put her into the speaking and debating classes. She fainted the first time she gave a public recitation to an audience, but Shaw persisted; she participated avidly in school debates, recited poetry, and even acted in theatrical performances.

Shaw's speaking skills attracted the attention of a certain Dr. Peck, an elder in the Methodist Church, who wanted to be the first to have a woman licensed for the ministry. To Shaw's surprise, he asked her to preach the quarterly sermon at Ashton. Because there was no church in Ashton, she preached her first sermon in a little schoolhouse, which was packed with people who were curious about the girl who was defying conventions and preaching the word of God. As she started to preach, she quivered so badly that the kerosene in a lamp standing at her elbow shook in the globe. But to her relief, this feeling of anxiety subsided, and she successfully unfolded her message. Dr. Peck was sufficiently impressed by her talents to invite her to join him on his circuit to preach in thirty-six different places.

Shaw's preaching produced a public controversy, and Mary's husband denounced her course of action through an announcement in the local paper. Despite her family's alienation, Shaw persisted. The following spring at the Methodist Conference in Big Rapids, Shaw was voted a license to preach.

Throughout all this Shaw continued her studies at Big Rapids High School with energy and dedication. However, after two years of high school, she felt that her age made it critical for her to move on to college, and she matriculated at Albion College in the autumn of 1873. Without high school, she faced entrance exams. Although Shaw was behind the regular students in some subjects, she nevertheless did well enough to be admitted to school.

At Albion, Shaw continued to seek opportunities to hone her speaking skills. Her first year, she started speaking for temperance. She gave a series of lectures, where she received five dollars "to hold forth for an hour or two in the little country schoolhouses" of the area. She did considerable temperance work during her second year at Albion and continued to preach regularly. However, throughout the fall she struggled with a critical question: should she remain at Albion four years, where she now was earning enough money to be financially secure, or should she go to Boston to test the less certain conditions of being a theological student at Boston University Theological School? Now twenty-seven years old, she decided that it was necessary to leave her financial security, and she set out for Boston in February 1876. A stern test of her character lay ahead.

At theological school, Shaw's class consisted of herself and forty-two males. Discrimination against her on the grounds of sex was immediate and obvious. Males were given free dormitory accommodations: Shaw, as a female, was allotted an inadequate two dollars a week to support herself. She rented a small attic room with a pale skylight and no heat or running water. Here she lived, literally near starvation, the rest of the school year. She cooked her food over a coal-oil lamp and studied in bed to keep warm during the cold New England winter. For weeks she lived on milk and crackers; she was constantly hungry. Earning extra money was difficult because she had to compete with one hundred male seminarians. Under these conditions, her health deteriorated as her weight dropped to less than a hundred pounds. After a few months, such conditions not only sapped her strength, they eroded her confidence; her commitment wavered. Fate intervened. Mrs. Barrett, the superintendent of the Women's Foreign Missionary Society, who admired Shaw's pluck, offered her $3.50 a week if she would give up preaching to concentrate on her studies. Shaw accepted the arrangements gratefully. Her health and spirits quickly improved and she finished the course.

Graduation brought joy and satisfaction. Shaw graduated with no special honors and she had been no more than an average student, but she had persevered. She had battled hunger, family isolation, loneliness, and prejudice in the classroom that gave her a constant sense of being unwanted. But she had achieved the ambition of her girlhood when she proudly accepted the title, Reverend Anna Shaw. Her early life had provided her with the freedom of thought that had made it possible for her "to break away from established customs for women and to be among the very first women to start out in the study of the ministry."(8)

Shaw accepted a call to be the pastor of a little church at East Dennis on Cape Cod in October 1878, a time when women ministers were still highly controversial and a woman pastor a distinct curiosity. She had to deal with two warring factions in the congregation and with a controversy about dancing. In each instance she met the situation frontally, and enough faithful rallied to her side so that the board of trustees confirmed their support for her.

Shaw's recollections of this period reveal much about her personality. While she admits the controversies were sometimes emotionally painful, she was sustained by her convictions. She handled the situations with remarkable forthrightness and assertiveness. She was quite comfortable with the role of leader and did not compromise with those who questioned her authority. These qualities and this style of leadership remained characteristic of her in later life. Undoubtedly her successes at East Dennis built Shaw's confidence in her abilities and in her rhetorical and leadership styles.

As a licensed preacher, Shaw could officiate at weddings and funerals, but could neither baptize nor receive church members. So in 1880, she applied to the Methodist Episcopal Conference for ordination. Although she received the top grade on the qualifying examination, the Bishop refused ordination. Upon the advice of a young minister in the Methodist Protestant Church, she applied for ordination to that group. After considerable debate and close examination of her, on October 12, 1880, they ordained her.

Despite having added a second congregation to her responsibilities, in 1882 Shaw decided that a medical degree would complement her ministerial training. Her brother James, who was now a medical doctor, had been urging her to study medicine, even if she did not take a full course. She had often wished she knew something about medicine, so she decided to enter Boston University Medical School. Her abundant energy allowed her to serve two congregations, work three nights a week in the Boston slums, and in 1885 to complete her medical training. At that point she began thinking of broadening her horizons. She found so many avenues of life opening up before her that she wrote a friend, "My Cape Cod environment seems almost a prison where I am held with tender force." Motivated by a burning conviction of the injustice of social conditions and an unshakable faith in the ultimate conquest of right over wrong, Shaw made a typically quick and somewhat radical decision to resign her pastorate and speak full-time for suffrage, temperance, and social purity.(9)

After doing free-lance lecturing for a year, her reputation grew to the point where the Redpath Lecture Bureau invited her to join them. Under their auspices, Shaw lectured almost daily, week after week, mostly at Chautauquas in the summer and wherever the bureau could schedule an appearance for her in the winter. Shaw focused on two general topics: temperance and suffrage. Her work in these areas soon attracted the attention of the leaders of organizations promoting those causes. Frances Willard, who had met Shaw at a Moody revival meeting, asked her to serve the Women's Christian Temperance Union (W.C.T.U.) in the suffrage department. Anxious to utilize Shaw's oratorical skills, the Union also offered her the post of national lecturer. A warm letter from the national office explained that the position was purely honorary, but that she could keep all lecture earnings. The letter added, "The lecturers are free lances and we are glad to know in making you one we appointed one of the best free lances that ever threw a javelin." In 1887, the American Woman Suffrage Association, in which her friend Mary Livermore was deeply involved, hired Shaw as their national lecturer. In this capacity Shaw met Susan B. Anthony while on a speaking tour in Kansas. This meeting proved eventful, for shortly thereafter Shaw and Anthony became inseparable co-workers, a relationship that greatly sustained Shaw in her activities. In 1890, the newly merged National American Woman Suffrage Association appointed Shaw national lecturer,   an appointment that broadened her speaking responsibilities and commitments. Then in 1892, the association designated her vice-president-at-large. Her primary responsibility, however, remained lecturing for the association. In this capacity Shaw traveled widely throughout the United States addressing a great variety of audiences. Her name was widely recognized, and reporters nationwide praised her oratorical talents after hearing her speak. For example, *The Morning Oregonian*, June 29, 1905, exuberantly proclaimed, "Dr. Shaw is easily the best and foremost woman speaker in the world." Individual listeners also tended to respond enthusiastically to Shaw. Perhaps the most colorful comment came from a cantankerous old lady in the audience at Greensboro, North Carolina: "There are just two things in which I have not been disappointed--Niagara Falls and Dr. Anna Shaw."(10)

In 1900 Susan Anthony resigned the presidency of the national association. At first it seemed that Shaw might be chosen as the next president (she was Anthony's choice), but Carrie Chapman Catt, with Shaw's full support, was picked instead. However, in 1904 Catt herself resigned and Shaw, by now a reluctant candidate, was chosen. For the next eleven years Shaw served in that capacity.

Shaw's presidency received a mixed review. Her personal style and lack of administrative acumen alienated some of the members, especially certain members of the national board. From 1910 on, an annual effort was made to oust her as president. At the same time, her administration compiled a relatively favorable record. During her tenure the number of states with full suffrage rose from four to eleven, and Illinois added presidential suffrage. She had moved the association out of the doldrums and into a period of renewed strength and activity. The membership rose during her tenure from 17,000 in 1904 to 183,000, a very impressive leap. Moreover, other suffrage groups had added still more women to those pressing for suffrage. The annual budget rose from $5,000 to nearly $50,000, and the organization moved from one campaign in ten years to five to ten annually. Shaw had also encouraged and supported many activities for which others got full credit. She participated in suffrage parades, visited states to help workers plan strategy and activities, supervised the distribution of literature, and continued her own lecture efforts, which were almost always successful. In short, while she was not a perfect leader and administrator, she was a stalwart advocate for woman suffrage during a challenging and difficult period.(11)

By 1915, however, Shaw herself felt that changing political conditions made it prudent for her to resign and allow new leadership to emerge. She committed herself to "unstinting loyalty" to her successor, Carrie Chapman Catt, and gracefully assumed the role of honorary president. The next two years she devoted herself to her usual activity of lecturing and campaigning for suffrage wherever the issue was contested.

Shaw's efforts to ease the transition for the new leadership and her desire to inspire other suffragists led her to write her autobiography, *A Story of a Pioneer*, which was published in September 1915. With a stenographer recording her recollections, Shaw recounted the events of her life to Elizabeth Jordan, who edited the reminiscences into a meaningful narrative. With a focus on her work for suffrage, the book is filled with anecdotes and amusing incidents from her lecturing and campaigning. It reads like her extemporaneous speeches. Overall, it provides a chatty and pleasant picture of her life, and it was favorably reviewed by the press.

A little over a year after her resignation as president of the national association, a new challenge came to Shaw. The Council of National Defense, eager to involve women in the war effort, created the Woman's Committee of the Council of National Defense. Shaw was selected to serve as chairwoman. She proved as efficient and effective in organizing the committee as her critics claimed she had not been with the NAWSA. Although Shaw encountered frustrations from time to time, because the committee's mission was never clear--it was basically what Shaw made it to be--nevertheless it functioned well enough that when the committee was terminated in 1919, President Wilson commended Shaw for the role she had played in the war effort. The country expressed its gratitude in May 1919 when it awarded Shaw the Distinguished Service Medal, the first living American woman to be so honored.

With the approval of the Anthony amendment by the House of Representatives on January 10, 1918, and the termination of her active leadership of the Woman's Committee, the time seemed ripe for Shaw to take at least a brief respite from her life as a campaigner. She was, after all, seventy-two years old, and she had maintained an incredibly active pace for all her adult life. But once again, her dedication to principles led her to postpone personal pleasures for service.

The cause that required her efforts grew out of her long-time commitment to peace, which she had frequently expressed in her speeches. Shaw's work with the International Suffrage Alliance and the International Council of Women had convinced her of the value and feasibility of cooperation between nations. In May of 1919 the League to Enforce Peace determined to wage a strong campaign to garner support for Wilson's peace plan and the peace treaty. They planned a series of ratifying conventions to show support for these proposals, especially the League of Nations portion of the treaty. Ex-president William Howard Taft and Abbott Lawrence Lowell, the president of Harvard University, were to be featured speakers. They, however, asked Shaw, as "the foremost leader of woman suffrage," to accompany them.   Reluctantly Shaw cancelled her plans for a rest and a European vacation and joined them for a proposed lecture tour between May 19 to June 5 through fourteen states from New Hampshire to Kansas.   As usual, Shaw entered into the work with great energy and dedication, sometimes speaking four or five times a day even though original plans had been that she should lecture only once.   Never had she been better received. *The Omaha Bee* advertised her coming to speak by enthusing, "Dr. Anna Howard Shaw!   The name stands for character, courage, intelligence, patriotism and--greater than all--service."(12)

Shaw literally died of overwork.   Having suffered a pleurisy attack a short time before, she was not at peak strength when she began the tour.   After a particularly gruelling day in Indianapolis, she collapsed at Springfield, Illinois, with a temperature of 104 degrees.   Doctors diagnosed the problem as pneumonia with inflammation of the liver.   She was taken home to Moylan, Pennsylvania, where she died on July 2, 1919.   The voice from the wilderness was at last still.   Her protests against existing conditions had, indeed, continued without cessation from the day she entered public life to the time of her death.

A SKETCH OF THE ORATOR

Shaw's reputation as a public speaker preceded her on lecture tours and other speaking engagements.   When she lectured for agencies such as the Redpath Lecture Bureau or the Massachusetts Woman Suffrage Association, these groups sent out advertising that   listed not only the subjects of Shaw's lectures but also contained pages of short testimonials about her ability to attract and impress audiences.   Moreover, newspapers, which published advance notices of her scheduled appearance, often mentioned Shaw's oratorical skill.   Shaw's reputation almost always assured a good crowd, eager to listen.

Clearly, Shaw was extraordinarily impressive as a lecturer in an age filled with other skillful speakers.   Since her ideas and causes were often not popular with the audience,   which invariably praised her as an orator, at least part of her effectiveness must stem from factors other than the substance of her speeches.   Understanding the sources of her skill and the elements that contributed to her effectiveness requires a brief consideration of several factors. We will consider her physical appearance, important features of her delivery, the tone and persona she projected in her suffrage rhetoric, and her rhetorical style.

Physical Appearance
Photographs, as well as observations by others, indicate that Shaw's physical appearance was not prepossessing.   At the same

time, her carriage and demeanor conveyed her dignity and authority on the platform. Of medium height, she had a pleasant face with exceptionally smooth skin and bright, prominent brown eyes. Throughout college, and even during her pastorate, she wore her short, brown hair, which sometimes tended to stand straight up, combed directly back. Her hair turned prematurely gray and later white, beginning in her thirties. These features led one journalist to write, "No one could look into those sparkling eyes, or see that majestic head, without being aware that he was in the presence of an unusual human being."(13)

While not vain, Shaw was conscious of the importance of the impression she made. When a Chautauqua critic asked her why she wore her hair short, she facetiously replied, "I was born with short hair!" Thereafter, however, she let her hair grow long. She confessed she had learned that "no woman in public life can afford to make herself conspicuous by an eccentricity of dress or appearance. If she does so she suffers for it herself, which may not disturb her, and to a greater degree for the cause she represents, which should disturb her."(14)

This surmise led her to dress very conservatively, for she almost always wore a black dress when she lectured or her ministerial robes when she preached. Shaw presented a solid presence on the platform. As a youth, her plumpness gave the impression of sturdiness; but in later life she grew stout. Still her size did not merit the sarcastic heading in the hostile *Wichita Daily Eagle*, "Very fat woman expounds her views before a slim crowd." On the positive side, Shaw's stoutness and bearing conveyed the impression she was in charge of the situation and would not yield to heckling or imprecations. Her solid stance suggested she was not easily bluffed or frightened, which was an invaluable asset on more than one occasion, especially with hostile audiences. One journalist summarized her appearance as: "Stout little old lady, dressed in a comfortable black gown, whose head was wreathed with a great crown of beautiful snow hair."(15)

Shaw's spirit and energy led observers to describe her as a person with "grit" or "spunk." For example, Frances Willard thought that her rarest quality was "pluck." Her auditors admired her enthusiasm and abundant vitality. This energy, coupled with her dignified appearance, sometimes won the respect of hostile listeners, who then accorded her a fair hearing. Although undoubtedly biased, Ida Husted Harper provides us with a good summary of Shaw's demeanor on the speaking platform and the impression she created:

> Her personality captured her audience before she had spoken. She was short, inclined to be stout, her white hair was combed back from her broad brow

and twisted over the crown of her head, her dark eyes twinkled under straight black brows and her cheeks dimpled with every word. She always came forward with a smile, her small pretty hands folded in front of her, or one, partly closed, resting on a table. Her audience smiled back, its prejudice, if it had any, was disarmed in advance and it was prepared for laughter or tears.(16)

DELIVERY

Although Shaw's delivery varied somewhat with the specific occasion, it was ordinarily quite animated. Her enthusiasm and energy translated into considerable facial and bodily expression. A paper in Arizona reported that she spoke with a "force and directness that many of her auditors, public speakers in Arizona for many years, wished they too possessed." She emphasized her words with gestures, which conveyed her earnestness. A Kansas journalist wrote, "Her addresses in print would be considered eloquent and logical but delivered from her lips, and hands--for she thoroughly understands the art of gesticulation-- they are simply irresistible."(17)

In part, Shaw's dynamic delivery came from her mode of speaking. She preferred to speak extemporaneously. Friends even chided her good-naturedly for writing her speeches on the tips of her fingers, because reportedly in planning a speech she first decided how many points she wished to make and what those points should be, then she named her fingers for each of her major ideas. Apparently, she did not even use notes while speaking, because no speech notes appear among her extant papers.(18)

Shaw found writing difficult, even distasteful. She once wrote, "It is hard for me to sit down in cold blood and work out a speech on paper--I am not used to that kind of speaking." Early in her career when she was approached to write a magazine article, she commented, "If I should stand on my head for a month not enough ideas would settle into it to enable me to write an article." On another occasion when she was asked why she never wrote, she replied, "I cannot write unless my private secretary takes it down as I walk up and down the room talking to an imaginary audience. I must have the inspiration of my hearers, real or fancied. Again and again different magazines have solicited work from my pen, but you would not recognize my stilted style of English as I write it, compared with my speaking."(19)

This extemporaneous style of speaking gave Shaw an opportunity to adapt to different occasions, even when she used the same basic content. Although she might be scheduled to give a speech she had given many times, each occasion demanded it be given somewhat differently, because a new occasion brought a new audience and a new source of inspiration. Shaw wrote to Lucy Anthony in 1892, "Aunt Susan [Anthony] says she does not see how I can twist a speech around so as to make it new every time. I don't, it just twists itself."(20)

Shaw had an unusual ability of being able to meet most challenges on the spur of the moment, a talent of great importance to the stump speaker. Sometimes she discarded her speech and spoke impromptu, or she reshaped her speech to fit the needs of the occasion. At other times she strayed from her planned speech and engaged in repartee with a heckler. Her autobiography is replete with examples of this, although such self-reports must be taken with some skepticism. For example, on one occasion Shaw discovered just before her lecture that she had been advertised to speak on "The Missing Link"--only she did not have such a speech. When she protested to the program manager, he told her she would have to speak on the "Missing Link" because they had sold all their tickets for that lecture. The whole town had turned out to hear it. Reluctantly, Shaw told him, "Very well. Open the meeting with a song. Get the audience to sing 'America' or 'The Star-Spangled Banner.' That will give me a few minutes to think, and I will see what can be done." Under the inspiration of the music the answer to the problem flashed into her mind: "Woman is the missing link in our government. I'll give them a suffrage speech along that line." Shaw later recalled:

> When the song ended I began my part of the entertainment with a portion of my lecture on "The Fate of Republics," tracing their growth and decay, and pointing out that what our republic needed to give it a stable government was the missing link of woman suffrage. I got along admirably, for every five minutes I mentioned, "the missing link," and the audience sat content and apparently interested, while the members of the committee burst into bloom on the platform.(21)

Shaw's extemporaneous delivery and the stimulation she got from interacting with her audiences undoubtedly enlivened her speaking.

Shaw apparently spoke very rapidly, but distinctly. One journalist reported, "So fast did her words flow that none but the most expert of stenographers could take her." But her rate did not seem to affect her audibility. Most reporters who heard her speak praised the quality, the clarity, and intelligibility of her voice. She was reported as the golden-voiced orator who was "never raucous though easily heard in the largest halls." *The Washington Post* asserted, "Her voice, while it is sweet, and musical, is strong and carries a tone of conviction." One impressed journalist said she possessed "a voice as clear and fresh as a mountain stream." Another proclaimed, "Her voice peals and rolls like a bell," while another declared that her contralto voice cast such a spell that it "was not to be evaded. Even in conversation her voice had the indefinable quality which makes the orator."(22)

Shaw easily projected her voice into "the back rows in the topmost galleries of such places as the Hippodrome in New York City and Albert Hall in London, while in outdoor speaking she could be heard at extreme edges of immense crowds." In *The Story of a Pioneer* Shaw relates that when she stood to speak in Vienna, Austria, an elderly, German man took one pained look at her, disgustedly arose, and snorted, "That old woman! She cannot make herself heard." Halfway down the aisle of the large hall he was arrested by the opening words of her address. Somewhat stunned by this power, he crowded into a pew and exclaimed, "Mein Gott, she could be heard *anywhere*." Harriet Grim concluded, "She was not a loud speaker but there was never any difficulty understanding her because of her good voice and enunciation."(23)

A clear picture of Shaw as an orator emerges from these accounts. All in all, she was a dignified, competent, energetic speaker. Her delivery, which resulted from a combination of natural ability, practice, and emotional commitment to her cause, was one crucial ingredient in her reputation as a platform speaker.

Tone and Persona

Shaw's sermons and eulogies reveal that she could adopt the solemn tone and pastoral persona appropriate on those occasions. But most of her speeches, particularly campaign addresses, do not reflect that approach. While Shaw was always earnest, she was aggressive and forceful like a debater rather than admonitory or pleading like a minister. Particularly in arguing the political bases of women's rights, Shaw was strongly assertive. An argument that appears with slight variations in several speeches reflects this forthright approach:

> Now one of two things is true: either a Republic is a
> desirable form of government, or else it's not. If it
> is, then we should have it, if it is not then we ought
> not to pretend that we have it. We ought to at least
> be true to our ideals, and the men of New York have,
> for the first time in their lives, the rare opportunity
> . . . of making the state truly a part of a Republic. It
> is the greatest opportunity which has ever come to
> the men of this state . . . If Woman Suffrage is wrong,

it is a great wrong; if it is right, it is a profound and
fundamental principle.(24)

Shaw's assertiveness was often coupled with a cool, reasoned
approach. For example, when she refuted the arguments of her
opponents, she often pointed out their inconsistencies and
contradictions, insisting "the anti-suffragists have the happy
faculty of answering their own arguments." Then she dispatched
the argument by answering each in turn. The impact was to
leave the opposition's case in shreds, a casualty of Shaw's closely
reasoned analysis. For example, with eyes twinkling, Shaw often
said in her speeches that one minute the anti-suffragists
contended that it was no use for women to vote, for they would
vote like their husbands--even if they had no husbands. In the
next breath these same speakers said that great discord, broken
homes, and divorce would be the consequence of equal suffrage.
A similar argument was the one that women do not really want
the ballot, and if it were given to them, they would not use it.
Later on these same anti-suffragists argued, Dr. Shaw pointed
out, that women would neglect their homes and families because
of the great amount of time spent in voting--just as though voting
would take several hours out of every day of the year.(25)

At times, however, Shaw strategically adapted her normally
rational tone to make an important point or to develop a moving
appeal. Nowhere is such adaptation clearer than in her
speeches shortly before World War I. For example, answering
allegations that woman suffrage would increase the likelihood of
war, Shaw, pointing to the headline indicating 250,000 deaths,
retorted, "No woman can comprehend the meaning of such
horrible slaughter! The horror of it would drive her mad . . .
there are miles of dead men, choking the rivers with their dead
bodies, filling the trenches with the dead and dying; their blood
mingling with the waters of rivers turning them to crimson."
She followed this emotional passage with a recounting of
mothers' reactions to the slaughter of the children they had
nurtured. This highly emotional depiction made her point
compelling.(26)

In a similar vein, Shaw often waxed patriotic in her speeches.
While she might castigate the actions of legislators, she was
patriotic to the point of sentimentality. One frequent strategy
was to refer to the flag lapel pin which she had received as
president of the NAWSA from Susan B. Anthony. It had a
diamond as a star for each state with suffrage. Shaw
characteristically alluded to it by observing, "I have here the
most beautiful flag in the world. It is the stars and stripes."
With the advent of World War I, Shaw became even more
patriotic, urging all-out support for the war effort.(27)

Although she was earnest, forceful, and rational in her tone,
Shaw was not aloof nor impersonal. She sprinkled her speeches

with anecdotes, often with herself as a central character. Many of these reflected a lively sense of humor. For example, she used a favorite story to answer claims that suffrage would increase the number of illiterate voters. Shaw drew on her childhood memories of elections in which ballots were imprinted with a rooster or an eagle designating parties to accommodate illiterate men. The officials assumed, she said, "that if a man has intelligence to know the difference between a rooster and an eagle, we could take the eagle out and put in the hen." While such stories amused her listeners, they also defused arguments that suffragists were cold and humorless. A Kansas newspaper commended Shaw's wit by writing, "Dr. Shaw's address was replete with apt stories and good natured raillery, entirely without bitterness or rancor." Another paper praised her 1908 presidential address by observing: "Anna Howard Shaw has set a new standard for womanhood. She is one of the most wonderful women of her time, alert, watchful, magnetic, earnest with a mind as quick for a joke as for the truth. She points her arguments with epigrams and tips the arrows of her persuasion with a jest."(28)

Shaw's tone and persona must be viewed in light of her physical appearance and delivery. She looked like a stolid matron but spoke with unusual vigor. Her voice possessed rare resonance and richness in quality. She combined reason, humor and earnestness to confront her opponents and advocate her cause. These elements coalesced to make her a rhetorical image of a new woman, the very embodiment of the cause she urged.

Style

While Shaw's extemporaneous delivery and dislike of writing contributed to her spontaneity on the platform, these practices produced flaws in her speeches when they were transcribed. Because most extant versions of her speeches are based on stenographic transcriptions, they preserve the grammatical errors, rough sentences, and generally unpolished style characteristic of all verbal presentations. Listeners, of course, would have been far less critical of these flaws than are readers. Thus, in examining Shaw's style, we must remember that some aspects that jar the reader would have been unnoticed by an audience, particularly one caught up with her dynamic delivery.

Even Shaw was quick to admit that her extemporaneous speaking fostered grammatical slips. She wrote to her private secretary, "When I began to preach one of the objections to me was my good grammar. One man said the Lord didn't care for it but I told him I did not believe the Lord objected to it. I am like the Lord in that, and I wish mine were as good as it used to be but extemporaneous speaking is as bad for grammar as taking lectures in shorthand is for writing and spelling." But for the most part Shaw's errors were not egregious. Often, for example, she used the singular "her" to refer to the plural antecedent "women," or she alternated past and present tenses inappropriately in a passage. Such minor lapses are insignificant in verbal delivery.(29)

Another noticeable but minor problem was Shaw's often convoluted syntax. Long, involved sentences, sometimes a page or more in length, with extremely loose construction, abound in the texts. For example, the last sentence of her 1909 New York State Suffrage Convention speech runs 451 words as transcribed; other samples run over 200 words. Many sentences have parenthetical expressions or are excessively wordy. "Now" is often used to begin many sentences without being a temporal reference. In short, Shaw's syntax reflects her informal verbal style.

While many of these flaws in the texts are the result of Shaw's extemporaneous style, some stem from stenographers' difficulty in recording her rapid-fire delivery. One stenographer remarked he would as soon take "chain lightning" as to report Dr. Shaw. The original manuscripts indicate that stenographers, who sometimes could not keep up, simply strung passages together in awkward, even meaningless constructions. At other points they left blanks to indicate their inability to follow her delivery.(30)

Shaw's language and style were those of a debater--plain, vigorous, and straightforward. She often introduced her arguments with a rhetorical question. For example, in developing one standard campaign argument, Shaw asked her audience:

> Now what is a Republic? Take your dictionary, encyclopedia, lexicon or anything else you like and look up the definition and you will find that a Republic is a form of government in which the laws are enacted by representatives elected by the people. Now when did the people of New York ever elect their representatives? Never in the world. The men of New York have, and I grant you that men are people, admirable people as far as they go, but they only go half way.

Shaw's direct, even aggressive style, when complimented by her adroit argumentation, produced a dynamic, forceful appeal. Her plea to one congressional committee, "The Nature of Democracy," is a case in point. The frequent notations of applause suggests her audience, too, was caught up by her energy and forcefulness. The plain, direct and forceful style of this speech leads the reader through at a rapid pace that undoubtedly resembles Shaw's rate of delivery.(31)

Although most of Shaw's addresses lacked stylistic polish because they were hard-hitting extemporaneous speeches designed to win a point, some texts reveal greater eloquence. Her eulogy at the memorial services for Susan B. Anthony, "All Absorbing Love," is quite impressive, while elements in "The Heavenly Vision" and her "Farewell" Presidential address reveal her facility with language. One passage from the eulogy suggests her ability to use an elevated style:

> There is no death for such as she. There are no last words of love. The ages to come will revere her name. Unnumbered generations of men shall rise up to call her blessed. Her words, her work, and her character will go on to brighten the pathway and the lives of all peoples. That which seems to our unseeing eyes as death is to her translation. Her work will not be finished, nor will her last word be spoken while there remains a wrong to be righted or a fettered life to be free in all the earth. You do well to strew her bier with palms of victory and crown her with unfading laurels, for never did a more victorious hero enter into rest.(32)

Because of her extemporaneous delivery and approach, Shaw's speeches contain relatively few figures of speech or carefully constructed sentences. Poetic language and fresh images were not her forte. She was, in short, plain spoken and direct. But her style, devoid of flowery language, enhanced her image as a rational, forceful advocate.

Shaw's one concession to figurative language was her frequent use of religious images and biblical allusions, probably because of her theological background. For example, in addressing her co-workers, Shaw often depicted them as reformers or missionaries carrying out a divine plan, which they ought to pursue with great zeal. A related reference suggested the "vision," presumably divine, which guides the reformer. For example, in *The Heavenly Vision*, Shaw inspired her listeners by picturing their role in the divine plan:

> All down through the centuries God has been revealing in visions the great truth which have lifted the race step-by-step until today womanhood, in this sunset hour of the nineteenth century, is gathered here from the East and the West, the North and South, women of every land, of every race, of all religious beliefs. But diverse and varied as are our races, diverse and varied as are our theories, diverse as our religious beliefs, yet we all come together

here with the harmonious purpose--that of lifting
humanity into a higher, purer, truer life.(33)

Religious allusions also produced one of the few rhetorical
figures in Shaw's speeches, an analogy that enfranchisement of
women was essential to make the voice of the people the voice
of God. Although she used this analogy quite frequently, one
case will demonstrate how she developed it:

> On the Fourth of July and other great patriotic
> occasions,   orators declare that the voice of the
> people is the voice of God, yet forget that, in the
> compass of the human voice there is the soprano as
> well as a bass. If the voice of the people is the voice
> of God, we shall never hear the voice of God in
> government until the soprano and bass mingle
> together, the result of which may be divine harmony.
> That time will not come so long as we are content to
> listen to a bass solo!(34)

While Shaw's campaign speeches were replete with such
religious allusions, the speeches were not generally sermonic in
tone. Rather Shaw deftly used her theological background to
build identification with her listeners and to warrant her
arguments in religious as well as political truths.

In conclusion, Shaw's plain and direct style complemented
her physical delivery. She expressed her ideas forthrightly and
simply, without resorting to bombast or elaborate language. This
style, coupled with her dynamic delivery and poise on the
platform, conveyed an image of a competent, rational debater.
Her matronly appearance made her seem formidable and
respectable. All in all, she embodied the responsible, intelligent
woman, who she argued deserved the ballot.   This image
accorded exactly with the substance of her arguments.

CHAPTERS TO FOLLOW

We will unfold Dr. Shaw's rhetoric both topically and
chronologically: we will recount the phases of her career and
analyze the kinds of speaking she did in each phase. Chapter
one will tell the story of Shaw as pastor, provide insight
concerning her preaching, and tell about her desire to expand
her horizons and address the nation's social problems. The
focus for analysis will be "The Heavenly Vision," a sermon that
Shaw delivered many times and that was listed on all her lecture
brochures with the notation "Sunday" placed in brackets before
it. Chapter two will narrate the excitement and the hardship
Shaw experienced on the lecture circuit and will examine her
best known lectures: "The New Man" and "God's Women." The

third chapter will focus on Shaw's campaigning for woman suffrage, will relate how she went from Susan Anthony's "Bonnet Holder" to "Queen of the Platform," and will analyze her three most complete suffrage addresses.   Three speeches will be examined in this chapter: "The Fate of Republics"--a lecture delivered many times, "The Other Half of Humanity"; and "The Fundamental Principle of a Republic."   Chapter four will deal with "The Orator as President."   It will recount Shaw's election as president of "The National," assess the numerous problems she encountered in leading the organization, and discuss the kinds of speaking she did as president, focusing upon her presidential addresses.   Chapter five will reveal how Shaw continued her efforts for woman suffrage after leaving the presidency, and then focus on her role as chairwoman of the Woman's Committee of the Council of National Defense during World War I.   We will examine the various activities of The Woman's Committee, assess Shaw's role in them, and discuss her speaking in behalf of the war effort.   Chapter six will tell how Shaw yearned to slow down, travel, relax, and enjoy herself after she resigned from the Woman's Committee at the close of the war; however, with the termination of hostilities in Europe she was again pressed into service by The League to Enforce Peace to accompany ex-President William Howard Taft and President Lowell of Harvard University on a speaking tour in behalf of Wilson's peace treaty--a plea she wanted to refuse but, because of her commitment to permanent peace, found impossible to do. She became ill and died before completing the tour.   The chapter will examine "What the War Meant to Women," an address that was reprinted as a pamphlet and still is available in many libraries.   It was Shaw's last speech.   The final chapter will develop a rhetorical portrait of Shaw as a woman suffrage rhetor. Her arguments and persuasive strategies will be summarized and assessed.

1

A "Gal Preacher": Shaw as Pastor

> I entered my new field as trustfully as a child enters a garden; and though I was in trouble from the beginning, and resigned three times in startling succession, I ended by remaining seven years.
>
> *The Story of a Pioneer*, p. 107

AMERICAN WOMEN IN THE MINISTRY

Although the ministry was not a common career for women in the nineteenth century, Shaw was by no means the first American woman to preach. In colonial times, Anne Hutchinson of Boston, who was probably the first woman in the United States to expound church doctrine, was banished from the colony for her efforts. Among the Quakers and Shakers, women such as Lucretia Mott and Anne Lee preached, but were not ordained; and among the early Methodists and similar church bodies, women were always permitted to exhort in meetings. The Society of Friends (or Quakers) always allowed women to preach; however, they usually did not have an ordained or settled ministry. Thus, women of various denominations prior to 1850 had been successful as evangelists and licensed itinerant preachers, but none had been formally ordained.

Although Clarissa H. Dansforth was licensed by the Free Will Baptist Church as early as 1815, the distinction of having the first ordained woman probably belongs to the United Brethren, which ordained Lydia Sexton in 1851. She continued in active service until 1890. When in 1853 the Congregational Church ordained Antoinette Brown Blackwell, a graduate of the theological department of Oberlin, she was mistakenly acknowledged in her day as the first woman ordained in the United States. Blackwell left her pastorate after only two years and achieved far greater fame as a speaker on slavery, temperance, and women's rights than as a member of the clergy, although she was always listed as the Reverend Blackwell. After these leaders, a few other women followed: Olympia Brown and Augusta Chapin in the Universalist Church in 1863; Celia Burleigh, Mary Graves, and Mary Safford in the Unitarian Church in the 1870s and 1880s. The Universalists ordained more women than any other denomination in the nineteenth century, ordaining about fifty women by 1911. As we know from Shaw's own account, she gained inspiration to pursue the ministry as a career from Mary Livermore, a prominent lecturer of the time, who saw nothing impossible or inappropriate in her ambition. However, Shaw's difficulties in gaining admission to the ministry in the Methodist Episcopal Church (including the refusal of a bishop to ordain her despite her outstanding performance in interviews with an examining committee and its firm endorsement of her as a candidate) suggests the prejudices women still confronted in seeking to preach.(1)

SHAW'S VIEWS ON WOMEN IN THE CHURCH AND MINISTRY

Shaw's early desire to preach and her pursuit of a theology degree forced her to consider carefully the history of women in religion and to consider biblical passages that seemed to delineate their role. She recalled with some gusto an early confrontation with a professor in theological school who opposed active roles for women in the church. Shaw questioned how he could explain the biblical verse, "Your sons and daughters shall prophesy," if Scripture enjoined against women's active participation in churches. His feeble response confirmed Shaw's conviction that no biblical basis existed for banning women from the pulpit.(2)

Shaw always remained a committed Christian, but she was forced to confront many opponents of women's rights who based their arguments on religious grounds. Since these arguments were common and effective and since Shaw often dealt directly with them, understanding her analysis of the roles of women as sanctioned by scriptural authority is important to understanding her general attitude toward women's issues. Although Shaw did not encourage young women to enter the ministry as a career because she perceived strong resistance to them in that profession, she argued that God intended women to preach. As early as 1879, her second year as pastor of a church in East Dennis, she drafted an address titled "Women in the Ministry," which she may or may not have delivered at that time. Evidence does indicate that she delivered at least the essence of it at the International Council of Women in Berlin, Germany, in 1904. In that address Shaw delineated her primary views about religious mandates governing women's roles. First, tracing the history of women as religious workers from the days of Israel, Shaw pointed to Miriam, the prophetess, Deborah, the judge and theocratic ruler, and Anna, the prophetess "who departed not from the temple," as biblical examples of the roles God had sanctioned for women. Jesus Christ, the founder of Christianity, Shaw argued, was extremely sympathetic and sensitive to women. "The three sublime events of his life, which form the basis of all orthodox creeds," Shaw pointed out, "were first revealed to women and announced by them to the world . . . the annunciation by the Angel to Mary, the declaration of his messianic mission by Jesus to the Samaritan woman through whose ministry many believed and followed him; and the manifestation of himself to Mary Magadelene after his resurrection, and her commission from the highest authority to preach a risen Lord." She noted that a woman was the last person at the cross and the first person at the tomb. While Christ was concerned with purity in relations of the sexes, he gave no directions about women's social or legal rights; and, more importantly, he did not relegate women to inferior positions. Thus, Shaw contended that religious history and Christ's ministry supported active roles for women in the church.(3)

In other speeches, Shaw also refuted generally accepted interpretations of many biblical passages. For example, in one campaign speech, after acknowledging that some "exegetes" urged that passages, most notably some of the Pauline epistles, were to be "accepted to-day exactly as they were uttered . . . hundreds of years ago," Shaw insisted that other scholars believed "that these things are not to be taken literally, but they are to be interpreted as we interpret all books published at that time, taking into account the circumstances under which they were uttered, the condition of society, and the needs of the people." Her analysis of these passages reflected this second attitude. First, she noted that Paul's commands for women's silence were contained in letters addressed to specific churches and persons. They were not given in a general sermon nor were they written, at least in the recorded Bible, to all his congregations. The particular circumstances of the churches to which Paul sent his dictum were also crucial to grasping his meaning, because in those churches women were creating undue disturbances. Finally, she contended that the passage exhorting women to be silent was not to keep them from preaching but to keep them from interrupting preachers with questions, a common practice at the time. Shaw concluded that an absolute command for women's silence would be out of harmony with the rest of the Bible.(4)

Although Shaw's analysis probably did reflect one strain of biblical exegesis, it also reflected selective perception. Shaw, like many persons, found in the Bible confirmation for her own attitudes. Still, she strongly believed that the Bible and religion were not impediments to women's rights but respecters and guarantors of them. Her knowledge of biblical scholarship and her experience with exegesis later proved very useful in her defense of women's rights, for she was able to answer challenges and arguments developed on religious grounds.

In her final analysis, Shaw felt that the aversion to women in the ministry stemmed as much from overly pious and disagreeable male ministers as from biblical injunctions. Reflecting the times, most male ministers were condescending to her. She once wrote that "a good deal of austerity passes for piety, and ugliness and conceit for deep religious emotion." She added, "I hope when I get to heaven--if I ever do--that I will not live near a deeply pious man; if I do I will move and try the society of jolly little devils for a while." With typical humor, she opined that churches and deeply pious male ministers needed to be taught a lesson, and that the best way to do this would be if women "let man pay the bills and run the church for a time while they sit back and fold their hands." The ensuing problems would prove the need for women's influence in church affairs.(5)

SHAW'S BACKGROUND AND TRAINING AS A PREACHER

Shaw's autobiography offers few clues as to the sources of her ambition to enter the ministry. As she admitted in her autobiography, as a youngster she used to preach to the silent woods in Michigan and felt the "stir of aspiration within her"; however, it was the opportunity to see a woman in the pulpit, Marianna Thompson, a Universalist minister, who visited Big Rapids, Michigan, which Shaw recalled, "thrilled my soul, all my early aspirations to become a minister myself stirred in me with cumulative force." A supportive and encouraging high school teacher not only provided Shaw with opportunities to develop her skills in speaking and debating, but also introduced her to a progressive Methodist minister, Dr. Peck, who invited her to preach at a quarterly meeting in a nearby town. Filled with trepidations and struggling to experience "conversion" herself before mounting the pulpit, Shaw spent six anxious weeks preparing her sermon. Her success on that occasion produced more opportunities to preach, but also led her brother-in-law to insert a brief announcement in a local paper, summarizing her family's reaction: "A young girl named Anna Shaw, seventeen years old, preached at Ashton yesterday. Her real friends deprecate the course she is pursuing." On the other hand, encouragement from Mary Livermore, who also came to Big Rapids during this period, confirmed Shaw in her decision to pursue a career in the ministry.(6)

The extant notes for this sermon, which she apparently delivered on other occasions, hint at Shaw's future rhetorical skills and practices. She used as a text John 3, verses 14 and 15: "And as Moses lifted up the serpent in the wilderness, even so must the Son of Man be lifted up; that whosoever believeth in Him should not perish, but have eternal life."   After a rather lengthy and erudite exegesis of the Scripture pertaining to Moses on which John was drawing, Shaw applied the text by comparing the effects of the venom of serpents to the effects of evil habits on humans, who can be saved by giving themselves over to God's mercy and accepting Christ as the Lamb of God. While the exegesis was logically unnecessary to the application Shaw made, it did serve rhetorically to enhance her ethos by suggesting her scholarship.   In the same way, the clearly organized and cogently argued text built her credibility.   The earnestness and even passion of her appeal revealed her commitment and concern for her hearers.   Thus, while the sermon was not notable for its substance, it did show Shaw's awareness of her audience and her need to build her ethos as a preacher.(7)

Although we know from her autobiography that Shaw continued to preach throughout her time in college and theology school, no copies of her sermons still exist, other than the initial one.   In the chapters about her years as pastor in East Dennis, Shaw focused on the controversies she handled and the personalities in her flock.   We learn nothing about her preaching, except her acknowledgment that church attendance improved during her tenure.   In later sections of her autobiography, Shaw mentioned times when she preached either at religious services held in conjunction with suffrage meetings or on occasions associated with her attendance at conventions. By her admission, she was usually well received despite occasional initial skepticism. Despite the paucity of texts and information about Shaw's preaching, the experience she gained in the pulpit was undoubtedly valuable preparation for her later work as a lecturer. Also, her training in exegesis influenced her later oratorical practices, for she became well known for her cogent arguments and skillful use of materials.(8)

SHAW'S SERMONS

Because Shaw's tenure as a pastor was relatively brief (about seven years) and because she delivered her sermons extemporaneously, no copies of her sermons are extant. We have complete texts of three sermons, all of which apparently were developed in conjunction with her work for suffrage; the rough notes for her first sermon preached as a girl in 1871; and fragments of two others, delivered at suffrage meetings. Despite this limited collection, Shaw's sermons merit some consideration because she was frequently asked to preach at services held in conjunction with suffrage meetings and because her sermons reveal the nucleus of many of her arguments for

Dr. Shaw in her thirties. The Schlesinger Library, Radcliffe College.

women's rights and the evidence she used to answer her opponents who drew on religious doctrine to oppose suffrage.

The text chosen for analysis here, titled "The Heavenly Vision," was one of Shaw's most popular and frequently delivered. Since she listed it on her lecture brochures, Shaw probably delivered it on many suffrage campaigns with slight variations and adjustments. Two copies of the text, both from stenographic records of the same occasion, are extant--in *The Woman's Tribune* of March 27, 1888, and in the *Report of the International Council of Women*. The substance of the two copies is quite similar, but since the *Woman's Tribune* version contains words and passages missing from the other copy and since it also includes additional pages at the end, it will be the version studied here.(9)

The *Report* of the Council's meetings, which had been assembled in Washington by the National Woman Suffrage Association, describes the March 25 occasion briefly:

> Long before the hour of opening (2:30 P.M.) had arrived Albaugh's Opera House was crowded and the aisles filled with persons standing. Rev. A. Handford made the invocation and read Samuel Longfellow's beautiful hymn of "Greeting." The audience joined in the singing. Rev. Ada C. Bowles read the 26th chapter of Acts, which was followed by the singing of "Nearer, My God, to Thee." Rev. Antoinette Brown Blackwell offered prayer, after which Rev. Annie H. Shaw delivered the sermon.

Shaw chose as her text chapter 26, verse 19 of Acts: "Whereupon, O King Agrippa, I was not disobedient unto the heavenly vision." Rather than engaging in exegesis of this text, Shaw applied the implicit lesson in Paul's conversion and his allegiance to the vision God sent him to the members of her audience in their work as reformers. Roughly, the text of the sermon falls into four parts: (1) establishing the appropriateness of women serving as conduits for visions to society as a whole; (2) describing the nature of contemporary women's visions, which demonstrates their divine sanction; (3) explaining the functions of divine visions and the responsibilities they entail; and (4) preparing the listeners for the problems visions impose on their bearers. Although this organization seems to be simply topical, in effect the sections form a rhetorical sequence. In the first two sections, Shaw empowered her listeners to be visionaries and agents of change, then she legitimized the causes for which they were to be active. In the final portions, she inspired and encouraged them to sustained action.

Perhaps because her audience had just heard the full chapter, Shaw did not immediately develop the context of the verse, although she did so a bit later. Instead, she referred to another biblical passage, Psalm 68, verse 11: "The Lord giveth the word, and the women that publish the tidings are a great host." In so doing, she developed a parallel between her audience and the women of Israel who rejoiced in God's triumphal ascent onto Mount Zion and His deliverance of His chosen people. One analysis of this psalm suggests that the reason David was singing God's praises was that "God was marching triumphantly on behalf of the oppressed." This reading of the psalm certainly accords with Shaw's interpretation, for she noted that women, who had been repressed and constrained, had, after years of struggle and pain, "beheld the vision of the grandeur and dignity of womanhood." Modern women, like those in the psalm, had the duty and right to publish their tidings.(10)

Rhetorically, this passage was significant because it legitimized the public activities of the audience. The biblical precedent for women as "publishers" of good tidings clearly supported the suffrage workers in their efforts to convey to others the "truth" of women's rights. As framed by Shaw, the passage also suggested women's unique ability to "intuit" truth and their importance as an effective moral force:

> The wisest and best people everywhere feel that if woman enters upon her tasks wielding her own effective armor, if her inspirations are pure and holy, the Spirit Omnipotent whose influence has held sway in all movements and reforms, whose voice has called into its service the great workmen of every age, shall in these last days fall especially upon woman, and if she venture to obey, what is man that he should attempt to abrogate her sacred and divine mission?

Interestingly, the translation of the psalm on which Shaw relied for her argument is from the Revised Version published in 1885, which translated the Hebrew source as "women" rather than the more usual translation as "host" or "company." Indeed, later editions of this translation, notably the 1952 version, do not retain this translation, nor does the King James translation. For Shaw's purposes, however, the then modern translation would have added force to her later argument that "truth" is a progressive process, which only gradually has an impact. That contemporary scholars had developed this "new" translation of the psalm only reinforced her claim.(11)

Having thus established the appropriateness of women as public bearers of truths and visions, Shaw moved into the body of her sermon. She provided a brief analysis of her text, observing that Paul "recognized that the purpose of his life could be fulfilled only when in obedience to that Master." In other words,

Paul could only fulfill God's purpose in his life by following the vision God offered. Shaw extended that lesson to her audience in a brief transitional statement:

> Permit me to use this vision, which is so familiar to us all, as a type of that which must appear to every one of us who is able to do anything for God and humanity. Every reformer the world has ever seen has had a similar experience. Every truth which has been taught to humanity has passed through like a channel. No one of God's human children has ever gone forth to the world who has not had first revealed to him his mission in a vision.

Shaw continued developing this theme by noting that the womanhood, consisting of those assembled in her audience and other's like them, "in this sunset hour of the nineteenth century, is gathered here from the East and the West, and the North and South, women of every land, of every race, of all religious beliefs, with diverse theories and plans. But . . . we come together here and now with one harmonious purpose--that of lifting humanity, both men and women, into a higher, purer, truer life." Like Paul, she implied, these women could only fulfill their God-ordained purpose in life if they followed their visions.

Among those worthy goals she listed visions of justice through political freedom, fighting "the rum fiend" to achieve social freedom, educational development, and social change such as that advocated by an unnamed Indian woman who sought to relieve the plight of widows who were deprived of status and comfort because of social custom. She concluded her summary of the inspiring visions of women: "And so we come, each bearing her torch of living truth, casting over the world the light of the vision that dawned on her own soul." All these visions, Shaw asserted, were part of a larger plan. God has given women these worthy goals not so that they might do their own work "but the will of Him who sent them." If women pursued these goals and served God as He intended, they need not fear any scorn nor oppression. Moreover, they would experience great serenity and confidence.(12)

Although this passage in many ways reflects rather commonplace sermonizing, it is significant on at least two rhetorical fronts. First, Shaw connected two strands of argument in her endorsement of women's allegiance to their personal visions. On one front, she suggested the distinctive nature of women. Her insistence on the unique sensibilities of women, their reliance on intuition and love rather than mere reason, and her list of visions clearly reflect an image of women as having a strong social consciousness. Within her contemporary society, this moral sense, allegedly most fully

developed in women, was the basis for society's limited support
of their public activities. They received full social sanction for
public activity only if their work was in the interest of the family
and moral causes. Such work elevated and purified the public
arena. This appeal embodied what one scholar has called the
argument from expediency, that supported women's rights
because of the constructive impact their involvement would have
on the moral climate of society. Of course, it also mirrored the
stereotypes of the day that held women to be more moral and
purer than men. On the other hand, in a manner similar to
Elizabeth Cady Stanton's plea in her "Solitude of Self," Shaw
contended that women as human beings have responsibility to
God and higher powers for their own lives. Thus, they cannot
abrogate the visions that God has sent to them. This dimension
of her appeal resembles the natural rights argument, which
insisted that women as individual persons should have full
rights.(13)

Second, and perhaps more significant rhetorically, this
analysis implicitly legitimized women's reform activities as
sanctioned by higher moral law. By comparing the allegiance of
suffrage supporters to their cause to Paul's devotion in following
his vision from God, Shaw transformed their efforts from a
political arena to a religious one. Implicitly, she suggested that
persons who advocated such causes, which were in the public
interest, belonged to a select group of visionaries who were
morally obligated to pursue their activities. Supporters became,
thus, what Hugh Duncan termed the moral guardians of society,
who were preserving and protecting the truest and best values of
the culture.(14)

Having justified women's involvement in activities like
suffrage, Shaw moved on to suggest that their perception of the
truth underlying their cause obligated them morally to act to
bring their wisdom to others. Noting that God does not expect
persons to whom He sends visions to use them for only their
personal good, Shaw argued that instead God intends that "they
to whom the truth is revealed may carry it to a waiting race, that
their eyes may be opened and that they may be turned from
darkness unto light and from the power of Satan unto God. This
then is God's lesson to reformers, God's lesson to you and to me.
He opens before our eyes the vision of a great truth, and for a
moment He permits our wondering gaze to rest upon it; then he
bids us go forth." In other words, the receiving of a vision
obligates one to spread the truth one has perceived. Labeling
such spreading of truth as obedience to God's plan, Shaw
insisted that such obedience was one secret of success of every
reformer, who must stand between "the world of truth on the
one hand and the world of men on the other" to become "the
medium through which these two find each other." Such
obedience and service brings spiritual rewards to the visionary,

whose inner life becomes richer and fuller ... the truth is shared. But Shaw warned, reformers and visionaries always confront difficulties, most especially from those to whom they were sent: "The world never welcomes its deliverers save with the dungeon, or the faggot, or the cross." Despite the energy and zeal of the reformer, she soon learns that "no form of slavery [is] more bitter or arrogant or brutal than error."

Persevering in the face of certain opposition, Shaw averred, was essential, for "the secret of success is in earnestness. The reformer may be inconsistent, he may be stern or even impatient, but if the world feels that the reformer is in earnest he cannot fail." Despite discouragements and failures, the reformer must persist because "apparent failure is oft times the grandest success." Again, while these words may seem cliched, they were rhetorically important for her audience, who as supporters of women's rights had scored few significant victories. Thus, Shaw's depiction of the disappointments and setbacks inherent in any progressive reform work was reassurance about the importance of their efforts and inspiration toward their ultimate success.

To persist despite failures required two qualities: infinite hope and infinite love. One must not succumb either to discouragement or to bitterness. In one of the few somewhat eloquent passages in the sermon, Shaw admonished her listeners to love and appreciate those they seek to persuade. Truth, like a flower, she insisted, grows slowly, so one must appreciate that those in error will only gradually come to recognize their mistakes. The reformer's task, she said, was to "bring them into clearer light; we must not despise them, for out of them we are to build a greater, newer and broader truth than that which the world has heretofore known."

She perceived that if one persists in spreading the truth and in maintaining a hopeful, loving optimism, the personal rewards will be great. But even more significantly, the reform one seeks will be achieved. "Out of the vision of truth which is within you He is able, by the influence of His spirit upon your life, to work a miracle and bring the truth therein to other lives." Shaw followed this encouragement with a passionate religious appeal to follow God's vision and dedicate one's life to conveying that truth to others.

In essence, in this sermon, Shaw turned the religious conversion of Paul into a parable for her auditors who were seeking greater rights and opportunities for women. By labeling them as visionaries and urging them to conceptualize their commitment to political and social change as obedience to a divine plan, Shaw offered her hearers a way to interpret and justify their work for a highly controversial agenda. Rather than opposing social stereotypes about women's moral natures, Shaw capitalized on them to suggest that women's intuitions and commitment to social causes were marks of their special status and role. She deftly transformed a political cause into a moral crusade, preparing her listeners for the difficulties they would confront by warning them that all visionaries, Paul and Christ among them, faced the same obstacles and abuse. Thus, within the sermon, Shaw empowered her listeners as agents of change and sanctified the cause to which they were committed.

Although this sermon was in many ways unremarkable and even cliched in its appeals, the evidence of Shaw's rhetorical skills must not be overlooked. As we have already noticed, her organizational pattern was quite subtle in its rhetorical process. Similarly, her use of Paul's conversion as a model for her listeners is particularly intriguing since Paul was the biblical source most frequently used against suffragists. Within the sermon, Shaw subtly urged her listeners to follow Paul's model rather than his edicts. Shaw's own earnest tone, her generous attitude toward opponents, and her clever linking of commitment to suffrage activities with following a heavenly vision, all made the sermon an excellent appeal for her audience. Rather than refuting religious arguments against her cause, Shaw turned to biblical sources to support the spirit of the movement. Thus, she avoided the perils of seeming to assault the values and beliefs of her contemporary society. She used biblical evidence to construct a mandate for her cause instead of responding to hostile arguments based on biblical sources. Her opponents became not caretakers for traditional values, but instead those who had not yet been vouchsafed a vision to reveal their error. Her supporters became prophets like Paul, who were commissioned to change their lives and speak out for the truth God had entrusted to them. Her constructive, knowledgeable, rhetorical persona added weight to the ideas she presented.(15)

2

On the Lecture Circuit: "My Real Work Had Begun"

> It would have been pleasant to go almost indefinitely, living the life of a country minister . . . . But all the time, deep in my heart, I realized the needs of the outside world, and heard its prayer for workers . . . . So it was that, in 1885, I . . . sent my resignation to the trustees of the two churches whose pastor I had been since 1878 . . . My real work had begun.
>
> *The Story of a Pioneer*, p. 147

When Shaw resigned her pastorate to join "the crusade of the men and women who were fighting" for the rights of women, she was already well established as a lecturer for suffrage and temperance. During the last two years of her ministry the Massachusetts Woman Suffrage Association had employed her frequently as a lecturer. They now offered her $100 a month to work as a speaker and organizer. Somewhat modest about her abilities, Shaw refused to accept that much, setting her own salary at $50 a month; one year later, convinced of her value, she asked for and received the original amount. But in her second year, Shaw resigned in protest because her request for a raise to $125 was met with the reply that, while she was certainly worth that much, funds were limited and the current wage was "a good salary for a woman."(1)

Standing on her principles, Shaw next turned to the commercial lecture circuit. Shaw asked her friend Mary Livermore to ask whether the Hathaway Agency might desire her services. Hathaway, however, declined to take Shaw on because he was not interested in new people. "Now," Livermore wrote to Shaw, "you must get out your own circulars and push yourself and we must all help you--the *Womans' Journal* and every other agency." Shaw was not greatly hampered by Hathaway's disinterest, for she was able to do considerable free-lance lecturing. Also, she apparently worked at least briefly with the Slaton Bureau of Chicago. A year later Shaw's reputation as a lecturer had grown to the point that the Redpath Bureau invited her to join them, making her such a good offer that she promptly accepted.(2)

Under the auspices of the Redpath Bureau, Shaw lectured almost daily, week after week, mostly in Chautauquas, in the summer, and wherever the bureau could schedule an appearance for her in the winter. Although Shaw usually received only $50 for a lecture, on one occasion she wrote exultantly, "Whoop la! Made $75 for a lecture." This income enabled her to save a small surplus that provided her with financial security the rest of her life. She maintained her rigorous schedule until she became president of the National American Woman Suffrage Association in 1904. At that point, she curtailed her commercial lectures to one brief tour a year, just enough to make her living. Only in 1908, when the officers of the association began to receive stipends, was Shaw able to abandon her commercial lecturing.(3)

THE RIGORS OF THE CAMPAIGN TRAIL

The lecture circuit and campaign work around the turn of the century required considerable dedication, courage, and fortitude. This task was not for the traditional "clinging vine"; it called for substantial physical stamina and mental toughness. Shaw's early years in the Michigan wilderness had prepared her for the hardships and deprivations she encountered as she toured state after state, moving from one town to another to follow a rigorous schedule. Lecture bureaus were insensitive to the comforts of their speakers and arranged schedules that disregarded rest, food, or sleep.

As a lecturer, Shaw had gruelling schedules exacerbated by primitive transportation. For example, on one tour she spoke in Toronto, Canada, on January 30 and the next day in Marcellus, Michigan; February 2 she appeared in Minneapolis, Minnesota, and two days later in Duluth; the next day, February 5, she spoke in West Superior, Wisconsin, and on the 7th in Oshkosh. Then after traveling for a day, she spoke three consecutive days in Ohio--in Cambridge, Marion, and Athens. She continued this gruelling pace month after month, usually ten months of the year. Travel under such conditions meant that Shaw frequently kept odd hours, perhaps getting up at 4 o'clock every morning for a week, since late arrivals and early departures were common. These gruelling schedules sometimes caused her to lament, as she did in a letter from Kansas in 1892: "It is hard to live this homeless life with no hope of it ending. Year after year of constant toil like a galley slave." From Erie, Pennsylvania, she wrote: "I am forming a habit of grumbling, and the dread of the work is growing on me. I must quit." However, she had an amazing ability to pull herself up by her bootstraps, as she reflected in a letter to Lucy Anthony from Madison, Wisconsin: "I think it is wicked for us ever to complain and I resolve that I never will again."(4)

All-night journeys in freight cars, engines, and cabooses were commonplace, and thirty- and forty-mile horse and buggy or sleigh rides in blizzards and rainstorms were routine. Often Shaw was unable to secure dry clothing. In the hinterlands of South Dakota, Wyoming, and Kansas, travel was always primitive. Although trains went to leading cities in these western states, they were not always passenger trains. More than once, Shaw traveled in the limited comfort of the cattle car.

Lodging accommodations were also often primitive, whether she stayed in a hotel or in someone's home. Hotels in South Dakota were especially bad. Shaw's letters to Lucy Anthony report her staying in tiny hotel rooms seven feet by eight feet; watching body lice crawl toward her; and sitting up all night in the heated hotel office because her room was too cold to sleep in. Shaw's experiences in private homes often were little better. When she stayed in farm homes, she confronted the family's early schedule. Once her hosts encouraged her to sleep late, but while she was still "sleeping like a top" they called her for breakfast at "a little after six!"(5)

Enduring such primitive conditions took its toll on Shaw's health. From early childhood, Shaw apparently was prone to respiratory illnesses; she was often referred to as sickly. Often in letters to Lucy Anthony she complained of a bad cold, sometimes with complications. She wrote from Wichita in 1892: "I thought the back of my head would be paralyzed before I got through speaking and my limbs were so heavy that I could hardly lift them or raise my arms to my head. I really thought I was dreaming and expected every moment to drop to the floor. But you see I did neither."(6)

Bad food and even ptomaine poisoning were other difficulties. On one occasion her food was prepared over burning cowslips. The odor permeated the food. At least twice, once in Canada and once in Ohio, she suffered severe cases of food poisoning. Because she was alone in stations waiting for her train on both occasions, she actually feared death because she could not summon help.

Not all travel was this hard. Shaw found some trips rewarding and pleasant. For example, in a letter from Yosemite Valley, Shaw spoke of the scenic beauties of California, and later in the year she wrote from Santa Rosa, California, "They are drying grapes for raisins, making wine and cider and it is full of the finest of alcohol. You can fairly breath it. Perhaps that is the reason one feels so hilarious." After the turn of the century, especially close to the end of Shaw's career, travel conditions in most places were greatly improved. Nevertheless, her speaking schedules remained gruelling, because she continued the practice of speaking several times a day, or several days in succession in different communities.(7)

According to estimates in 1893, an average year for Shaw, she traveled 28,000 miles. Shaw thrived on work, and although from time to time she would be badly exhausted, her endurance was considerable. She once remarked, "I count my endurance, and above all, my willingness to work the greatest of things I have to be thankful for. My work is my play, and the best thing that can happen to me is to have plenty to do."(8)

Because she never missed a chance to speak, Shaw often spoke under odd circumstances at unusual places. On one occasion she spoke virtually impromptu to a grandstand crowd before a race at a county fair. Once, on a snowbound train near Faribault, Minnesota, at the request of a cowboy who had heard her before, she addressed a group of rough cattlemen who stopped their poker game to give her their undivided attention. At Leavenworth, Kansas, she spoke at the Old Soldiers' Home, and at Pontiac, Illinois, at the Boys' Reformatory. She often spoke to labor audiences, making a case for labor in general and women in the work force in particular. Her speeches took place in town halls, opera houses, Y.M.C.A. auditoriums, school buildings, churches, Grange meeting halls, and a great variety of other facilities, some of which were less than ideal. In Kosiusko, Mississippi, in 1903, Shaw spoke in a "great big barn of a place fully thirty feet high" with two little fireplaces to heat it. "It was so cold that you could see the breath rise from every mouth . . . and as I talked my breath looked as if it were a steam engine. My feet were as cold as rocks and it seemed as if there was a stream of ice water running down my back." Of Pittsburg, Kansas, in 1890, in a tin-roofed opera house during a hailstorm, she recalled, "I tried to speak above the roar, but at last had to give it up and burst out laughing, as did the audience, at the queer race between myself and the hail." When the hail stopped, Shaw finished her speech.(9)

The audiences Shaw addressed ranged from a mere handful in remote places to as many as 6,000 at a meeting in Atlanta. Audience response also varied greatly. For example, Shaw wrote in 1895 that at Erie, Pennsylvania, "I had a hard audience last night and they took the very life out of me. I hate Teachers Institutes." By contrast, she wrote from Troy, Ohio, "My hand is so lame this morning from the grips of strong male and female hands, for I guess half the audience came up and shook it."(10)

During the years between 1885 and 1890 (when she decided to devote her skills solely to suffrage work), Shaw focused on two reform causes in her public lectures: temperance and suffrage. Her work in these areas attracted the attention of the leaders of organizations promoting those causes. In 1887, the

American Suffrage Association, in which her friend Mary Livermore was deeply involved, made Shaw its national lecturer. Shaw's temperance lectures impressed Frances Willard, the president of the Woman's Christian Temperance Union (W.C.T.U.). Soon two women, themselves very prominent and successful lecturers, were vying for Shaw's talents in the service of their organizations: first, Frances Willard and a bit later Susan B. Anthony of the National Woman Suffrage Association. Having strong allegiances to each cause, Shaw was delighted to continue advocating both reforms. Although her work during this period blended advocacy for both temperance and suffrage as well as general topics, the following discussion will examine her temperance speeches and general lectures. Her suffrage work, to which she devoted most of her life, will be the focus of chapter three.(11)

WORKING FOR TEMPERANCE

After Shaw met Frances Willard at a Moody revival meeting in the early 1880s their relationship grew so close that at one point the two vowed to meet weekly to point out to each other their most serious faults in an effort at self-improvement. Willard's correspondence with Shaw is replete with examples of affectionate intimacies. After Shaw resigned her ministry, Willard, who had realized her potential, asked her to serve the W.C.T.U. in the suffrage department, because the organization embraced that reform as a mechanism for achieving its other social purity goals. When Mrs. Ziralda Wallace resigned as head of that division, Shaw assumed charge of the suffrage division.(12)

Anxious not to lose Shaw's oratorical skills, the Union offered her the post of national lecturer as well. With encouragement from Mary Livermore, Shaw accepted. A warm letter from the national office welcomed her to the ranks and explained the stipulations: her position was purely honorary; she had complete freedom of movement, and she could keep all lecture earnings. The letter added, "The lecturers are free lances and we are glad to know in making you one we appointed one of the best free lances that ever threw a javelin."(13)

Shaw was not new to temperance lecturing. As early as her years at Albion College, temperance work had been a main source for her income. At first, she spoke on temperance to small audiences for five dollars per engagement. Later, during her pastorate at East Dennis, she gained prominence as a frequent temperance lecturer in that area. After leaving her ministry, one year she gave 215 temperance lectures for pay, 25 sponsored by suffrage associations and the rest by temperance and literary organizations. Her temperance lecturing went so well that in 1889 Willard wrote Shaw, "I heard some Southern women yesterday declaring that, next to me, you were the one for president of the W.C.T.U."(14)

SHAW'S TEMPERANCE LECTURES

Little of Shaw's temperance rhetoric remains for our inspection. Other than an occasional snippet in the press, we have only two lengthy excerpts. The first, apparently quotations from a lecture, survives in a pamphlet issued by the Ohio W.C.T.U. and, although it almost certainly began as a speech, we have no dates or places for its delivery. The second, titled "The Temperance Problem," was delivered at a sectional meeting of the International Congress of Women in London in 1899. Because this is also the title of one of her prominent temperance lectures, we can surmise that Shaw had used it earlier in her temperance work.(15)

Both pieces reflect the "home protection" theme that Willard developed within her W.C.T.U. strategy, and they complement each other in terms of their argument. Each asserts that women have the right to protect their homes and children, which were threatened by liquor. The speech given in London, for example, asserted, "It is the life of the home at which the legalized liquor traffic strikes its deadliest blows, blighting its dearest hopes." Within that speech, Shaw traced women's efforts to combat the liquor foe first through efforts to get men to sign a non-drinking pledge (which proved ineffective), then through attempts to ban saloons. Gradually, women realized that since saloons operate with official sanction, only direct governmental action in the form of national prohibition would alleviate the problem. Thus, in this speech Shaw focused on defending women's public advocacy for temperance and their efforts to secure national prohibition on the grounds that other measures had proven ineffective.(16)

In the Ohio pamphlet, Shaw developed the home protection theme quite vividly and linked temperance to the need for woman suffrage directly. She began by asserting, "For thirty-five years women in this country have been crying aloud to God and crying aloud to men to redeem their homes from the curse of the saloon without avail. These women empty-handed with only the power to pray in their hearts, are year after year appealing to Congress and to State Legislatures and their appeals are denied." Noting that men had been unable to protect their homes from the evils of alcohol and arguing that women had a sacred duty to "protest against the iniquitous conditions which surround the home and child-life of the land," Shaw concluded, "It is the right, and ought to be the purpose, of all women of this country to demand every bit of power which will enable them to do for their children the very best and noblest service which can be done by free women in a free country." This argument lead directly to her concluding call for suffrage, "The homemaker, the child rearer, is powerless against such a foe without the ballot . . . . Every principle of justice, divine or human, demands the enfranchisement of women."(17)

These brief excerpts have little of the appeal of Shaw's suffrage rhetoric, probably because of their abbreviated written form. But they suggest quite clearly the basis of Shaw's link between temperance and suffrage. In essence, Shaw's primary concern was women's ability to control their own lives and to protect their families. Because alcohol had undermined many families, Shaw supported temperance. Increasingly, however, Shaw saw suffrage not only as a means to gain prohibition but as an end in itself, because women needed political power for reasons other than temperance activities.

GENERAL LECTURES

The brochure pictured on the next page identifies some other topics of Shaw's lectures in the 1890s. Significant fragments of two of the most prominent ones, "Fate of Republics" and "The New Man," remain for our inspection as does a text of another of Shaw's most popular lectures, "God's Women." Because "Fate of Republics" will be discussed later with her suffrage rhetoric, this examination will be confined to the other two to provide insight into how she interwove women's issues into her general interest lectures.

"The New Man"

According to Shaw's diary, she delivered "The New Man" lecture most frequently in the late 1890s, presenting it at least forty times in 1898. The following year at Pittsburgh, Pennsylvania, the master of ceremonies mistakenly introduced Shaw as speaking on "The New Woman." She was in an awkward situation, but her quick wittedness rescued her. "I began on the New Woman and her discoveries, greatest of which was the New Man," she told Lucy Anthony in a letter, "and I told what kind of a man she had discovered him to be." Thereafter, she began "The New Man" lecture with a brief discussion on the "new woman" and then related her to the new man issue.(18)

To begin this lecture Shaw contrasted the "new woman" as men pictured her with the real new woman. For example, men always saw the new woman as invading "his prerogatives in dress." To which she replied, "This is a useless fear, as the real new woman will always want to look as well as she can, and no human being could look well in men's clothes, and the new woman will not wear them for that reason if for no other." The actual new woman was an improvement on the old because she enjoyed all the advantages of education and culture, together with opportunities for acquiring trade and professions. The

Mary Carnell, Photographer.

REV. ANNA H. SHAW

SUBJECTS

"THE NEW MAN"

"THE FATE OF REPUBLICS"

"THE POWER OF THE INCENTIVE"

"THE NEW DEMOCRATIC IDEAL"

"THE AMERICAN HOME"

"COLONIZATION AND CIVILIZATION"

"THE RELATION OF WOMAN'S BALLOT TO THE HOME"

"WOMAN SUFFRAGE ESSENTIAL TO A TRUE REPUBLIC"

"THE TEMPERANCE PROBLEM"

(Sunday) "THE HEAVENLY VISION"

(Sunday) "STRENGTH OF CHARACTER"

The Redpath Lyceum Bureau
Boston and Chicago.

LUCY E. ANTHONY, Private Secretary.
7443 Devon St., Mt. Airy, Philadelphia.

"problem for the new woman to solve," Shaw said, was "how to blend her broader, larger culture of the present with the devotion to duty, the loyalty to family, and the best service of life." The new woman must balance her head and heart to become the ideal human woman.

In the balance of the lecture Shaw addressed the question of what manner of "new man" would be required to be a fit mate for the "new woman." First, the new man would have to be a sound physical organism. This, of course, meant that he would have to rid himself of all habits that interfered with his physical development. She cited statistics compiled in institutions of learning that showed the young men of the day were continually deteriorating physically. "The reasons given by those who have studied the subject," she attested, "are insufficient nourishment in childhood among the poor, and the excessive use of tobacco and liquor among the growing youth of all classes." As a corollary, the new man must also "be intellectually developed to be the fit mate for the new woman." Tragically, Shaw told her audiences, statistics showed that the nation's high schools and grammar schools were graduating nearly two girls to one boy. The remedy was not to bar young girls from graduating, but to insist that young men also educate themselves for life's service. They must be made to discover that material wealth is a false value and that intellectual development is "more important than a bank account."

Moreover, Shaw said, the new man would try to determine "what God meant women to do, or rather not to do." Each person of both sexes should do what he or she was fitted to do. Women's working, Shaw explained, was not new; they always had been engaged in ceaseless, grinding toil. It was only when women demand fair compensation for their work that men objected. The only appropriate remedy, according to Shaw, was "equal pay for equal quality and quantity of work."

The new man must also be a moral man. The double standard would no longer do. The new woman should not be expected to degrade herself by lowering her moral standards to those of men; rather she should expect the new man to elevate himself to her level. "The new man and woman must stand upon the same moral plane," Shaw stated, "and it must be the one which men have erected for women." The new woman, would, of course, assume control of her physical substance, and hence men would no longer be able to dictate moral terms to her. Lastly, the new man must be just and "refuse to accept for himself either political or other privileges which he denies to women." Among the privileges shared by both sexes would, of course, be the right to vote. When both men and women were enfranchised, the country would have a republic that derived its power "from the consent of the governed women as well as governed men."

"God's Women"

"God's Women," a standard lecture that was one of Shaw's most amusing as well, appears in the report of the National Council of Women meeting held in Washington, D.C., from February 22 to 25, 1891. Apparently, the speech was initially stimulated by Shaw's reaction to an essay by a minister in which he defined what God's women were like and educed biblical examples to demonstrate his point. For her part, Shaw not only refuted his arguments, offering examples of her own, but also reacted to the efforts of religious leaders to reduce women to subservient positions within the church and in society. The extant text notes several points at which the audience responded with either laughter or applause, clear indications of their positive response to Shaw's arguments and wit. Shaw, who was seldom enthusiastic about or pleased with her own efforts, wrote to Clara Osburn:

> Never in my life did I make the success I did there at the Council with my Speech "God's Women." The audience cheered, stood up and waved their handkerchiefs and then broke out singing "Praise God from Whom All Blessings Flow," It was a perfect oration. I wish Father and Mother had been there. I thought of them all the time and how glad they would be.(19)

Beginning with a reference to a minister's essay, Shaw asserted that, while men in the nineteenth century had presumptuously defined women's roles and females had simply acquiesced, twentieth-century women would define themselves and identify their rights independent of men's interference.

> It has always seemed to me very remarkable how clear the definitions of men are in regard to women, their duties, their privileges, their responsibilities, their relations to each other, to men, to government, and now to God. . . . The woman of the nineteenth century has taken to definition, and she has come to the conclusion that it may be quite possible for a woman as well as a man to comprehend the relations of women to each other, to their homes, to the Church, to the State, and listen for the voice of God themselves, to know what the relation of women to the Divine God is.

She located the minister's attempt to constrain women in limited roles as part of a second phase through which any innovation must pass. In the initial phase, a reform was labeled impossible and ridiculous; in the second phase, theologians and other persons fearful of human corruption of divinely ordained religion raised strong objections to the proposed innovation, citing biblical texts and exegesis to confirm their views. The movement for suffrage, she noted, had been "passing through this phase for some time." Shaw next turned her attention to refuting the claims against women's greater freedom.

First, she used the example of Deborah to answer arguments that women should not be allowed to be ministers within the church. Not only did God select and ordain Deborah to fill this role for the Israelites at a crucial point, but also her influence brought forty years of peace to the nation. "We have never known such a period since that day," Shaw proudly pointed out. Next, she cited the example of Miriam to demonstrate again God's choice of a woman to exert great power in a crisis and to refute claims that women have only limited ability to reason. In the following section, Shaw responded to "the Ruths," "Rachels," and "Marys," the minister had presented as examples of God's women, either to note their limitations as "God's women" or to show how he had misconstrued their activities.

Finally, having presented Vashti, a dynamic, independent woman as her model for God's woman, Shaw responded to the minister's claim that motherhood is a woman's greatest glory. Motherhood, she averred, may be a dishonor as well as an honor and must have something behind it to make it a crown of glory; and that something is "*womanhood*--true, noble, strong, healthy, spiritual womanhood; the daughter of the King, the child of God, equal with the Bishop or of any man in the world. If the woman is first of all a woman, all things shall be to her a crown of glory, whether it be motherhood or spinsterhood."

Shaw's personal enthusiasm for this speech and her hearer's approval of it suggest the saliency of the topic for a contemporary audience. Certainly early in Shaw's career, some of the strongest opposition to women's rights was from established religious groups. In fact, a few years after this address Elizabeth Cady Stanton attempted to overcome these barriers with *The Woman's Bible*, which refuted passages that suggested inferior roles of women. While that document proved extremely controversial, Shaw was often successful in deftly refuting religious arguments through a combination of wit and exegesis, as her "God's Women" speech indicates.(20)

While neither of these speeches represents Shaw's best efforts, each reveals some features of her rhetorical practice quite well and conveys something of the flavor of her oratory. "God's Women," for example, shows her skills as a debater. Not only did she provide evidence that clearly refuted the unnamed minister's thesis but she also challenged his examples, proving their flaws and weaknesses. In so doing, particularly in her listing of possible "Marys," Shaw reduced her opponent's argument to rubble. She pointed out, for example, that one of the Marys was a "theological student with Christ" while her sister wanted her to stop that nonsense and cook the meal, but Christ rebuked Martha, not Mary. Another Mary stood by the tomb of the risen Lord and was given "the first divine commission from the Divine one himself to go out into the world and preach the gospel of a risen Lord." Finally, the Mary who was the mother of the Savior, Shaw averred, was absolutely the wrong Mary for the Bishop to prove his case, because God and woman gave the Redeemer to the world--man had nothing to do with it. The above example of the different Marys shows how Shaw co-opted the Bishop's arguments and turned them against him. Her clear-headed analysis made his argument and use of examples seem careless and even distorted. Furthermore, her discussion revealed her knowledge and mastery of biblical history, a significant asset to her ethos. The examples she proffered as "God's women" forcefully developed her argument that biblical sources confirm both the appropriateness of women's public activities and their skill as leaders. Providing evidence for her own claim in addition to refuting the minister's examples developed a strong case for her cause.

If Shaw revealed her skills as a debater, she also crafted an engaging rhetorical persona. Her humor and deft sarcasm conveyed good-natured amusement at the minister's apparent bigotry and demagoguery. In her treatment he became, despite his trappings of office and prestige, a pompous fool, more prejudiced than knowledgeable. Shaw, in contrast, emerged as bright, assertive, and good-humored. In addition, the final passage, which portrayed the "mother-heart" of women, affirmed her appreciation for women as nurturers and persons with strong social consciences.

> The mother-heart of woman, the mother-heart that reaches out to the race and finds a wrong and rights it, finds a broken heart and heals it, finds a bruised life ready to be broken and sustains it,--a woman instinct with mother-love, which is the expression of the Divine Love; a woman, who finding any wrong, any weakness, any pain, any sorrow, anywhere in the world, reaches out her hand to right the wrong, to heal the pain, to comfort the suffering,--such a woman is God's woman.

By emphasizing women's roles as servants of God, Shaw implicitly suggested her own piety and commitment.

The "New Man" also provides glimpses of how Shaw built identification with her audience by affirming their values and connecting her ideas with those values. For example, the qualities she insisted on for the "new" man were certainly not controversial: good physical conditioning, sound intellectual development, and high moral standards. By emphasizing the importance of these factors and their social implications, Shaw suggested the high-mindedness and constructive attitudes of the "new women," many of whom of course were suffrage supporters. Far from repudiating accepted social standards, Shaw asked a more elevated and stringent application of them to men as well as women.

Furthermore, Shaw connected "new women" and their activities to efforts to improve and purify society from, among other ills, the perils of alcohol and tobacco. Indeed, she castigated "false social ideals," including the valuing of material wealth above character, which does not serve the greater social good. If her tone and stance seemed at times a bit strident and moralistic, they also served to depict her cause as an almost "moral" crusade, led of course by women, to improve public social life.

Together these texts suggest why Shaw came to enjoy such high ethos, in spite of her devotion to the controversial cause of suffrage. Her good humor, earnestness, good sense, and allegiance to approved civic virtues reflected the components of ethos delineated by Aristotle.

As lecturer, Shaw dispelled many of the stereotypical traits of the nineteenth century "true" woman. She was a woman capable of doing things, including public speaking. She met lecture dates, despite the numerous adversities of the frontier, and demonstrated herself a woman not weak and prone to fainting, but strong and courageous; she did not have to look to man as her strength and shield, but was able to stand by his side and account for herself. Shaw was, in essence, the model for the new woman she advocated.

3

Campaigning for Suffrage: From "Bonnet Holder" to "Queen of the Suffrage Platform"

> Many of the noble women of the day were coming to East Dennis to lecture, bringing with them the stirring atmosphere of the conflicts they were waging . . . They were fighting great battles, these women--for suffrage, for temperance, for social purity--and in every word they uttered, I heard a rallying cry.
>
> *The Story of a Pioneer*, p. 147

When Shaw left the ministry, her goal was to devote herself to the great causes of her time. Initially, as we have seen, she worked as a general lecturer, although she spoke out especially forcefully for the causes of temperance and women's rights. Understanding Shaw's later primary devotion to and work for suffrage requires understanding both the links between these two movements and her relationship with Susan B. Anthony.

TEMPERANCE AND SUFFRAGE

Shaw's perceptions of a link between suffrage and temperance were not unique. Historically, the two movements had many ties and enrolled many of the same members. Most leading suffragists had prohibitionist sentiments. The early suffrage association, struggling desperately for a place in the sun, was at first glad to get the help of the well-established temperance union. In 1889, Susan Anthony, seeking an alliance with the Women's Christian Temperance Union (W.C.T.U.), went to one convention to help sway them to woman suffrage. Despite some sympathy, the W.C.T.U., perhaps wary of the radical new movement, refused to let Anthony appear on its platform. Willard, herself an ardent suffragist, fought resistance to suffrage inside the Union. By 1892 she was successful enough so that when Shaw (by then a member of the National American Woman

Suffrage Association) spoke to the Denver W.C.T.U. Convention, she was received with tumultuous applause and the characteristic waving of handkerchiefs.(1)

In the early days of the suffrage struggle, the W.C.T.U. was an important ally. Willard, an excellent organizer, brought together a large group of women under the innocuous slogan of "home protection." As her biographer noted, "Every new idea was interpreted in the light of home protection, every fresh endeavor was clothed in the romantic garb of safeguarding the home. The whole world, she announced, must be made more 'homelike.'" Gradually she fused prohibition and the franchise. Support from the W.C.T.U. with the motto "home protection" worked against the "home breaking" stigma that was sometimes attached to suffrage. Moreover, the temperance union had strong social approval; the clergy, prominent socialites, and many dignitaries aided their cause. Some of this prestige transferred to the suffrage movement.(2)

But this alliance also had drawbacks. For one thing, the liquor interests became alarmed. The endorsement of woman suffrage by the W.C.T.U., the temperance sentiment of most suffragists, and the general feeling that women were the nondrinkers caused the brewers and distillers to begin mobilizing to fight every attempt of the suffragists to win a legislature or a popular vote. Often, they were successful; a number of times they wrested apparent victory from the suffragists. Later, when the prohibition amendment became law, a Senate investigating committee uncovered an extensive and well-financed anti-suffrage organization. Thus, while the suffragists' marriage with the anti-liquor forces brought numbers and organizational machinery to their cause, it also brought a most potent foe.(3)

Some early suffragists perceived the dangers of this intermixing of suffrage and temperance. Abigail Scott Duniway of Oregon sensed that the connection would prompt liquor interests to mount strong opposition to suffrage initiation. At the 1889 national suffrage convention she gave a dramatic plea against the affiliation with temperance groups, declaring, "This humble leader must sound an alarm. She sees that her ships are being scuttled." This pugnacious leader ultimately became Shaw's greatest critic. She was concerned when in 1888 Susan Anthony persuaded Shaw, a national officer in the W.C.T.U., to join the suffrage forces. She curtly told Anthony that "this alliance would create a conflict between the two opposite extremes of force and freedom, that would defeat them both." Even after Shaw resigned her national temperance office, Duniway remained suspicious of her affiliation. Years later she charged, for example, that the W.C.T.U. "became a convenient receptacle for the meetings of Dr. Shaw and her hired auxiliaries in Oregon during the National Campaign of 1905-6, which swamped and wrecked us, and held us down for six successive years." From that point forward, Duniway made every effort to keep Shaw out of Oregon.(4)

Others were also concerned about Shaw's split allegiances. Before embarking on a South Dakota tour Susan Anthony declared, "If Miss Shaw will not proclaim herself a Methodist minister and an officer in the Women's Christian Temperance Union at every meeting, I'll pay her double what I would any other speaker." Anthony wanted Shaw fully dedicated to suffrage and as early as 1888, began to pressure her to work exclusively for suffrage. Shaw herself began to set clearer priorities for her work. In 1889, Shaw wrote to Lucy Anthony, "Aunt Susan is mistaken if she does not think I am already gone to woman suffrage, head, heart and hand, and that I am not now in the Temperance Union save in the interest of suffrage. . . . It is the only thing I would live in a grip-sack for and tramp this world over, homeless and houseless and alone. No, there doesn't live, not accepting Aunt Susan, a more thoroughly radical suffragist than I am."(5)

Shaw maintained an affiliation with the temperance union because she felt that there she could reach people that she could not reach through the suffrage association alone. She wrote to one friend that suffrage work was needed far more than temperance, for without the franchise, the temperance effort was useless. "When we ask men who love whiskey," she said, "to stop the sale of it and refuse to let women who do not love it have any voice in the matter we are simply putting the cart before the horse. Until women have a voice in protecting their homes and themselves, neither will have proper protection."

Finally, at Anthony's repeated urgings, Shaw decided to devote her efforts entirely to suffrage. In 1890, she resigned her official position as national superintendent of franchise in the W.C.T.U., although she remained as an honorary officer.(6)

Despite her other activities, Shaw never fully divorced herself from temperance interests. For example, in 1904 Shaw spoke at state W.C.T.U. meetings in Massachusetts, Pennsylvania, Wisconsin, and Illinois. The *Portland Morning Oregonian* reported that Shaw spoke at an interstate meeting of the W.C.T.U. June 28, 1905. In 1912 she spoke at a W.C.T.U. meeting in Columbus, Ohio. Moreover, throughout her career, Shaw reverted to temperance themes, often urging suffrage so that women could protect themselves, their homes, and society from the perils of liquor. Later, as president of NAWSA she welcomed W.C.T.U. assistance for suffrage campaigns. Moreover, she maintained her admiration for and friendship with Willard until the latter's death.(7)

SHAW AND ANTHONY

In 1887 when Shaw made her first speaking tour in Kansas, a state that women leaders were always hopeful of winning despite repeated failure until 1912, she met Susan Anthony. Although each woman knew of the other's work, they had never met. For her part Anthony had expressed reservations about Shaw because she was a Methodist minister, was involved with temperance, and was affiliated with the American Woman Suffrage Association (rather than the National Association founded by Stanton and Anthony). But Shaw's rhetorical skill in a local debate with Senator John J. Ingalls impressed Anthony, who was also very pleased by the wide publicity given to the encounter. The meeting was fortuitous, for Anthony was seeking new co-workers. Many of Anthony's closest friends and workers had become inactive because of age or death; even Elizabeth Cady Stanton, her closest companion, curtailed her activities. Anthony, herself nearing seventy, was looking for someone to continue her work. Her first meeting with Shaw lessened her prejudice and Shaw's considerable talents increased Anthony's interest in her. Later that year at the International Council of Women meeting in Chicago, after a night-long conversation, the two welded a relationship.(8)

After 1890, when Shaw began to work exclusively for suffrage, she and Anthony became permanent companions on the campaign trail, and, until Anthony's age forced her retirement, the two were seldom separated. Not only were they a source of support for each other, they got to know each other's mental processes so thoroughly that each perceived what the other was going to say in speaking situations. Thus, when Anthony sometimes suffered momentary strangulations because of throat contractions, Shaw, to the astonishment of the audience, would pick up her train of thought and finish. At first Shaw was somewhat in Anthony's shadow, but by 1895 she could write Lucy Anthony that she was receiving so much praise on her own account that she no longer felt that she was Aunt Susan's "bonnet holder." In 1900 she wrote: "I live and am happy. Such a meeting! Mr. Whelpley introduced me as the peer of Elizabeth Cady Stanton, Mary A. Livermore and Susan B. Anthony." Anthony thought so highly of Shaw's platform skills that she encouraged her to raise the price of her suffrage lectures, feeling that if she charged the standard rate people would never hire other lecturers.(9)

The relationship with Anthony, whom she called "Aunt Susan," was central in Shaw's life. In fact, she devoted two full chapters of her autobiography to "Aunt Susan." Besides praising her fortitude, stamina, and dedication, Shaw also extolled her character. Having described a night-long conversation in 1888, Shaw concluded in her autobiography:

In the eighteen years which followed I had daily
illustrations of her superiority to purely human
weaknesses. To her the hardships we underwent
later, in our Western campaigns for woman suffrage,
were as the airiest trifles . . . To me she was an
unceasing inspiration--the torch that illumined my
life. We went through some difficult years together
. . . but I found full compensation for every effort in
the glory of working with her for the Cause that was
first in both our hearts, and in the happiness of
being her friend . . . now it is of her I wish to write--
of her bigness, her manysidedness, her humor, her
courage, her quickness, her sympathy, her
understanding, her force, her supreme common-
sense, her selflessness; in short, of the rare beauty of
her nature as I learned to know it.(10)

Probably, the strong affection between the two women, which
was cemented by their experiences of the campaign trail,
deepened Shaw's already strong commitment to suffrage work.
Undoubtedly, the relationship was the core of Shaw's emotional
life. Recalling her presence at Anthony's death, Shaw declared,
"Kneeling close to her as she passed away, I knew that I would
have given her a dozen lives had I had them, and endured a
thousand times more hardship than we had borne together, for
the inspiration of her companionship and the joy of her
affection. They were the greatest blessings I have had in all my
life."(11)

Shaw's relationship with Anthony and her success on the
lecture circuit fostered reconciliation and later encouragement
from her parents. Her father, who had watched with some pride
the development of her career, was amazed by her success. In
February 1894 Thomas Shaw wrote his daughter: "It is now
forty-seven years since you were presented to me, a lovely little
valentine. Could I have seen your future as it now is how amazed
I would have been! Why, everything about you is phenomenal." A
year later he reminded his daughter that she probably owed
some of her success to Anthony who "is a passport wherever the
English language is spoken and most of the rest that know
anything." He closed the letter by telling Anna that he would
like to hear her views on the present status of the country, and
noted that "Grandma and I join in love to you."(12) As a lecturer
for suffrage, Shaw traveled throughout the United States,
addressing a wide variety of audiences. In 1890, the newly
merged National American Woman Suffrage Association
appointed Shaw national lecturer, an appointment that
broadened her speaking responsibilities and commitments. At
the 1892 national convention the Association designated her

vice-president-at-large, but her primary responsibility remained lecturing for the association. Even after assuming the presidency, she remained a stalwart on the campaign lecture circuit.

SHAW'S SUFFRAGE SPEECHES

Close examination of Shaw's suffrage speeches reveals considerable repetition and overlap. At least two factors account for this. First, because of the rigors of campaigning over a long period of time, Shaw, like many other speakers, did not always have the time or energy to prepare a fresh speech for every occasion. Instead, she developed stump speeches, which she varied slightly for particular audiences. Second, during the period from 1885 to 1910, the campaign for suffrage focused almost entirely on referenda in individual states. Thus, Shaw and other suffrage workers repeatedly confronted the same arguments from opponents and offered the same reasons for their position. Quite literally, they were forced to repeat themselves. As a consequence, Shaw relied on another standard rhetorical ploy: commonplaces that she inserted in various speeches. In her case, these were usually anecdotes or examples, often with a humorous edge. But also entire lines of argument recur in different speeches.

Another feature of these speeches is their rather loose organizational pattern. Although, as her sermons and other speeches indicate, Shaw could develop tightly reasoned and organized arguments, in her stump speeches she tended to a loose, sometimes almost rambling format. At times her discussions seem at best tangential to her central argument; at other points, particularly with her anecdotal materials, they seem to serve as almost comic relief in what were often quite long presentations. Evidence indicates that Shaw spoke invariably extemporaneously, using at most minimal notes. Her own reports also indicate that she enjoyed interaction with her audience and, like many good stump speakers, played to the crowd. Thus, the organizational looseness of these speeches probably does not reflect a lack of rhetorical skill, but rather the exigencies Shaw faced and her pragmatic, even shrewd adaptations to them.

"The Fate of Republics"

One of the first lectures on women's rights Shaw composed, this speech remained one of her most popular. Apparently, she chose it for her debut presentation at the first National Suffrage Convention she attended in 1889 and she continued to use versions of it for many years. A rough copy of this speech appears in Shaw's papers, but the most complete version of the text is in a report of a Congress of Women meeting in 1894, which is undoubtedly an abbreviated and condensed copy.(13)

Perhaps because it is probably condensed, the extant text differs from Shaw's other suffrage speeches in having a very succinct, clearly organized argument and in having far fewer anecdotal and humorous elements. Briefly, in the speech Shaw argued that since all republics reflect the character of the voters in them and since all have limited the franchise to men, their rather rapid declines follow a similar pattern. All have failed because they have aggressive and warlike spirits and because they lack the special qualities associated with women: morality, purity, temperance, religious loyalty, obedience to law, and love of peace. Shaw then addressed the question: "Is there anything in the nature of woman, differing from the nature of man in such a manner, that if women were permitted to vote it would enable them to affect the government differently from the way in which men affect it?" Her answer was, of course, in the affirmative and she offered several ways in which women differed from and were superior to men: they were more moral, more peace-loving, and more law-abiding. She supported her claims with varied evidence, including statistics on church attendance, the biblical example of Deborah, and statistics on prison inmates. She concluded by noting that the areas in which women were superior to men were precisely those that produce the fatal weaknesses in most republics. Enfranchisement of women could, she claimed, strengthen the United States Republic and, "for the first time in history the voice of God shall be crystallized into the laws of the republic."

While neither the ideas nor the arguments advanced in this speech are outstanding features, three that recurred throughout her later works do merit comment. First, Shaw skillfully managed to take certain stereotypes associated with women during the period and turn them into reasons for enfranchising women. In so doing, she avoided antagonizing her audience and also developed a rather clever twist on the expediency argument for suffrage. Women's influence was needed not just to achieve particular social reforms, but to act as a counterweight to the influence of men. One analogy she used to make this point here became a commonplace in her suffrage rhetoric: if the voice of the people is to be the voice of God as politicians claimed, it must include both the bass and the soprano registers. In effect, Shaw implied that both men and women were needed to constitute an effective citizenry for an enduring republic. Without belaboring the point, it is worth noting that modern feminist theorists have made similar claims about the differences between women and men and their impact in our social life.(14)

Second, the speech revealed Shaw's ability to master a variety of evidence to support her claims. While some of this material was not rigorous (e.g., Clara Bewick Colby's survey), Shaw's use of it was often quite effective. For example, her support of the claim that the nature of voters affected political decisions involveed two cases: cranberry farmers in the Northeast and the liquor interests nationwide. Both cases neatly and effectively proved her thesis and both rang true to even an unsympathetic listener. On another front, her use of Deborah as a biblical example, which she had used before, and her endorsement of the golden rule as a principle to govern political life added a religious flavor to her arguments, which built her ethos with many in her audience and defused some criticisms of suffrage supporters as irreligious.

Finally, the speech clearly showed Shaw's skill as an advocate. Her ability to construct cogent arguments and to use the attitudes of her audience to her advantage made her ideas appealing. Moreover, while she was forceful and direct, even her sarcasm (e.g., in pointing out the neglect of the women Pilgrims) was tempered with good humor. She attractively combined strong logical arguments with emotional appeals to construct a compelling case for suffrage.

"The Other Half of Humanity"

Although Shaw delivered this address in Birmingham, Alabama, on April 16, 1915, it reflected many arguments she had used throughout her advocacy for suffrage. Our copy of the speech is derived from a stenographic transcription; it was reprinted as a pamphlet and widely distributed by suffrage workers, who saw it as one of Shaw's best efforts.(15)

While this speech was much more disjointed and loosely organized than the preceding address, it had two clear, central thrusts. First, granting that a republic was a desirable type of government, if her audience accepted the definition of a republic as a form of government distinguished by rule by its citizens, then they had to admit that the United States did not currently qualify as a republic because women were citizens but were not allowed to participate in making political decisions. Disenfranchisement of women could not, Shaw contended, be defended as a proper qualification or limitation of the right to vote because sex was an insurmountable barrier unlike literacy or ownership of property. The United States was, in her terms, an oligarchy of sex.

On a second front, Shaw refuted the arguments of her opponents. In a fashion typical of her suffrage rhetoric, she attacked their arguments by pointing out the internal contradictions of anti-suffragists, who frequently made opposing claims. Their arguments, she jibed, "generally come in pairs. The anti-suffragists have the happy faculty of answering their own arguments." So, for example, Shaw noted that her opponents argued both that, since women would vote as their husbands did, enfranchisement would only double the count, and that allowing women the ballot would produce dissension and disorganization within families because of disagreements about issues and candidates. On another tack, she ridiculed the absurdity of other arguments. Among these was the claim that voting was unladylike. As Shaw observed, putting a ballot in a box was considerably more decorous than the lobbying efforts many of her opponents were already vigorously pursuing.

Shaw's refutation was characterized here and in other speeches not only by its logical force, but also by its use of ridicule and sarcasm. In answering opponent's arguments, Shaw frequently targeted unnamed persons (the young woman who had left her home to campaign against suffrage on the basis that women belonged at home and had no time to vote) to demonstrate the inconsistency and absurdity of their attitudes. But in these passages Shaw never seemed mean-spirited; rather her tone was one of friendly amusement. While she personalized her arguments with these individuals, her attack was on their ideas and attitudes, not on them as persons.

Among the other examples of Shaw's wit in this speech, two suggest how her humor functioned rhetorically. First, in the opening passage, which plays off of her ministerial background, she labeled her supporters saints and her opponents sinners and she offered her seat to any "sinner" so that the sinner might be comfortable during the speech, a state Shaw realized was essential for conversion. She continued in this vein, refering to the past when she was forbidden to speak on suffrage, in contrast to "today when I should be forbidden to speak on anything else." If these remarks produced chuckles and smiles in her audience, they also undoubtedly built her ethos with her listeners because they demonstrated that her serious intent and commitment did not produce pomposity or severity.

Later in the speech she reported how she answered an opponent's claim that voting would remove the bloom of femininity from women. First, Shaw turned this metaphor into an opportunity to comment on the cosmetic wiles of women before extending it to make a more serious point. Admitting that if one rubs the bloom from a peach, as her opponent has argued, it cannot be replaced, Shaw added, "I am glad to be able to assure the gentleman . . . there *is* a difference between the peach and the woman; for, give the woman five minutes and the opportunity, and the bloom will be restored just as it was before." By retelling the incident as a lively exchange, Shaw highlighted her own quick-wittedness and her good humor. By extending the metaphor to praise the bloom of womanhood that comes from within, Shaw was able to contrast his false ideal of femininity with the God-given moral character of women. Thus, Shaw's humor served both to enhance her rhetorical persona and to advance a serious, emotional argument.

Although many passages in this speech closely paralleled sections in "The Fundamental Principle of a Republic," which will be discussed in the next section, Shaw's discussion of her own gradual realization of the necessity of enfranchisement was distinctive. In relating her personal journey from the ministry to medicine and finally to public advocacy as means of helping women, Shaw was able to suggest quite forcefully the futility of stopgap measures to improve the plight of women. Her admission that she finally recognized that women were "a branded sex," who would have no fair chance until the stigma of political inferiority was removed, indicated to the listener a need for fundamental changes to achieve the American ideal of equal opportunity. Couching this argument in terms of her personal journey toward enlightenment added force and poignancy to her claims.

Also in this speech Shaw developed an implicitly racist argument. She warned American males about the domination of women by "every and any class of men under the sun!" While she disavowed any prejudice toward immigrants, noting she herself was one, her attitude was unmistakable when she declared adamantly: "It is time for us all to think that, if we are to save America's womanhood, if we do not wish to see it overwhelmed by external forces, we must give American women the power to save themselves." Undoubtedly, this argument was effective for many of her listeners, because it played to their fears and prejudices toward immigrants. Unfortunately, however, such arguments served to divide women along racial and ethnic lines, probably impeded the progress of women's rights in the long term. The problems of modern-day feminists in gaining support from minority groups and the widespread image of feminism as a white, middle-class movement may have roots in this argument from expediency developed by early suffragists.

"The Fundamental Principle of a Republic"

As references in the speech indicate, the text we have of this popular lecture is from a New York suffrage campaign. Although the particular setting was the City Opera House in Ogdenburg, New York, there is little doubt that Shaw gave versions of this text many times before and after, for it contains many of her standard suffrage arguments, her typical answers to opponents' claims, and her anecdotes and humorous passages.(16)

The name of the speech indicates one of its major arguments. Here, as elsewhere, Shaw advanced the claim that the United States was not a true republic, but an oligarchy of sex, because it deprived one group of citizens, women, of the right to participate in the electoral process. Shaw coupled this natural rights argument with one of her standard contentions that the wisdom and characteristics of both men and women were necessary for the best interests of the state. In a form of the expediency argument, she particularly emphasized the qualities of women-among them their love of peace--which would be useful to the nation and the world. Shaw also offered her typical refutation of opponents, using many of the same examples and much of the same language found in other efforts.

Although not limited to this speech, two other rhetorical strategies that are apparent here merit mention. First, Shaw developed a motif of consistency to undergird her arguments. This theme or motif is apparent in at least three areas. For example, in a humorous play with words Shaw jibed men for their consistent inconsistency in regard to the ballot. Noting that the nature of a republic requires rule by its citizens, Shaw pointed out how, despite their avowed allegiance to this principle, men in the United States had consistently tried to abridge this right on various bases, among them religion and ownership of property. Shaw, of course, argued that only systematic, consistent application of the fundamental principle of a republic could make the voice of the people the voice of God as politicians claimed. On another front, Shaw observed, as she frequently did, the inconsistency in her opponents' arguments. Furthermore, in contrast with the contradictions within the anti-suffragists, Shaw suggested the unanimity of her supporters; "We have our theories, our beliefs, but as suffragists we have but one belief, but one principle, but one theory and that is the right of a human being to have a voice in the government under which he or she lives, on that we agree, if on nothing else." In a minor point, she also contrasted the efforts in the ongoing war to end the notion of the divine right of kings with her side's efforts to end the divine right of sex. Taken together, these elements constituted a strong implicit argument and appeal for suffrage. Only that measure was consistent with the principles of a democratic republic.

Another significant theme in this speech was Shaw's pacifism. In a rather lengthy passage, Shaw also discussed the war and women's attitude toward it. While she fully supported the principles that were at stake in the confrontation, she also deplored the loss of lives and the emotional costs to all concerned. Later, she remarked on the ability of women at an international conference to come to accord without warfare on key issues of the day. Shaw's point seems to have been that women's inherent natures lead them to seek peaceful solutions and alternatives. While this was in one sense a form of the expediency argument, it also suggested Shaw's own pacifism. In large part, Shaw's strong commitment to suffrage lay in her conviction that women would not only be concerned with issues of social purity but also that they would seek to preserve the peace. Certainly, Shaw's emotional depiction of the costs of war was rhetorically expedient and persuasive to many in her audience. But at the same time it reflected Shaw's perception of the inherent difference between the sexes and her conviction of the salubrious effect women would have as voters.

Shaw gave several thousand speeches in behalf of woman suffrage. As Susan Anthony's hand-picked successor, she was unflagging about her commitment to carry the woman's question to tiny, remote hamlets as well as to major cities, often wearying of the hardships she had to endure in the process, but never relenting to bodily complaints. Her speeches were seldom polished orations, but were free-flowing and extemporaneously adapted to the audiences she was addressing. During the course of her career her argument shifted from expediency to principle, as is illustrated by the speeches examined in this chapter. She saw suffrage as an inherent right of an adult citizen in a democracy; to disfranchise women on the grounds of sex alone, she argued, produced a tyranny of sex that defied all principles of a republican form of government.

4

President of the National: Eleven Eventful Years

In the work I now took up I found myself much alone.

The Story of a Pioneer, p. 286

ASSUMING THE REINS

As early as 1896, Susan Anthony had expressed her intention of retiring as president of the national association when she reached the age of eighty. Soon a friendly but clear rivalry emerged between Carrie Chapman Catt and Anna Howard Shaw to become her successor. Although Shaw described the contest as the "unusual spectacle of rivals vigorously pushing each other's claims," she also acknowledged "my highest ambition had been to succeed Miss Anthony, for no one who knew her as I did could underestimate the honor of being chosen to carry on her work." For her part, Anthony had a strong preference for Shaw, who had been vice-president-at-large for eight years and who had been her sturdy co-campaigner before that. But she was determined to adopt a "hands-off" policy regarding her successor.(1)

Although few dispute Anthony's opinion of Shaw's contributions and value to the movement, Catt had important assets for the job and the strong support of the *Woman's Journal* through editorials by the Blackwells. On a pragmatic level, Catt could afford to take the position without remuneration because her financially successful husband was very supportive of her work. Shaw, in contrast, was still dependent on her lecturing to support herself. Moreover, Catt's background as head of the organization department had honed her natural talents as an effective fund-raiser and organizer. Shaw herself commended Catt's organizational and executive abilities. She later recalled, "Mrs. Catt had been chairman of the organization committee, and through her splendid executive ability had built up our

organization in many states . . . . In my mind there was no
question of her superior qualification for the presidency.   She
seemed to me the logical and indeed the only possible successor
to Miss Anthony; and I told 'Aunt Susan' so with all the
eloquence I could command."   Finally, Shaw withdrew her name
from consideration to expedite Catt's nomination.   Later she
admitted that "in urging Mrs. Catt's fitness for the office I made
the greatest sacrifice of my life." Without a serious rival, Catt was
selected almost unanimously.(2)

During the four years of her tenure, Catt proved an able and
effective leader.   But in 1904 some health problems and her
growing commitment to international suffrage work led her to
refuse to stand for reelection.   Anthony, concerned about the
future of the organization, wrote to Shaw: "I don't see anybody in
the whole rank of our suffrage movement to take her place but
you. . . . We must not let the society down into *feeble* hands. . . .
Don't say *no*, for the *life of you* . . . we must *tide over* with the
best material that we have, and *you are the best*." Out of
devotion to and respect for Anthony, Shaw obeyed her
command. But she wrote, "I yielded with the heaviest heart I
have ever carried, and after my election to the presidency at the
national convention in Washington I left the stage, went into a
dark corner of the wings, and for the first time since my
girlhood 'cried myself sick.'"(3)

PROBLEMS AT THE NATIONAL

Shaw's ascension to the presidency of the NAWSA came at a
difficult time for the movement.   Suffragists later dubbed the
period between 1896 and 1910 "the doldrums" to describe the
stymied progress in gaining suffrage.   Before 1904 only four
western states with a total of seventeen electoral votes had
granted full suffrage to women and no new states had been
added to the list since 1896.   In Washington, the suffrage bill
had not received a favorable committee report from either house
since 1893 and no report had left a committee since 1896.
Efforts to press for a national amendment had been largely
abandoned after that time. Despite yearly conventions to sustain
enthusiasm, membership in 1904 stood at only 17,000, perhaps
a solid base for activities but hardly an impressive enrollment
after the many years of suffrage work.   Thus, interest in the
movement, as reflected in membership growth, was low.   In
contrast, for example, the Woman's Political Union, organized in
January 1907 in New York by Harriet Stanton Blatch, had
19,000 members by October 1908. Blatch, in explaining her
reasons for establishing the Union, described the state of the
suffrage movement in New York.   Her comments probably
reflected conditions and sentiments in other areas: "The
suffrage movement was completely in a rut in New York State at

the opening of the twentieth century. It bored its adherents and repelled its opponents."(4)

In addition, the NAWSA itself had substantial problems, which were to plague Shaw throughout her tenure. In the first place, the National struggled to continue its activities on many fronts while chronically short of funds. State organizations eagerly sought financial help from the national association for their campaigns, but were less enthusiastic about their contributions to NAWSA. Even more problematic was the structure and organization of the National. Until 1909, the center of operations for the organization was Warren, Ohio, simply because it happened to be the home of Harriet Taylor Upton, the treasurer. The lack of a national headquarters produced considerable inefficiency that added to Shaw's work. As she once reported to the Executive Board, "The difficulty in our work is that much of it is done twice over. Much of it comes to Mrs. Upton at Headquarters [then Warren, Ohio]; some of it comes to me and when I am at home I immediately attend to it, and in that way, it is given double attention and creates some confusion." A generous gift in 1909 enabled the organization to establish a national headquarters in New York, which alleviated some of these difficulties.(5)

In addition to the lack of a national headquarters, the officers and executive board of the organization were widely dispersed. Because the president's powers were officially rather limited, many decisions about fairly routine matters, such as dispersing funds for office functions, had to be resolved by polling persons by mail. Catt, during her tenure, had exercised considerable executive power, only infrequently consulting the board. In contrast, Shaw adopted a more democratic approach. Thus, she wrote to the officers frequently, sometimes long letters more than once a week, to report on activities and to poll them on decisions. This correspondence was time-consuming, cumbersome, and unsatisfactory as a means of discussing issues and resolving problems, particularly in the light of the growing number of members and the scale of activities. In 1911, Shaw complained to the national board that "to attempt to conduct business of the Association by correspondence, is an absolute impossibility."(6)

During Shaw's tenure, tensions within the association also mounted and sapped her energy. As individual states mounted campaigns, they turned to the national association for financial support and speakers and workers to help with their efforts. But when the national association tried to coordinate efforts and exert some control over the activities they were assisting, state groups became belligerent. On one level the cleavages were geographical. Women in the South, Midwest, and West were increasingly critical of the eastern-based national association that they felt did not understand their problems or how to work

effectively in their regions.   For example, many southern and
western workers supported efforts to push for suffrage for white
women only, recognizing that the prejudices toward and fears of
blacks and Mexicans made many politicians very uncomfortable
with full female suffrage.   National leaders, however, were more
reluctant to pursue such opportunistic approaches.   Even
sensible and well-intentioned efforts by the national association
to overcome the administrative chaos by scheduling bi-monthly
meetings of the board at the New York headquarters exacerbated
tensions because the required quorum of five members could
easily be obtained with no representatives from the South or
West.(7)

On another level, the largely futile efforts of the national
association to gain endorsement for suffrage within states
frustrated many younger women, who favored more militant and
aggressive action.   Harriet Blatch's conclusion that "a vital idea
had been smothered by uninspired methods of work" and her
frustration with the stagnation she perceived in the national
association led her to organize what became known as the
Women's Political Union.   At a meeting with like-minded
women, Blatch concluded, "We all believed that suffrage
propaganda must be made dramatic, that suffrage workers must
be politically minded."   Others took even more dramatic actions.
When Woodrow Wilson won the 1912 election, defeating
Theodore Roosevelt's Progressive party, which had included a
suffrage plank in its platform, Alice Paul and Lucy Burns
organized and conducted a parade on the day before Wilson's
inauguration.   The rough treatment of the marchers garnered
public sympathy and support for the suffragists.   At first with the
support of the NAWSA, Paul, who even retained her post as head
of the Congressional Committee, formed the Congressional
Union, which focused on obtaining a suffrage amendment to the
Constitution.   Although relations were at first harmonious, the
Union's increasing insistence on concentrated efforts toward the
amendment and its disagreement with the National's
relationship to state organizations produced great tensions.
Shaw strongly disliked any militant tactics, and became
suspicious and critical of the Union and its leaders.   At one
point, she wrote to an officer in the Virginia state association, "I
consider it [the formation of the Union and its activities] the
greatest blow that has been struck at our movement for many a
year. . . . I think the Congressional Union is the greatest foe that
suffrage has ever had in its history-much more damaging than
the anti-suffragist associations, and its methods are the most
unprincipled of any body of women I have ever known."(8)

Matters reached a critical point in 1914 over the proposed
Shafroth-Palmer amendment, which had been developed by a
member of the NAWSA leadership without the Executive Board's
knowledge.   Briefly, the proposal would have required any state

to hold a referendum on woman suffrage if eight percent of the voters in the last election signed an initiative petition to do so. Supporters saw this approach as expediting the process of getting state referendums and believed it would gain the support of senators who saw a national amendment as infringing on states' rights. To Paul and the Congressional Union, the proposal conflicted and undermined their pressures for a national suffrage amendment. Shaw, who was not by any means enthusiastic about the measure, nonetheless supported it. When the issue became a point of controversy at the 1914 Convention, Shaw somewhat unfairly became the focus of disgruntlement. A bungled effort to allow Shaw to resign gracefully--the petition reached the press before Shaw had a chance to consider it-- angered her and she stubbornly refused to step down. But by 1915, tensions within the association and the need for a more skillful administrator at the helm forced Shaw to resign. Catt, with Shaw's strong endorsement, resumed the post for which she was in truth much better suited.(9)

SHAW'S PRESIDENTIAL ORATORY

Circumstances forced Shaw to continue her regular lecturing during the early part of her tenure as president. In fact, Shaw herself had foreseen that necessity and realized the problems it would create for her as president. She responded to Susan Anthony's urging that she take the job, "If I continue to earn my living, I cannot do the work of the presidency and if I attend to that I cannot earn my living." Fortunately, in 1906 a fund was established to pay the officers of the NAWSA and a bequest in April of 1908 provided a modest stipend. Later, Shaw labeled the gift "a most welcome help," but in a letter to Lucy Anthony at the time she described her reaction more candidly: "I could scarcely keep from fainting. . . . I know what I need; it is not treatment but rest and freedom from heartache and worry . . . . To think I am on a salary! My, but I am rich."(10)

Some relief from the pressures of lecturing for a living was undoubtedly welcome to Shaw, although she continued to campaign vigorously as much as her duties would permit. But the office itself introduced new speaking demands and opportunities. While much of Shaw's oratory during this period closely resembles her earlier efforts, the slightly different contexts produced some new opportunities and strategic adaptations that merit consideration. In addition to her standard campaign speeches, as president Shaw was expected to appear before legislative bodies that were considering any actions on suffrage and to give presidential addresses at the conventions of the NAWSA. These particular audiences and situations presented Shaw with new rhetorical challenges.

Dr. Anna Shaw speaking at Sea Cliff, Long Island, New York, August 31, 1913. The Schlesinger Library, Radcliffe College.

Legislative Addresses

Before assuming office she had appeared before legislative bodies several times to speak in behalf of suffrage, although versions of only four such speeches are extant. As president and afterwards until her death, she appeared at least eleven times, five times before United States Senate committees, four times to House of Representative Committees, once to a Pennsylvania commission, and once to the New Jersey legislature. None of these is a great speech and most, because of their abbreviated form, lack the liveliness and wit that characterized Shaw's best efforts. The best presentation was probably Shaw's appearance before a 1913 Senate committee. Not only did the committee give a favorable report about the suffrage amendment, but the Anti-Suffrage Association prohibited its members from engaging in debate with Shaw. Other legislative speeches do, however, contain strategies which were not common in Shaw's other speeches.(11)

First, they pay more attention to the impact and functioning of woman suffrage in areas like the western states where it had been adopted. Shaw's repeated points in these passages were that granting women suffrage had often had a salubrious effect and had never produced the problems opponents claimed. For example, in her 1902 appearance before a Senate Select Committee on Woman Suffrage, in the closing speech of the hearing, Shaw urged the appointment of a group to investigate the results of woman suffrage where it had been enacted. Noting that in earlier years supporters had been forced to rely on theory to urge suffrage, Shaw observed that the twenty-one years that had elapsed in some areas since women had been allowed to vote "at least is a long enough time to measure the effect of a mode of action upon the life of an individual or that of a company of individuals. We women are perfectly willing to let our case rest upon the result of suffrage in those States."(12)

Second, most of the speeches specifically urged an amendment to the Constitution to guarantee women the right to vote. (This proposal, dubbed the Anthony amendment, was first urged as the Sixteenth Amendment, but as time passed without action, its numerical order changed until it was finally the Nineteenth Amendment.) Not only did Shaw offer her standard arguments for suffrage to support this appeal, but she also drew attention to the difficulty supporters faced in trying to achieve suffrage on a state-by-state basis. For example, in her 1908 appearance before another select committee, Shaw pointed to Finland, Norway, and Denmark as having granted women the vote. "This so-called Republic," she added, "stands almost alone among progressive nations in continuing to withhold from women political enfranchisement." Her analysis of the causes for that situation was compelling:

The reason is not hard to discover, for we can not believe it is due either to the fact that the men of this nation are less just than those of other countries, not that our women are less patriotic or less capable of exercising the suffrage than are women of other lands. It is due rather to the more difficult method by which suffrage is conferred. In the nations of the older civilizations where suffrage has been conferred upon women it is necessary to obtain a majority vote of the parliament, which has the power within itself to grant it, while in this nation each State has its separate legislative body, in which not only is a majority demanded, but in some States a two-thirds majority of one and sometimes two consecutive legislatures, not to grant the law, but to submit an amendment to the State constitution to the electors, where again a majority, and in some cases a two-thirds majority, vote of all electors voting at the election is required to carry it. When we consider the character of our electorate, educated and ignorant, good and bad, wise and otherwise, foreign and native born, white and black, such a task is indeed formidable. Still, these are not all the obstacles with which we are met. Powerful influences, with which the gentlemen of the committee are familiar, hedged about by vast organizations, unlimited wealth, and political party machinery, smother the bill in the committees, prevent the measure from being reported to the various legislatures, much less from being submitted to the voters. It is because of these almost insurmountable obstacles which impede the progress of woman's political freedom that we make our appeal to Congress, asking for a seventeenth amendment to the National Constitution, forbidding the disfranchisement of United States citizens on account of sex.

Her plea in many of these appearances was simply that the committee in question report the proposal out of their hearings and allow the full House or Senate to consider it. Such a report would, she contended, both allow fairer, fuller consideration of the proposal and expedite the process of granting women their citizenship rights.

In a related vein, in many of these speeches, Shaw alluded directly to the sustained, long-frustrated efforts of women to gain a fair hearing. For example, in her 1915 statement to the House Judiciary Committee, she began: "This, I believe is the forty-fifth year since the first introduction of the resolution of which I wish to speak. . . . We come again this year with the same hope and same expectation which we have had in our hearts all these 45 years, and as I look over your committee and over the ladies present I find that I am the only woman alive and the only person alive who was present at that first meeting." Later she pointed out that she had labored the longest of any suffragist for "this fundamental principle of freedom and justice." Although these points were logically irrelevant to a consideration of the merits of the proposal, they may well have had a psychological impact on her hearers. Not only did they suggest the dedication and determination of the supporters but they also took advantage of Shaw's considerable public ethos at this time. Her physical demeanor and rather grandmotherly appearance lent the comments a special poignancy.(13)

What was largely missing in these speeches were the anecdotes, the detailed refutation, and the humor of her campaign efforts. Her tone was quite sober, often almost pleading, rather than aggressively assertive. Shaw clearly was not angry with nor humbled and intimidated by the legislators; but one does get a clear sense of her frustration with the repeated delays and the powerlessness of women to overcome or circumvent this procedural obstacle.

Presidential Rhetoric

As president of the association, Shaw was expected to give a formal address at their annual conventions, somewhat similar in tone and substance to a state of the union speech by our national chief executive. Of these official speeches, we have a partial copy of her 1904 acceptance speech and complete versions of her 1905 and 1906 presidential addresses to the conventions, as well as her 1915 farewell presentation. The passages of the 1904 and 1910 speeches, which are from transcriptions, reflect the usual problems stenographers had with Shaw's rather rapid delivery. But the 1905 and 1906 speeches, both published in the *Woman's Journal*, are probably based on Shaw's own manuscripts, as is the pamphlet that contains her farewell address.

Undoubtedly, Shaw's sense of the seriousness and formality of these occasions prompted her to abandon her usual extemporaneous delivery and to develop a full manuscript. A report in *The Morning Oregonian* of Shaw's 1905 speech, given at the convention in Portland, specifically refers to this departure from her standard practice: "The annual address of the president, Rev. Anna H. Shaw, did not disappoint the large audience, which packed the church in anticipation of hearing this famous speaker. An unusual press of business made it necessary for her to read her address, which slightly detracted from her usual charm of delivery, but what she had to say was clear and to the point, and time and again she had to wait for the applause of the enthusiastic audience to subside." Regarding her 1906 address, *The History of Woman Suffrage* observed, "Although it was a statesmanlike document the audience missed the spontaneity, the sparkle of wit, the flashes of eloquence that distinguished her oratory above that of all others, and there has been a general demand that hereafter she should give them in the spoken instead of the written word." Shaw, apparently as sensitive as ever to the requirements of her audience, acceded to this demand in her future speeches.(14)

Like her legislative speeches, none of her presidential addresses is memorable in its own right. Stylistically, because they were fully composed before delivery, these speeches show more polish and clear attempts at eloquence than many of her other efforts. For example, the two presidential addresses for which we have complete copies show considerable rhetorical flair in their introductions. Both begin with a reference to the convention locale and discuss historically important, but somewhat underrated women from those areas--in Oregon it was Sacajawea, the Shoshone who guided the Lewis and Clark expedition, and in Baltimore she mentioned both Margaret Brent, who was the first woman to own land in her own right, and Mary Catherine Goddard, a Revolutionary War newspaper printer. Shaw used these examples both to inspire her audiences about the past contributions of women and to emphasize how the contributions of women had been and continued to be overlooked by many in society. This approach paved the way for her further discussion of issues and concerns that confronted the organization in their efforts to gain political equality for women.

Some passages contained more carefully crafted language than was typical of Shaw's extemporaneous works. For example, the conclusion to her 1905 speech developed what was for her a rather lengthy parallel series:

> If you think our organization worth while, come and help us make it worth while. If you believe the ideal of self government is a good one; if freedom is worth having; if work for the public good is worth doing; if the problems of human development are worth solving; if it is worth while to be one with the infinite in bringing to pass order and peace and justice in human governments, then our ideal should be our life; the very breath of our body.

In addition to being more stylistically polished, these speeches differed from her other efforts in tone. Although Shaw was always earnest in her lectures, her presidential addresses contained little of the reported repartee and few of the anecdotes that enlivened other efforts. Shaw was not more earnest in these speeches; rather, her earnestness was less frequently relieved by her usually characteristic wit and humor. This consistently serious tone was certainly appropriate to her position and the occasion, but, as the reports cited above reveal, it was not suitable for Shaw. Her strength as a rhetor was due, in part, to her spontaneity and platform charm. These speeches were almost stolid in comparison to her better efforts.

Substantively, the speeches displayed many features of an incumbent president's state of the union address. In the first place, they treated many of the same topics. They discussed progress made by the movement, they highlighted continuing concerns and issues, and they made at least some suggestions for future action. For example, in 1905, Shaw declared that the women's movement had made amazing progress since its inception at Seneca Falls. She avowed, "More has been accomplished for the betterment of the condition of women, for their physical, economic, intellectual and religious emancipation, by these 57 years of evolutionary progress, than by all the revolutions the world has known." In 1908, attempting to rally women during a period when little progress was being made, Shaw even more forcefully delineated the progress of the movement as she listed the changes wrought by the efforts of the suffragists in sixty years. To answer charges that the progress had been minimal, Shaw observed that even Christianity in nineteen hundred years had not been fully successful in bringing about peace.(15)

As real progress began to occur, Shaw was able to be even rosier in her assessments. By the 1911 speech, Shaw could point with pride to the success of referenda in California and Washington. Enthusiastically, she exclaimed, "The eighteen months which have elapsed since our last convention have been permeated with suffrage activity. Never in an equal length of time has there been such rapid progress in the enlistment of recruits and the development of active service." In her farewell address in 1915, partially in defense of her own tenure as president, Shaw went into some detail about the organization's accomplishments during the previous twelve years. With some eloquence, she concluded, "But why stop with a recital of our victories? Why not recount what we have lost? Because there is nothing to recount on the lost side. We have lost nothing, not an inch of the territory we have won. Ours is a winning, not a losing game. We have only victories, successes, and more victories to recount."(16)

The issues she mentioned that concerned women were often far-ranging. Included in her 1905 address, along with the somewhat predictable topic of marriage and divorce, were discussions of an educational movement known as the school city, which she commended as being an ideal training ground to prepare males and females for citizenship, and of an agricultural conference, which she saw as paving the way for peaceful cooperation among nations. One function of introducing such diverse topics and locating them within the realm of concerns for suffrage supporters was to suggest the areas in which women's influence through the ballot would have an important impact.

Her 1906 address suggests how skillfully Shaw was able to use current issues for her own rhetorical purposes. In that speech, she referred to a section of Theodore Roosevelt's state of the union address that called for an investigation of the condition of women in industry to introduce an issue she saw as a continuing concern for women. Endorsing such investigation wholeheartedly, since suffragists had been urging it for years, Shaw continued to disagree with the president's claims that the introduction of women into industry had produced "change and disturbance in the domestic and social life of the nation" and that "the decrease in marriage, and especially in the birth rate, have been coincident with it." With typical forcefulness, she questioned and refuted his claims. In Shaw's analysis, the presence of women in industry supplied another reason for granting them suffrage: "One can not but wish that with his recognized desire for 'fair play' and his policy of 'a square deal,' it had occurred to the President that, if five millions of American women are employed in gainful occupations, every principle of justice known to a republic would demand that these five millions of toiling women should be enfranchised to enable them to secure enforced legislation for their own protection."(17)

Although presidents in state of the union addresses often recommend particular legislative actions, Shaw's situation required a slightly different tack. Because the goal of her association was clearly delineated, she had to focus on the means to achieve the agreed upon end. Thus, she often made general calls for sustained work on the part of supporters rather than specifying particular actions. For example, in 1905 she urged the need for greater organization to produce a target of 100,000 members before the close of the next decade. After clearly explaining why that number was feasible, she concluded: "There is hope for the future success of our work only in organization adequate to its needs, active, persevering, aggressive, determined. In that word lies hidden the secret of all success. Organize in every direction. Do not take for granted that the people of any community or race or nationality or creed are wedded unalterably to past prejudices, and refrain from seeking their aid. Organize, not a month before a campaign, but now, and keep at it continually." Her farewell address in 1915 included a list of four "lines of campaign," two of which again called for organizational efforts; the other two recommended sustained work toward a national amendment and toward state referenda.(18)

The parallel between Shaw's speeches and presidential state of the union addresses must not, however, be overdrawn. Despite the similarities, the audience for and context of Shaw's speeches placed different constraints on her and she responded accordingly. Because her audience was fully supportive of her position, Shaw did not need to generate an audience for her cause as a president might be required to do. But she had to inspire her supporters and sustain them in their efforts. She did this not only by optimistically predicting the triumph of their cause, but also by reiterating the significance of suffrage. Thus, for example, she pointed to problems with controlling "vice" (e.g., prostitution) and to the decline in civic responsibility as evidence of the need for women to be able to vote to protect their homes and society as a whole. She insisted that women would be more sensitive to and would support measures to correct the plight of many children.(19)

These speeches also differed in substance and focus from her other efforts. For example, she spent some time in each of her speeches responding to critics of the movement. In contrast to her campaign speeches, which dealt with the arguments typically presented by her opponents, Shaw's presidential addresses discussed current objections to and threats confronting the movement. Thus, for example, in 1905 she responded to an essay by Mary St. Leger Kingsley Harrison, published under the pseudonym Louis Malet, which explored the "retrograde" movement against women's rights. Shaw drew attention to areas such as education and employment in which this movement had had an impact. These occurrences, she explained, proved the need for sustained effort and renewed vigilance by suffragists. But she also cleverly used the vehemence and visibility of the opposition and the activities of the retrograde movement to prove the vitality of her organization. After listing a group of their attackers, Shaw quite forcefully observed:

> A dead movement does not arouse the antagonism of great sensational magazines, nor would it pay to employ expensive writers to impede its progress. A decaying cause does not demand redoubled energies to stop its onward movement. The Church does not step aside from its purpose of regenerating human souls to block the march of a funeral procession. Great ex-statesman do not give up the joys of hunting and fishing to produce labored philippics on the Garden of Eden, and issue divine edicts against the dangerous aggressions of a cemetery. The movement which calls forth such frenzied opposition is not dead; it is not even sleeping.(20)

In 1906, besides responding to Roosevelt's concerns about women in industry, Shaw confronted comments made by an unidentified "Oracle of Baltimore," who argued that women should remain in the home. She refuted this viewpoint, arguing for a new notion of the home and a more modern attitude toward family life. She concluded that "woman is more than a home-maker; she is an individual, and as such she needs for her protection and development all that any other individual needs home-maker, or citizen, she needs the ballot, the only power known in a republic by which a citizen may protect his interests and the interests of the State." In the section following this firm avowal, Shaw urged her listeners to take themselves and their cause seriously. She had once told an author that she saw self respect as the greatest need of American women; Shaw now argued that in some ways the attitudes conveyed by the "Oracle of Baltimore" reflected women's acquiescence in their subjugation. "The time has come," she asserted "when women must question themselves to learn how far they are personally responsible for this almost universal disrespect, and then to set about changing it. They should refuse to submit to being referred to as unthinking, irrational and hysterical beings, petty and uncontrolled by reason and common sense."(21)

As these passages indicate, Shaw was aware of the need both to inspire and empower her listeners. Particularly during this bleak period in the history of suffrage work, the frustrations and lack of progress in gaining suffrage sapped the energies of even devoted workers. Shaw's strategies of highlighting the significance of the cause and of insisting that women had both the responsibility and power to promote change were rhetorically well-conceived. Although these speeches do not reveal Shaw at her oratorical highpoint, they do reveal her keen sense of audience and her rather skillful adaptation to different rhetorical constraints. Probably, the limitations of these speeches stem more from the genre itself than from Shaw's skills. Certainly, the fit between genre and rhetor was not a good one. Shaw's forte was argument; her best arena the campaign platform. But her presidential addresses suggested both her rhetorical sensitivity and her skills.

ASSESSMENT OF SHAW AS PRESIDENT

Although she remained without peer as a campaign orator and although the members of the association retained great respect for her and appreciated her unstinting efforts for the cause, Shaw's tenure as president of NAWSA ended on an unpleasant note. Her resignation at the 1915 convention came only after tremendous tensions with the governing board of the association and earlier efforts to oust her as president. A full assessment of the problems Shaw inherited as president and those she created within the association are beyond the scope of this work.   In fairness, however, some points do merit attention.

First, Shaw became president of an extremely poorly organized and coordinated organization. A bitter fight in 1900 had resulted in the disbandment of the Organization Committee, which had been headed by Catt and which had been very important in coordinating efforts within the organization. Because the lack of such a committee handicapped Shaw administratively, holding her solely responsible for the problems of coordination and organization during her tenure is unfair.(22)

In the same way, the very cumbersome structure of the organization of the association and the lack of a national headquarters made Shaw's work almost impossible. The sheer volume of correspondence was daunting and as the number of state initiatives grew, this burden increased. Since Shaw was also in demand as a speaker and in fact earned her living during her first year as president by lecturing, the workload engendered by the association's structure was almost impossible to manage. Shaw herself realized this and often complained about the endless demands on her time.

On the other hand, Shaw had little training or aptitude for administrative work. Within the association her responsibilities had always been campaigning, in contrast to Catt, who had worked in organizing and recruiting. Shaw was also not a political strategist; her forte was argument and her usual style was confrontation. Nothing in her background had ever encouraged her to think strategically; instead she had relied on candor and determination to work her will. Her hard won confidence in her own abilities and a firm conviction that she was right, both of which served her well as a campaigner, often became liabilities in her dealings with her peers within the association. Often she was impatient with those with whom she disagreed and she developed "a tendency to greet any and all signs of awakening initiative in the ranks as political insurgency." Finally, Shaw, like all people, was a product of her own generation. While she saw herself as a progressive thinker, she was not in tune with the younger generation of suffragists and was often critical of their efforts. Thus, she remained firmly opposed to confrontational tactics and deplored many of the activities of persons like Alice Paul, although she was forced to acknowledge their final success.(23)

Despite the problems she confronted as president and the difficulties she engendered, her administration compiled a relatively favorable record. During her tenure the number of states with full suffrage rose from four to eleven, and Illinois added presidential suffrage. She had guided the association out of the doldrums and into a period of renewed strength and activity. The membership rose during her tenure from 17,000 in

1904 to 183,000, a substantial increase.   Moreover, other suffrage groups had added still more women to those pressing for suffrage. The annual budget rose from $5,000 to between $40,000 and $50,000, and the organization moved from sponsoring one state campaign in ten years to five to ten annually.(24)

Shaw had also encouraged and supported many activities for which others got full credit.   She participated in suffrage parades, visited states to help workers plan activities, supervised the distribution of literature, and continued her own lecture efforts, which were almost always successful.   Under her guidance the Men's League for Woman Suffrage was organized, which proved quite helpful in New York.   Moreover, she remained a staunch, uncompromising advocate of full suffrage for women. She never faltered in her dedication to that cause and never considered partial or attenuated reforms. In short, while she was not a perfect leader and administrator, she was a stalwart advocate for woman suffrage during a challenging and difficult period.(25)

5

Helping Win the War: Recipient of the Distinguished Service Medal

> This call of your country is not one you may or may not answer at
> your will. It is as obligatory as is the call of the men to the field.

Woman's War Service, Linkugel, vol. 2, p. 894

Shaw's resignation from the presidency removed her from the
daily pressures and the hectic pace of the national office. The
role of honorary president permitted her greater freedom and
leisure. At sixty-eight, with thirty years of vigorous campaigning
behind her, she merited some relaxation. In 1908 she had built
a lovely house on eight acres in Moylan, Pennsylvania, the
"realization of a desire I have always had--to build on a tract
which had a stream, a grove of trees, great boulders and rocks,
and a hill site for the house with a broad outlook, and a railroad
station conveniently near." She looked forward to spending
more time there because she was, as she claimed about all
suffragists, very fond of her home. She insisted that the
conviction that one was fighting for the home inspired all
suffragists and that the privations of campaigning made them
think "most tenderly of home." In a 1918 speech on women's
war efforts, she admitted that "I frankly confess I had expected
when I reached the ripe young age of seventy to give up work
and do anything I liked the rest of my days, and I resigned the
position which I formerly held for the special
purpose of having a real good time from seventy to eighty and
then to begin thinking on the after life."(1)
   Although stepping down was difficult for Shaw, she
accomplished it with some grace. With admirable magnanimity,
she gave Carrie Chapman Catt what one scholar termed
"unstinting loyalty." She wrote something of her reactions to the
new leadership to Lucy Anthony. "The new group is taking hold
and doing things splendidly . . . . I realize that my day except for

speaking and 'inspiring' has gone by, and this is all right; I will speak and 'inspire' my best. I might do worse, I suppose."(2)

CONTINUING THE FIGHT

Shaw's efforts to ease the transition for the new leadership and her desire to inspire other suffragists led her to write her autobiography, *Story of a Pioneer*, which was published in September of 1915. Elizabeth Jordan, in a tribute to Shaw after her death, recalled the events surrounding the writing of the book. Jordan, as literary advisor to a publishing house, approached Shaw about writing her autobiography, which she felt would be "extremely interesting reading," because Shaw's life was so interwoven with the woman suffrage cause that the history of one would be the history of the other and would inevitably help the cause.

With a stenographer recording her recollections, Shaw recounted the events of her life, some Jordan called "intensely painful," others "almost intolerably bitter, with the splendid frankness of her nature." Unfortunately perhaps, Jordan, for her part, felt entrusted and responsible for editing the transcriptions. Frequently, she signaled the stenographer to stop transcribing when Shaw rehearsed some particularly "intimate experience" that Jordan saw as a result of Shaw's lapsing into "subconscious speech." Jordan was determined not only to let Shaw tell her story but also to assure that "there should be no word in the book which she would regret." The reminiscences were then organized chronologically to develop a coherent personal narrative.(3)

The substance of the work reflects Shaw's attempts to transcend the increasing tensions in the NAWSA about her leadership. Rather than offering a vindication of her role and activities, she provides a chatty, pleasant picture of her life. With a focus on her work for suffrage, the book is filled with anecdotes and amusing incidents from her lecturing and campaigning. It is almost totally without animosity. After prolonged contact with Shaw during the writing of the book, Jordan insisted Shaw's "soul sincerity . . . made it impossible for her to affect admiration or liking which she did not feel." Still Jordan averred: "I never heard Anna Shaw express active dislike of anyone." Instead, Shaw perceived her enemies like "her occasional sufferings from poison ivy--as the inevitable results of injudicious association." In only one paragraph does she mention the efforts to unseat her. Because it suggests the persona Shaw and Jordan wished to convey at this critical juncture, the whole paragraph bears quoting.

I do not claim anything so fantastic and Utopian as universal harmony among us. We have had our

troubles and our differences.   I have had mine. At
every annual convention since the one in Washington
in 1910 there has been an effort to depose me from
the presidency.   There have been some splendid
fighters among my opponents-fine and high-minded
women who sincerely believe that at sixty-eight I am
getting too old for my big job.   Possibly I am.
Certainly I shall resign with alacrity when the
majority of the women in the organization wish me
to do so. At present a large majority proves annually
that it still has faith in my leadership, and with this
assurance I am content to work on.(4)

The rest of this chapter, titled "Vale," and the others that
summarize her career as a suffrage worker, are replete with
praise for her comrades and with optimistic assessments of the
movement. The chapter concludes by affirming Shaw's faith in
the value of the movement and her place in it:

I sometimes feel that it has indeed been hundreds of
years since my work began; and then again it seems
so brief a time that, by listening for a moment, I
fancy I can hear the echo of my childish voice
preaching to the trees in the Michigan woods.
    But long or short, the one sure thing is that,
taking it all in all, the struggles, the discouragements, the failure, and the little victories, the fight
has been, as Susan B. Anthony said in her last hours,
"worth while."   Nothing bigger can come to a
human being than to love a great Cause more than
life itself, and to have the privilege throughout life of
working for that Cause.
    As for life's other gifts, I have had some of them,
too.   I have made many friendships; I have looked
upon the beauty of many lands; I have the assurance
of the respect and affection of thousands of men and
women I have never even met.   Though I have given
all I had, I have received a thousand times more than
I have given.   Neither the world nor my Cause is
indebted to me--but from the depths of a full and
very grateful heart I acknowledge my lasting
indebtedness to them both.(5)

In other arenas Shaw conveyed the same attitude.   For
example, in a speech to a convocation of students at Temple
University in 1917, Shaw urged them to choose a cause to which
to dedicate themselves. Hers, she admitted, had been suffrage.
"Only two things made the struggles, pains, losses, joys, and
victories of life worthwhile: First, to be so possessed by a

fundamental principle of right that it becomes consuming fire. The other is to have a heart filled with a great love for humanity."(6)

Reviews of the work were almost entirely positive.   The American Library Association *Booklist* praised it warmly, even adding it to its list of works recommended for small libraries. *The New York Times* observed her frankness and her "ardent" wish for human betterment. Including the review with a series of others, generally and significantly titled "Fighters Who Win Success Against Odds," the assessment concluded, "no one could read it without awarding to its author hearty admiration for her courage, her abilities, her determination, and her never failing sense of humor."   The impression Shaw made with the work undoubtedly not only inspired her supporters, but also may have calmed the fears of those uncertain about her and the organization she headed.   Her personal tone, humor, and especially her emphasis on her love of her own home may have dispelled some myths and misconceptions about her and her cause.(7)

Whatever her personal disappointments and animosities at the developments that forced her out of leadership in the NAWSA, Shaw did not falter in her work for suffrage.   She continued public lecturing and worked to advance the policies and approaches of the NAWSA.   She still opposed the militancy of women like Alice Paul and their activist confrontations with public officials.   In a letter to Caroline Bartlett Crane, she opined that if an attempt were made to assassinate President Wilson, the National Woman's Party would be largely responsible for it because they were stirring up discord and trouble.   In another case she openly stated that "picketing and any other unnecessary means to gain publicity is hurting the suffrage cause."(8)

Despite her qualms about such public demonstrations, Shaw did not shrink from direct challenges in the proper forum.   For example, Catt credited Woodrow Wilson's conversion to support for suffrage to Shaw's response to his 1916 address to the national convention.   Therein Wilson commented that he felt and rejoiced in the rising strength of the suffrage that "I have not come to fight anybody but with somebody" and that he "would not quarrel in the long run as to the method of it." Shaw responded with an expression of the association's frustration. "We have waited long enough for the vote, we want it now and we want it to come in your administration."   This answer prompted the entire audience to rise silently and turn to face Wilson.(9)

A NEW CAUSE

In a little over a year after her resignation, however, a new challenge faced the country and Shaw became deeply involved.

With the growing menace of war facing the nation, Catt summoned the Executive Council of One Hundred of the NAWSA to Washington to meet on February 23 and 24, 1917, to discuss the crisis. Shaw delivered one of the principle addresses at the meeting, which affirmed the patriotic commitment of all American women yet called for explorations of alternatives to war as a means of settling international disputes. After deliberations, the council sent representatives to President Wilson assuring him that women were eager to do their part in the event of war.(10)

The association's offer came at a propitious time. The Council of National Defense, created in 1916 to help prepare the nation for war, had decided that women could play an important role in preparing for the national defense. They created the Woman's Committee of the Council of National Defense. On April 19, 1917, W. D. Gifford, Director of the Council of National Defense, telegraphed Shaw, who was in Atlanta lecturing for suffrage, about meeting with the Council in regard to the Committee. Shaw, reluctant to interrupt her suffrage activities, agreed to meet with them on April 27 when she returned to Washington. At that time, eager to do her part for the war effort, Shaw agreed to serve as chairwoman. Two women were added to the eleven other members at her request: Agnes Nestor, an officer of the National Women's Trade Union League, as a representative of labor, and Hannah J. Patterson, who had been an extremely effective executive officer with NAWSA. On May 2, 1917, the committee was organized. After taking the oath of office and swearing allegiance to the government, the group set up headquarters in Washington.(11)

Although Shaw was eager to set to work on war efforts, her commitment to suffrage remained firm. Together with other suffragists, she determined to continue pressure for suffrage despite demands from some quarters that such activities were inappropriate. In fact, on March 26, 1917, she wrote directly to President Wilson, assuring him of her loyalty ("Believe me, Mr. President, a loyal citizen and a consistent Democrat") and urging him to take action on suffrage. She asked rhetorically, "can the government without shame, call upon its women citizens to perform patriotic duties while depriving them of the fundamental right of all free people in a Republic--the right of self Government?" To Shaw's credit, she made clear to all concerned her intention to continue working for suffrage. She reported to Lucy Stone:

> In talking matters over with the ladies of the Woman's Committee today I took occasion to say that while on the Committee I intended to speak for suffrage, of course, and that if there was any objection on the part of the members I would tender

my resignation at once. When I talked with the
Secretary of War, head of the Council of National
Defense, he said that he hoped I would continue
to speak for suffrage, and I told him it was my
intention to remain active in the suffrage work all my
life. None of the ladies objected and they were
very nice in every way.(12)

As we shall see within her speeches for the committee, Shaw
developed suffrage issues subtlety but effectively.

Shaw proved as efficient and effective in organizing this group
as her critics claimed she had not been with the NAWSA.
According to her accounts in her speeches for the committee,
she first determined the charge of the committee; it was "to
become a clearing house to coordinate and make efficient the
woman war work of the whole country." In a speech probably
given in late 1917, Shaw was even more explicit in explaining
the committee's work. "The instruction given our Woman's
Committee as to the form of work which it should undertake was
not that it should create new organizations or build up
machinery for the woman's work, but that we should coordinate
all existing women's societies which were engaged in doing any
form of war work for the purpose of preventing overlapping,
duplication, and unnecessary work." The committee also was to
be "a channel through which the government's orders might be
delivered to the womanhood of the country."(13)

To accomplish this task, the committee moved in two
directions. First, it organized a state division of itself in every
state, which "under one head should bring together all women's
societies of that state and beseech them to coordinate their
work." This plan was so effective that Shaw claimed that every
state was fully organized, sometimes down to the local voting
precinct in a state and even, in the case of Illinois at least, down
to "the very block in each city." This organization was so
efficient that the committee could, Shaw declared, "put women
upon any drive which the government requires." Eventually, the
organization embraced 18,000 units capable of reaching 82,000
women.(14)

Second, the committee set up ten departments headed by an
expert. These persons, cooperating with the national
departments of the government, were the connecting links to
state divisions and individual women. The departments were:
registration, food production/home economics, food
administration, protection of women in industry, child welfare,
Americanism in education of children, and maintenance of
existing social agencies. Through these departments, state
organizations instituted work in everything from encouraging
general thrift to counteracting propaganda "intended to
undermine our institutions and laws, especially pertaining to the

home and family life." In her interviews and speeches Shaw supported the diverse activities. For example, a report on a speech she gave to the Germantown Cricket Club indicates the range of her topics. She emphasized the need for women to learn to dry fruits and vegetables because of shortages of canning containers ("'Dry your fruits and vegetables' will be one of the urgent recommendations for women through the country") warned against exploiting child labor, and urged all women to undertake useful war work. Apparently, Shaw kept in direct, personal touch with the chairwomen of the state divisions. For example, on November 19, 1917, she wrote them asking about observing Christmas with restraint by refusing to give or receive presents that were not real necessities.(15)

The work was demanding and frustrating. Shaw wrote a friend on August 18, 1917, that it was "the hardest thing I have undertaken in my life, and, so far, the least satisfactory but I am hoping in the end our service will prove valuable." Frustrations with the work and the travel involved to and from Washington for meetings led Shaw to broach resigning to Ida Tarbell, herself a member of the committee. In a letter to Lucy Anthony, Shaw quoted Tarbell's reply, which apparently encouraged her to remain:

> I will tell you not only my own but Mrs. Lamar's opinion: we are both agreed that if we had the whole country to choose from we would select you, and I can not think of another woman who could bring the prestige to the Committee that you can; there is not another woman in the country who has the love and confidence of so many women, or who is more respected or whose judgment is considered more by men; then you are broad-minded and fair and generous and human in your attitude toward other people and other societies; in fact, I could not work on the Committee if you did not remain Chairman; Mrs. Catt is a remarkable woman but she has not the broad human vision. No, do not think of giving up, it would be a calamity.(16)

As chairwoman of this committee, Shaw also took to the platform to explain its role and to gain support for it. Two of her speeches from this period, which remain in complete texts, reveal how she approached these tasks. Although the speeches themselves are not distinguished, Shaw's rhetorical strategies in them are notable in how they implicitly develop strong arguments for women's rights in the context of explaining and urging cooperation with the Woman's Committee. Time and again Shaw managed to develop points that reinforced her earlier suffrage appeals or that enhanced the credibility of the movement without mentioning it directly.

First, Shaw reiterated emphatically how patriotic all women were and how dedicated they must be. All citizens, women and men, must, she urged, be ready to do whatever was necessary for the war effort. Shaw emphasized the need for dedication and work by all the citizens. "The women have no more right to disobey the command of the government than have the men in the country. The government has a right to conscript us to do any kind of service it needs, if we are able to do it." In one passage she explicitly delineated the need to focus on the common war concern rather than divisive issues like suffrage. Retelling the story of a woman co-worker who admitted she opposed suffrage, Shaw repeated her own response. "Well, what of that; that does not disturb me in the least; we have nothing to do with that here. Our business here is to coordinate woman's work for war, and we are not talking about suffrage . . . we don't even know on this committee who are suffragists and who are not." Although this willingness to rise above one's particular concerns to focus on more significant issues was admirable, it was also rhetorically shrewd. Shaw, as a leading suffragist, could hardly have chosen an approach that did more to enhance her ethos and the credibility of the NAWSA.(17)

A second strategy that Shaw employed was to argue strongly that women were not only willing to perform whatever tasks were necessary for the cause, they were also able to do so. For her own part, she stressed her desire to do the work most needed and useful. To suggestions that she aid the war effort by making bandages and pads, she responded: "Why that kind of work is for old women and for old men and for children. Every vital active woman like myself should be doing real work in the world. I am going to be a plumber." Besides her own willingness to train as a plumber, Shaw insisted that women should be trained as draftsmen because that was a skill that the country needed and that women could perform. In another case, she pointed to Great Britain, where women had built a "man-of-war without the assistance of a single man, from beginning to end-- and they can do that." At one point, she contended, "There is no longer such a thing as man's work and woman's work."(18)

While she agreed women should not be drafted to perform such labor unless absolutely necessary, Shaw contended that the government should provide the educational opportunities and training to prepare women for whatever jobs were useful. Interestingly, the text notes that there was applause when Shaw opined that women should not be required to perform tasks for which they were not suited short of a crisis. A report of Shaw's remarks at a vocational conference in Wisconsin reflects how forcefully she developed this point. The government, which demanded trained women for war work, had spent "millions upon technical schools for boys but nothing for the training of women." Thus, forcefully but rather indirectly, Shaw again raised a suffragist issue, equal educational opportunity, but clothed it in patriotism. Moreover, she had implicitly argued for rejecting the sexual stereotypes that had limited what women could do.(19)

Shaw further masked her implicit feminist argument by warning women to be realistic and practical about their desires to do meaningful war work. At first, she admitted, women wanted to do "spectacular work, work that they read about as being performed by heroes and heroines in the war . . . one request that the Woman's Committee would like to make of the men who control public opinion very largely through the press, is that they would impress upon the women of this country that the one vital purpose and object of the woman's work is not spectacular, it is not unusual work, but it is to maintain existing conditions in the country itself, to do the things that men can't do, and to fill the places which are made vacant by men, which are adaptable to the nature of women."(20)

In a similar vein Shaw argued that women must try to maintain the social order. Women must demand that the schools remain open, despite some arguments that the children could work for the war effort or that coal shortages made heating the schools impossible. Because the war would not last forever, she contended that continuing the education of children was vital to assuring the future of the nation. Women must also strive to maintain the charitable and philanthropic institutions vital to the country. "The work of women, their first work," she averred, "is to maintain existing standards of education among the children, to keep up their health, and see that no women enter upon any work that would interfere with the health of the women and the integrity of the home." At one point, Shaw insisted that all women should be drafted into the war effort except two groups: mothers and schoolteachers, who were already performing socially crucial tasks. Again this approach was not only commendable and farsighted, it also functioned to build the ethos of the suffrage movement, for Shaw as a leader of that group was reaffirming the value of the traditional roles and activities of women.(21)

By the mid-teens, Shaw's reputation had become far-reaching and people were aware of her struggle from wilderness obscurity to national recognition as suffrage leader and chairwoman of the Woman's Committee of the Council of National Defense. She thus was sometimes asked to tell her life story in a speech. In 1917 she was invited to address a student convocation at Temple University in Philadelphia with the request that she speak about her life's experiences and make a few comments about the work of the Woman's Committee. The speech that she gave contained her finest statements about her resolve to break with custom and tradition and step out of the gilded cage in which women were confined.

She began the speech by extolling the virtues of youth and warned the students that as they entered the arena of life they would no longer have the guiding care of the faculty of Temple University, and unless they understood the challenge they were confronting and "selected their principle of life" resolutely, they would someday lament, "Oh if I were but twenty-one, what might I not do with my life." To inspire her listeners (and because she was asked to do it) Shaw told her Temple University audience how she came to select her principle of life.

By age thirteen, she said she realized that she would not pattern her life upon the same plan laid down for all women. "So in the midst of a dense forest, by the side of a swift-rushing stream, I spent a day making up my mind whether or not I should defy all conventions." She knew that she could not make a half-way decision, one that could be easily changed or reversed. Absolute resolve would be essential. "So I faced the vastness of the great calm of a dense forest, and faced myself as I looked at my little anxious face in the waters of the brook, and waited all day long. When night came the decision was reached, and it was I WILL." It was the hardest day's work she had ever done, and she likened it to Christ in the Garden of Gethsemene. She went home looking for sympathy, but was scolded instead for having been gone all day. The reproach filled her with the heroic fire for martyrdom. She "flashed forth with my purpose," and "the soul within me refused to beat out its life against barred doors, and I rebelled."

She then told the story of her life, from the Michigan wilderness to her current position as chairwoman of the Woman's Committee for the Council of National Defense. Throughout her narrative, she re-iterated the hardships she faced and indicated how her resolve was tested. She concluded:

> There are two things in life which makes its struggle, its pain, its losses, its joys and its victories worthwhile. They are, first, to be so possessed by a fundamental principle of right that it becomes consuming fire. The other is to have a heart filled with a great love of humanity.
>
> Possessed by these two passions, no struggle can become too severe, no waiting too wearisome, no life useless. In the midst of a multitude or alone with God, at home or abroad, with friends or with enemies, life is worthwhile.(22)

Shaw then told the students about the great cause for which she had given forty years of her life--woman's enfranchisement. She said that she had come to the belief that democracy was not

merely a form of government but the "divine law of life
emanating from the heart of the Infinite entering into the souls
of men and transforming human character until some day it will
respond in like spirit to the source from whence it springs."
This dictum provided her with a transition to her war work. "It
is in this faith and from this spirit, I believe, that we are
entering into this war, to make the 'world a fit place for
democracy.'" She briefly outlined the structure and mission of
the Woman's Committee, wishing to create a "civilian army of
women to enhance the nation's war efforts." She ended her
speech abruptly: "To fight is not more noble than to inspire."

Shaw was at her best in the rough and tumble of debate,
including the refutation of opposing arguments when the
opponents were not physically present. She may, however, have
been nearly as effective as an inspirational speaker. This
explains why her sermons at suffrage conventions around the
world were so immensely popular and so thoroughly motivating
to her listeners. Almost all of Shaw's rhetoric was instrumental.
It was entirely oriented toward her immediate audience in
behalf of a cause. Her speeches never addressed the ages, as did
Elizabeth Cady Stanton's "Solitude of Self." Shaw's Temple
University speech, also principally for the students present,
came as close to a timeless, universal application as she ever
came. Her advice of selecting one's principle for life is
doubtlessly as relevant today as it was for her time.

In essence, throughout the speeches Shaw gave as
chairwoman of the Women's Committee she reiterated her belief
in the patriotism, abilities, and successes of women in
supporting the war effort. While her arguments were focused on
explaining the work of her committee and garnering support for
it, she also was indirectly enhancing the credibility of her
movement and her own ethos.

Because of her effectiveness, Shaw was in great demand in
addressing a wide variety of war efforts. For example, she
reported to Lucy Anthony that Herbert Hoover had asked her to
speak at the opening of the Food Campaign in Baltimore on
October 27, 1917. She also spoke frequently at Liberty Loan
Conferences. Typically dedicated, Shaw tried to fill all the
lecture requests. In addition, she responded patriotically and
magnaminously to a request from the editor of the *Ladies Home
Journal*, who had been a staunch, even vicious opponent of
suffrage, to write a monthly column on women's war work.
Although apparently her willingness did not bear fruit, her
reaction to the editor's request demonstrated her dedication to
the war cause. In 1918, she toured the South, lecturing each
day in a major city. In Nashville, she reported more than 7,000
people heard one speech. Public response was strong and
positive. One anti-suffragist wrote her reaction: "God bless you
for your speech at the Liberty Loan Conference. I wish every

woman in the country could have heard it. I was never so moved
in my life."(23)

But some anti-suffragists were wary of Shaw's motives and
questioned her integrity.   One group circulated a rumor that
Shaw had stated, "What is the American flag but a piece of
bunting?" Frank E. Woodruff of Bowdoin College asked her to
clarify her statement in light of her government position.
Deeply insulted, Shaw responded:

> Everybody who knows anything about me or about
> woman suffragists knows very well that I said the flag
> is "but a piece of bunting" I said it in such a
> connection that part   of the sentence extracted
> from its context is worse than a deliberate falsehood.
> I made this statement in the presence of several
> members of the President's Cabinet at a great public
> meeting where Senators and members of Congress
> were also present, and it was after this speech that I
> was selected by the President and the Council of
> National Defense as the head of the Women's
> Committee.   Do you think it would have been
> possible for them to choose me for that position if I
> had made any disrespectful reference to the
> American flag, or if in any way I had shown a disloyal
> attitude toward the Government?(24)

The anti-suffragists had clearly lifted the "piece of bunting"
passage out of context, for she had used it in talking about loyalty
and patriotism and the ideals of our form of government, saying
that although our government had not yet reached its ideals, it
nevertheless stood for them. This is how Shaw usually used the
passage:

> This is the American flag. It is a piece of bunting and
> why is it that, when it is surrounded by the flags of
> all other nations, your eyes and mine turn first
> toward it and there is a warmth at our hearts such as
> we do not feel when we gaze on any other flag? It is
> not because of its artistic beauty, for other flags are
> as artistic. It is because you and I see in that piece of
> bunting what we see in no other. It is not visible to
> the human eye but it is to the human soul.
> We see in every stripe of red the blood which
> has been shed through the centuries by men and
> women who have sacrificed their lives for the idea of
> democracy; we see in every stripe of white the purity
> of the democratic ideal toward which all the world is
> tending, and in every star in its field of blue we see
> the hope of making that some day the democracy

which that bit of bunting symbolizes shall permeate
the lives of men and nations, and we love it because
it enfolds our ideals of human freedom and
justice.(25)

Indeed, this passage was a commonplace in Shaw's speeches and
the anti-suffragists' efforts to impugn her loyalty on the basis of it
were certainly based on deliberate misconstruals.

Overall Shaw's management of the committee was as
successful as her rhetoric was skillful. Among its diverse,
effective activities were the publication of a pamphlet, *War Work
For Women*, which provided information and addresses of
women eager to support the country's effort, cooperation with
the Medical Women's National Association to promote the
development of hospitals in France; and drives to sell Liberty
Bonds. In all these activities, the committee proved not only the
skill and dependability of its members in coordinating important
work but also the reliability and dedication of thousands of other
American women.(26)

Still the work had many frustrations and disappointments. In
a report on her southern tour of 1918, Shaw berated the "very
shallow, and loosely collected" groups "without any definite
aims" she found in some places. The difficulties of gaining
cooperation among themselves and with men's groups also were
problems. In fact, Shaw began to favor placing all women's war
work under "military rules" to facilitate cooperation and
efficiency.(27)

Shaw's observations about organizational confusion and
overlapping efforts were reported to President Wilson by
Secretary of War Baker. As a result, a series of conferences
between the Council of National Defense and the Woman's
Committee created a new plan under which the Woman's
Committee became an advisory unit, meeting only to discuss any
emergency related to women's war work. A field division of six
men and six women was to conduct the war effort on the home
front. Shaw was named a member of this division.(28)

After September of 1918 when the greater part of the
Woman's Committee was merged into the field division, the
committee gradually terminated its affairs. On February 12,
1919, Shaw wrote the secretary of war that she thought the
committee's work was at an end and the committee members
tendered their resignations. On February 27, President Wilson
accepted the committee's resignation and paid it an eloquent
tribute: "It would be difficult to overestimate the importance of
the function the committee has served in being both a vast
bureau for the dissemination of information, and itself a
wellspring of inspiration and zeal." Secretary of War Baker noted
that Shaw and the committee "wrought a work the like of which
has never been seen before and her reward was to see its

success." For her part Shaw wrote to Lucy Anthony, "Well, I am honorably discharged and I feel a great relief."(29)

The country expressed its gratitude more formally. In May 1919 Shaw received the Distinguished Service Medal, the first living American woman to be so honored. In her comments on the occasion, she admitted with gratitude and characteristic candor that she was "prouder to wear this decoration than to receive any other recognition save my political freedom, which is the first desire of a loyal American." In fact, she did treasure the medal and it was pinned to her lapel in her coffin.(30)

Shaw's work was distinguished and merited recognition for its contribution to the war efforts. But equally significantly, she brought increased respect and stature for the organization she represented. Tracing the role her wartime leadership played in altering public attitudes toward the suffrage movement is impossible. But there can be little doubt that all but her staunchest enemies were impressed by her patriotism and zeal. Such positive impressions probably transferred in some measure to the suffrage movement as a whole. One supporter did suggest her impact in a letter thanking Shaw for a note of commendation she routinely sent to workers:

> I have already had my reward for any small service which I may have rendered the Woman's Committee, for I have counted every moment of my association with you a privilege. I know that you can never realize until you get to Heaven, what your leadership has meant to the women of the country, and I am afraid that not even then will you fully understand what it has meant to one humble but loyal follower.(31)

6

The Last Campaign: Advocate for the League of Nations

> A lifetime seems short at best, but what may not take place in a lifetime.
>
> *Partial Autobiography*, Shaw papers, box 19, folder 436

With the approval of the Anthony amendment by the House of Representatives on January 10, 1918, and the termination of her active leadership of the Woman's Committee a year later, the time once again seemed right for Shaw to take at least a brief respite from her life as a campaigner. She was, after all, seventy-one years old and had maintained an almost incredibly active pace for all her adult life. She was, of course, firmly committed to working for ratification of the amendment she had so long espoused. Still realizing that others could carry that effort forth while she enjoyed at least a brief vacation, she planned a trip to Europe before beginning her fierce campaigning for ratification. But once again, her dedication to principles led her to postpone personal pleasure for service to ideals.

The cause that required her efforts grew out of her long-time commitment to peace, which she had frequently expressed in her speeches. Shaw often argued that women were innately pacifists because of their clear realization of the costs of war. Her speeches after the beginning of World War I had consistently included passages that emotionally depicted the psychological costs of war for women, when they saw their husbands and sons sacrificed to the cause. Despite her intense patriotism and loyalty during the war effort, Shaw never glorified the conflict and insisted that women work arduously to protect the social fabric that war often threatened. Although the war had summoned forth her best efforts, she remained convinced that such conflicts must be avoided in the future.

Shaw's work with the International Suffrage Alliance and the International Council of Women had also convinced her of the value and feasibility of cooperation among nations. On numerous occasions she participated in meetings of these groups, often preaching a sermon for their conventions. She also had made a point in these trips of bringing back a fir tree from each country to be added to her "Forest of Arden" at her home in Moylan. The friendships she had developed because of these meetings and her positive experiences at them had made her a staunch supporter of international initiatives toward peaceful cooperation.(1)

These attitudes attracted her to the peace movement, which had gained momentum as the war drew to a close. In 1918 she had been named to the executive committee of the League to Enforce Peace, a group that had its roots in the New York state peace movement and that antedated the war. As the war neared an end, the League sought to pressure the government to cooperate in the founding of an international organization to protect peace and promote international cooperation. With President Wilson's success in developing a proposal for a League of Nations to be included in the Treaty of Versailles to end the war, the group moved to generate support and congressional endorsement of the treaty and the League of Nations.(2)

In May of 1918, Shaw addressed a "Win the War for Permanent Peace" Convention held in Philadelphia under the auspice of the League on the topic, "The Degradation of Childhood and Womanhood." The speech summarized many of her attitudes and views toward the problems of world peace. In it she argued that the ethical codes of communities determined the moral status of their inhabitants. Using Prussianism as an example, she averred that "the enthronement of might, of arrogance, of physical force creates within the human spirit a disregard for justice, of human sympathy, and of personal obligations on the one hand, and on the other, it breeds a spirit of cowardice, or servile submissions and of sullen degrading acquiescence in injustice and wrong." The events in Germany proved the corruptive and destructive impact of militarism. Not only must Germany be conquered militarily, but it must be taught that other nations would never condone the disregard for human rights that it had displayed. The choice confronting the United States and all nations was, she insisted, to become "a world military camp or a world without a military camp. The former is the ideal of the Prussian militarism; the latter that of our own and our allied nations. There is no neutral ground between these two opposing ideas. There is only a battleground." To accomplish our ideal, we must, she contended, turn to some organization like the League of Nations to protect small nations and safeguard the peace. Only through education and devotion to ideas could the world be saved from "the debasing results of a military spirit."(3)

In the spring of 1919, the League to Enforce the Peace determined to wage a strong campaign to garner support for Wilson's plan and the peace treaty. They planned a series of ratifying conventions to show support for these proposals. Careful planning would allow the most prominent leaders of the League to address many or all of the conventions. Ex-president William Howard Taft and Abbott Lawrence Lowell, the president of Harvard University, were among those to be featured as speakers. They asked Shaw, as "the foremost leader of woman suffrage," to accompany them. Reluctantly abandoning her plans for a European vacation, Shaw cancelled her other engagements and joined them for a lecture tour between May 19 and June 5 through fourteen states from New Hampshire to Kansas.(4)

"WHAT THE WAR MEANT TO WOMEN"

The only extant text of Shaw's speeches in behalf of the League was printed in pamphlet form titled, "What the War Meant to Women." The foreword notes that the revised manuscript, which had been received the day before Shaw's death, was her "last message to the women of this country, to whose service she devoted her life and by whom she was singularly revered." Since we know that Shaw, like campaigners, often relied on a standard stump speech, which was varied extemporaneously to fit particular audiences, it is reasonable to assume that this pamphlet represents the substance and tenor of her speeches on the tour.(5)

Although the pamphlet does address briefly some arguments offered by opponents of the treaty and although Shaw does use her typical wit and sarcasm against her adversaries, the tone is exhortative and impassioned rather than coolly rational. Shaw's sense of urgency, almost desperation, colors the work throughout. Appealing directly to the women of the United States, Shaw spoke as both peer and stern advocate. Both frustrated and disappointed with government leaders' actions on the treaty, Shaw encouraged women to become active in the struggle to assure a lasting peace. Because the work is not a carefully constructed argument but instead an ardent plea, its organization is rather loose. The work's unity stems from its emotional tenor rather than from coherent argument.

The pamphlet began by immediately addressing the target audience, the women of the United States, with two rhetorical questions: "What are we women to do in this matter of a League of Nations? What part are we to play in it?" Insisting that women's war service had won them an unusual opportunity to have a voice in world affairs, Shaw briefly but emotionally emphasized their sacrifices for the war. "But when we speak of the cost of life in this war we enumerate only the men who died. We have made no enumeration of the women. We have made no enumeration of the children. We do not know the vast bodies of women and children who have been slaughtered, women who have been outraged and who today are filling the mad-houses of France and Belgium and Serbia and all other nations which have been overrun by the armies." These sacrifices and their devoted service, Shaw implied, not only earn them the right to participate in discussions about the peace, but also should impel them to consider why they acted so bravely.

Her answer was simple. Women were willing to unite and work so arduously because they believed that war would be "the war to end war." While she affirmed the valor and importance of the men who died, Shaw insisted that efforts to make a permanent peace were vital, if survivors were to prevent the United States from becoming "a dishonored nation" that did not understand the need for international cooperation. Praising Wilson's generous spirit toward the defeated nations, Shaw added that women did want something from the war: "We want Peace now and Peace forever." Only a devotion to that cause could, she opined, offer hope to the nations devastated by war.

With that noble end in view, Shaw expressed exasperation with senators and others who were quibbling about terms in the Treaty. Admitting the League of Nations might not be perfect, Shaw nonetheless emphasized that some such arrangement was essential and the League was the best available alternative. Her plea combined pragmatic politics with emotional appeal:

> There are a lot of other people who want this nation to go alone in the world. But the time has gone by when any country can stand alone. The time has gone by when a country no more than an individual can live to itself or die to itself. We have come to the place now where we can fly in a day from this country to any other country on the earth, almost, and we have become so closely interallied that national interests merge the one with the other, in such a manner that we cannot go alone. We must look facts in the face. All humanity is one. The world is one. And no nation can suffer unless all nations suffer. No nation can prosper without all nations prospering. We have got to take facts as they are and we have got to find out the best thing we can have. The best thing that has been given us and the only thing we have before us is this League of Nations. We have no other League of Nations. We have only this one. We must take this one or no one can tell what will come. We have no midway point.

> We have no purgatory. We have to choose Heaven or
> Hell. We must take it or we must reject it.(5)

Shaw discounted the possibility of a Senate amendment as a
means to improve the treaty. Such action, she argued, would
prolong the process indefinitely. On the other hand, refusing to
sign would simply isolate the United States economically and
politically. To women who had been canvassing to sell Liberty
Bonds to bring troops home, the wrangling would be particularly
frustrating since the money they had raised might have to be
diverted to maintain forces along the Rhine.

With clear sarcasm, Shaw turned on the senators who had
been talking pointlessly without acting. She ridiculed their
objections based on fears that the League would have a "super-
sovereignty" and on allegations that the proposal was
unconstitutional. Such words, she argued, like earlier terms
applied to women who sought suffrage, frightened listeners
because they were unfamiliar.

Finally, in a discussion of the "meaning of a League," Shaw
ended with a strong emotional plea. Referring to the recent
devastating flu epidemic, she warned that other such diseases
might sweep the country because of the unsanitary conditions in
military trenches and the impoverishment of civilians. Only
concerted international efforts could prevent such disasters.
Women, who as "mothers of the race have given everything, have
suffered everything," must now demand that their voices be
heard. They must work daily to express their will and to let
their senators know their opinion. If the senators remained
unresponsive, then voters must deny them reelection.

If the pamphlet does not represent Shaw's best rhetorical
efforts, it does reflect her commitment to principle and her
high idealism. The fervor with which she urged ratification of
the Treaty mirrored her deep concern for the future. While the
pamphlet contains little of the good humor that often
characterized Shaw's efforts, it does convey the humanistic
impulses that motivated all her work.

THE END OF THE CAMPAIGN

In some senses, Shaw literally died of overwork. Having
suffered a pleurisy atack a short time before, she was not at peak
strength when she began the tour. While on the tour, she
traveled and spoke for two days with a high temperature, until
finally, after a particularly gruelling day in Indianapolis, she
collapsed at Springfield, Illinois, with a fever of 104 degrees.
She was taken to a hospital, where doctors discovered that she
had pneumonia with inflammation of the liver. She remained
hospitalized in Springfield until June 12 when she was
transported to her home in Moylan. There, nursed by Lucy

Anthony, she improved temporarily. After a sudden and unexpected relapse on June 30, she died on July 2, 1919. The voice from the wilderness was still at last.(6)

Condolences and tributes came from around the country. Taft observed, "Her going is a great loss to the community." President Wilson, who admitted he had only known her during the last years of her life, expressed his admiration for her work and praised "the extraordinary quality of her clear and effective mind." Vice-President Thomas R. Marshall was more personal: "The world is infinitely the poorer by the death of so great and good a woman." Shaw had become the best known woman in the United States, and nationwide newspapers noted her passing, invariably paying tribute to her dedication and commitment, not only to her cause, but the nation as well. Many women and women's groups expressed their grief. But none spoke more eloquently and accurately than one who signed herself, "Elizabeth C. Carter, President of the Northeastern Federation of Women's Clubs (colored)": "Truly all womankind has lost a faithful friend."(7)

Honors continued to come to Shaw posthumously. Alumnae of the North Carolina College for Women, where Shaw had given her last commencement address in May 1919, requested that the residence hall for women be named the Anna Howard Shaw Building. Under her name, chairs of political science were established at Bryn Mawr College and at Barnard College, and a chair of preventative medicine was designated in her honor at the Woman's Medical College of Pennsylvania. In December 1926, the Beckman Avenue Methodist Protestant Church at North Tarryton, New York, the church at which she had been ordained, unveiled a memorial window for her. During World War II, the S.S. *Anna Howard Shaw* was launched on August 29, 1943, by the New England Building Company in Portland, Maine. Finally, honor came to Shaw near her childhood home. In October 1988, the Mecosta County Council for the Arts and the Mecosta County Woman's Historical Council dedicated a life-sized sculpture of Shaw and placed it in the park next to the community library in Grand Rapids. With this action, the journey of this remarkable woman was complete. She had come from the Michigan wilderness to preach social justice to the nation, and her image now stands immortalized at the scene of her youth.(8)

Conclusion:
A Rhetorical Portrait

Her talent as an orator is unsurpassed; as a public speaker there is
none of either sex today upon the stage that can hold an audience
more securely with such pleasurable attention or carry more
intelligent conviction.

Boston Post, November 25, 1915

THE QUEEN OF THE SUFFRAGE PLATFORM

Anna Howard Shaw's brilliance as an orator is clear in the
testimony of both friend and foe. Women of the suffrage
movement paid her glowing tribute. For example, Carrie
Chapman Catt wrote, "There is one woman who without question
is the greatest orator produced among women in all ages . . .
since history began men have been orators, yet with all the
prestige behind them I do not know one man today who is more
than peer to our own Anna Howard Shaw, in wit, eloquence and
magnetic power. Wherever her voice has been lifted the cause of
liberty has been strengthened." The authors of volumes four and
five of *The History of Women Suffrage* refer frequently to Shaw's
oratorical skills, always praising them profusely. But suffragists
consistently spoke glowingly of virtually all their co-workers.
Even mediocre speakers were described as having spoken
"gracefully"; no woman gave an ordinary speech.(1)

Of greater value than sympathetic testimony in assessing
Shaw's skill are comparisons of Shaw as an orator with the other
women in the movement. Susan B. Anthony and Ida Husted
Harper concluded that Shaw "is beyond question the leading
orator of this generation." Other authors hold that Dr. Shaw
"stood unchallenged throughout her career as the greatest orator
among women the world has ever known. Carrie Chapman Catt,
who was not a member of the Shaw-Anthony-Harper faction,
wrote Shaw, "It must be a wonderful thing to know that you are

the only orator our movement has had in its three generations and 26 nations. It is a tragic thing to know there are no more coming on. Apparently you are to remain the one and only which the completed history can record." Even her antagonist, Abigail Scott Duniway of Oregon, who once notified Shaw that she would have her arrested if she tried to cross the border into Oregon, described Shaw as "an oratorical genius of the highest order."(2)

People outside the suffrage movement also confirmed Shaw's oratorical skill.   Newspapers labeled her "a magnificent speaker," "brilliant, clever, and humorous," "the foremost orator of her generation," and "Queen of the platform."   The *North American* asserted, "Doctor Shaw was without an equal as an orator among women. She is generally conceded as the greatest woman speaker who ever lived. Some believed her to have been without peer in either sex among orators of her day." Even newspapers hostile to Shaw and her cause, while discrediting her views, commended her oratorical skills. For example, an unfriendly *Burlington Independent* noted that despite Dr. Shaw's views, which were becoming progressively worse, she was one of the most remarkable platform speakers in the United States.(3)

Outside the press, other prominent persons extolled Shaw's speaking ability. George W. Bain, himself an eminent lecturer, considered "Rev. Anna Howard Shaw equal to the very best on the American platform." Ex-President William Howard Taft, with whom Shaw campaigned for the League of Nations, was greatly impressed with her "persuasive eloquence." President Woodrow Wilson, observing "the extraordinary quality of her clear and effective mind," described her as a powerful and persuasive advocate.(4)

Shaw's reputation as a public speaker preceded her on lecture tours and other speaking engagements.   When she lectured for agencies such as the Redpath Lecture Bureau or the Massachusetts Woman Suffrage Association, these groups sent out advertising that listed not only the subjects of Shaw's lectures but also contained pages of short testimonials about her ability to attract and impress audiences. Moreover, newspapers that published advance notices of her scheduled appearance often mentioned Shaw's oratorical skill. Shaw's reputation almost always assured a good crowd, eager to listen.

In her career, Shaw spoke more than 10,000 times on many sorts of occasions for a host of causes. Her speeches ranged from sermons to eulogies to campaign speeches and legislative addresses. Obviously, no brief survey nor simple generalizations can do justice to the characteristics of all her speeches. We have already examined dominant features of her physical appearance, her delivery, the tone and persona of her rhetoric, and her rhetorical style. In this chapter we will examine her basic line of argument, organization and design of her speeches, and her persuasive strategies. We will limit ourselves to her woman suffrage rhetoric found in speeches delivered after the turn of the century. Thus, we will be able to draw some comparisons and contrasts with her 19th-century lectures, and determine what, if any, evolution occurred in her rhetoric. Because two speeches she gave in 1915, one in Birmingham, Alabama, and the other in Ogdenberg, New York, are far and away the best and most typical, we will draw heavily from these in our analysis.

Argument

Throughout her speaking career Shaw used a variety of arguments to construct her case; however, her most powerful was the argument from definition. As Aristotle described it, in arguing from definition one "defines his term, gets at its essential meaning, and then proceeds to argue from it on the point at issue." In selecting this form of argument, Shaw rejected the approach of the anti-suffragists who opposed the measure on the basis of circumstances and consequences. For example, the anti-suffragists frequently argued that women did not need the ballot because their husbands could vote for them or because they had no time to take care of their family duties and vote. They also pointed to the consequences of women's voting. For Shaw, the consequences or circumstances, good or bad, were irrelevant to the fundamental issue of the question. The question, Shaw insisted, must be addressed on the basis of democratic principles.(5)

In her most cogent and frequently reiterated argument for suffrage, Shaw turned to exploring the definitions of "democracy" and a "republic" to build her case. The belief that "a republican form of government is desirable was the whole ground of contention that women should be enfranchised. If a republican form of government is not desirable, then our contention might be debatable; but if a republican form of government is desirable, then there can be no debate upon the question whatever." Inquiring into the nature of a democracy confirmed her point. Democracy, Shaw held, was linked with the sublime and the divine. It was not merely a form of government, but a "great spiritual force emanating from the heart of the Infinite, permeating the universe and transforming the lives of men." Democracy was not man-made, rather man inherited it. Predating humankind, democracy always existed in the soul of God. Since democracy was a greater than human creation, a spiritual force, it belonged to all of God's human children.(6)

To understand the essential characteristics of a democracy Shaw turned to the words of America's founding fathers, quoting from the writings of James Otis, Benjamin Franklin, Samuel Adams, and others. She also delighted in citing the prominent contemporaries opposed to woman suffrage such as Woodrow Wilson. These sources confirmed the principles of democracy in powerful phrases: "Governments derive their just powers from the consent of the governed," government "of the people, by the people, and for the people," "The voice of the people is the voice of God," and "Under God, the people rule." If these principles described the nature of democracy, Shaw reasoned, then the essence of a republican form of government was that laws were made only by representatives of the people.(7)

But the United States did not reflect those democratic principles. Laws were being made by only half the human family. Women, who had no voice in government, were expected to obey all its laws and pay taxes to support it. This situation was not democracy; it was tyranny, an aristocracy of sex. After the Civil War such an aristocracy had proven to be the most degrading in history, for their former slaves became the masters of their female owners.(8)

While she felt the right to vote was inherent to citizenship, Shaw did not oppose restrictions on that right. For example, age or residency were acceptable qualifications because they could be met by all humans. In contrast, sex was not a qualification, but an insuperable barrier, and therefore, out of harmony with the nature of democracy. To exclude women from the ballot was by definition to bracket them with criminals, the insane, idiots, and children, who were all excluded because of irresponsibility. In a number of speeches, Shaw pointedly traced the development of voting qualifications in the United States, showing how from the days of the Puritans to the Civil War democracy had increased. Only one important step remained for the country to fulfill the definition of democracy, the enfranchisement of women.(9)

To arguments that women had "virtual" representation through their husbands, Shaw replied that "virtual" representation did not fall within the definition of a republican form of government. With characteristic wit, Shaw asked what husband was representing her, a single woman. Moreover, she questioned how men had acquired this power to subject women to virtual representation; certainly women themselves had not conferred it. With James Otis she insisted that no virtual representation could exist, because the concept preposterously assumed that husband and wife never had differences. To insist one person could vote for another, she quipped, was as silly as pretending one person could eat for two.(10)

Thus, thorough analysis and completely logical argument from definition permeated Shaw's twentieth-century suffrage rhetoric and complemented the expediency arguments for granting women the ballot she had used extensively in other earlier, lectures. In her "The Fate of Republics" she presented advantages to be gained from suffrage through a detailed inquiry into the question, "Is there anything in the nature of woman, differing from the nature of man in such a manner, that if women were permitted to vote it would enable them to affect the government differently from the way in which men affect it?" Her inquiry lead her to the conclusion that women were more moral, more temperate, more religious, more peace-loving and more law-abiding than men. If the nature of the voting class could affect the government, she concluded that permitting women to vote would improve the government and all of society.(11)

In her later years, Shaw sometimes returned to expediency arguments to maintain that women voters would be more sensitive to social issues and the welfare of children than men. Thus, their votes would sustain the family and improve conditions, particularly in relation to child labor laws and education. Women's votes were crucial, she argued, to help correct the abuses in employment and labor. In answering the charges that suffrage would destroy the home, Shaw contended, "I believe in the ballot for women if for nothing but the protection of the home itself."(12)

On a less admirable note, Shaw sometimes lapsed into another implied argument based on expediency that reflected some of the dominant fears and tensions in American society. Although she believed in basic rights for all, she appealed to racial and ethnic prejudices, by pointing out to her male listeners that American women were in an unusually "humiliating political position" because they were "governed by every kind from black to white, from red to yellow, there is not a race, there is not a nation, which has not contributed men to be our sovereign rulers." Giving immigrants the ballot, she contended, was grossly unfair to American women who had sacrificed much for the country. She concluded with a blatantly racist challenge: "It is time that American men should think where American women stand politically. It is time for us all to think that, if we are to save America's womanhood, if we do not wish to see it overwhelmed by external forces, we must give American women the power to protect themselves." While contending that she did not oppose foreigners, since she was one herself, Shaw insisted more moderately that "what women object to is that men who are not American, who are not of our race, should have the power to deprive American women of their right to a voice in their own government."(13)

After women gained the ballot in some states, Shaw added arguments based on consequences to her repertoire. While she agreed that women's voting would not solve all problems, she pointed with pride to the changes in labor laws that reduced child labor and established limits for a work week in states that had enfranchised women. In sum, she concluded, "The

Legislatures in most of the suffrage states have shown greater readiness to protect women from over work than the Legislatures in most of the non-suffrage states." In addition, suffrage states had passed laws granting women access to professions and the right to their children in divorce cases. While the ballot was not a panacea, Shaw did argue that its impact had been largely positive.(14)

In short, Shaw relied heavily on a fully developed, logically supported argument from definition as her primary basis for urging suffrage. While she refuted the arguments from circumstance and consequence developed by her opponents, she supplemented her definitional argument with materials based on expedience and later consequences to build her case. Whatever the particular form of argument she employed, Shaw's speeches were solidly supported and clearly reasoned. Both her skill at argument and her adeptness at refutation enhanced her reputation as a rational, forceful debater.

Organization

The organizational tightness of Shaw's extant speeches vary considerably. Some are almost without a perceivable pattern. In part her discursiveness and lack of organization may reflect the demands on her. Because listeners expected her to touch all issues related to suffrage, her campaign speeches frequently lasted an hour or more. Such lengthy performances, done extemporaneously, made careful organization virtually impossible. Moreover, Shaw's fondness for and extensive use of anecdotes, which enlivened her speeches, often led her to depart from any simple plan of organization. Still Shaw's speeches were not confusing or incoherent. The individual points were often closely reasoned, although the wholes were often broad topical surveys unified only in that each topic related, however indirectly, to her call for woman suffrage.

Despite their internal discursiveness and loose topicality organization, Shaw's suffrage speeches tended to have five major divisions. She usually began with a few brief introductory remarks, stated the basic premise from which her argument would be developed, clearly unfolded her constructive argument, refuted opposing arguments, and ended with a concluding affirmation of her cause. To begin, Shaw frequently referred to the occasion or location. For example, to adapt what became her standard stump speech to one particular audience, Shaw recalled her last appearance in that arena some twenty years before. In a speech given in Birmingham, Alabama, in 1915 she began with a direct, light-hearted reference to the audience:

> There are two classes of people here this afternoon--
> saints and sinners; the sinners are the people who
> do not agree with us, and the saints are the people

want the sinners to be seated. I am a
aving been a Methodist for years, I
nt to convert a man, he must be
vhile you are attempting it, so
comfortable, let him come

At Ogdenburg, New York, Shaw began with a reference to an
earlier time when she and Susan B. Anthony had spoken in the
same meeting hall and that anti-suffragists still weren't
answering her basic arguments.

> When I came into your hall tonight, I thought of the
> last time I was in your city. Twenty-one years ago I
> came her with Susan B. Anthony, and we came for
> exactly the same purpose as that for which we are
> here tonight. Boys have been born since that time
> and have become voters, and the women are still
> trying to persuade American men to believe in the
> fundamental principles of democracy, and I never
> quite feel as if it was a fair field to argue this
> question with men, because in doing it you have to
> assume that a man who professes to believe in a
> republican form of government does not believe in a
> Republican form of government, for the only thing
> that woman's enfranchisement means at all is that a
> government which claims to be a Republic should be
> a Republic, and not an aristocracy. The difficulty
> with discussing this question with those who oppose
> us is that they make any number of arguments but
> none of them have anything to do with Woman's
> Suffrage; they always have something to do with
> something else, therefore the arguments which we
> have to make rarely ever have anything to do with
> the subject, because we have to answer our
> opponents who always escape the subject as far as
> possible in order to have any sort of reason in
> connection with what they say.

Shaw then stated the basic premise from which she was going to
argue: "Now one of two things is true: either a Republic is a
desirable form of government, or else it is not. If it is then we
should have it, if it is not then we ought not to pretend that we
have it."(16)

Shaw's conclusions were often forceful affirmations of her
cause or dynamic assertions of her position. In one repeated
stump speech, she ended by insisting, "When woman has her
free rights then the voice of the people shall be the voice of God
and a republic shall be born." In another, much later, she

echoed the same theme. "Whether in war or in peace, the man is not complete without the woman; and as it is impossible to conceive of an ideal home without the man, so it is equally impossible to conceive of our ideal Republic without the woman."(17)

A word of caution is necessary about assessing the success of Shaw's opening and closing strategies. Because her extant speeches are so often stenographic transcriptions, one cannot be certain how accurately they convey her rhetorical practices. Still, these transcriptions strongly suggest Shaw spent little time in elaborate introductions; rather she launched directly into her basic argument. Her conclusions do not summarize her material nor review her main ideas. Instead they reiterate the theme or central ideas. While such techniques may seem rough or abrupt, one must recall that Shaw spoke extemporaneously and that directness was one facet of persuasion she consciously crafted on the platform.

Persuasive Strategies

One key to Shaw's effectiveness on the platform was her concrete vivid material. She eschewed abstract or theoretical discussions for direct exposition of her ideas. While at some point she used almost every form of supporting material and adopted almost every rhetorical strategy, her most characteristic techniques included use of personal anecdotes and example, direct rebuttal of opposing arguments, and appeals to key American values of democracy.

Illustrations, particularly personal anecdotes, appeared often. Her experiences and confrontations as a lecturer provided much grist for her rhetorical mill, especially stories at the expense of her opponents. When a story demonstrated a point, she repeated it often. For example, she reiterated the slippery technique of one New Jersey anti-suffragist on a western speaking tour. Adapting to her audience in dry states, Shaw could offer statistics to prove that women voters would vote dry states wet while in wet states she cited facts to prove females would return the state to a dry column. Shaw used this story not only to undermine the credibility of the opposition, but also to show their tendency toward hyperbole and foolish hypothetical argument.(18)

An important feature of such anecdotes was their humor, often tinged with gentle sarcasm. Shaw usually depicted herself as basting an opponent with her sharp wit in a lively retort. For example, she recounted the story of a "mere lad of 21" who approached her after a speech to observe she apparently endorsed woman suffrage. "I said, 'My boy, I should hate to think that I had attained my age without looking intelligent.' He answered 'I do not believe in woman suffrage. . . . The reason . . . is because I love women so.' Just think of a lad of 21 talking to a

I would gladly g[...]
for women if I could get [...]
ridicule of the opposition wrap[...]
[...] [19]

Early in her career Shaw was pron[...]
later sweetened her satire and modified [...]
Carrie Chapman Catt observed in her eulogy of [...]
her cutting ridicule and biting sarcasm she could cut [...]
wide open until its fallacies lay bare for all to see. But [...]
cause gained she put aside this ridicule and sarcasm a[...]
assumed a gentler and sunnier humor."[20]

In other cases, Shaw referred directly to cases or instances to prove her point. For example, one allegation made against suffrage was that women would neglect their children if they were granted the ballot. Not only did Shaw point out that women who made this claim frequently left their children to go play whist, but she also mentioned her experience in Colorado, where women could vote. Her recitation of her observations also suggests her typical humor:

> I went to Denver and I found that they took care of their babies just the same on election day as they did on every other day; they took their baby along with them, when they went to put a letter in a box they took their baby along. If the mother had to stand in line and the baby got restless she would joggle the go-cart--most every one had a go-cart--, and when she went in to vote a neighbor would joggle the go-cart and if there was not a neighbor there was the candidate and he would joggle the cart. That is one day in the year when you could get a hundred people to take care of any number of babies.

Shaw's use of such concrete, amusing examples and anecdotes undoubtedly impressed many audiences who expected suffragists to be fanatic and humorless.[21]

Although Shaw occasionally relied on facts to make her points about desirability and impact of suffrage, the limited number of states that had granted women the ballot made such materials scarce. Instead of building her case in that way, Shaw refuted claims and arguments of her opponents. At times she even turned the materials of her opponents against them. For example, she mentioned one young anti-suffragist who had gathered a mass of statistics to prove her points. Ridiculing the woman's claim that her statistics proved her case because figures do not lie, Shaw retorted, "Well, they don't, but some liars figure." She continued to answer the argument that women would not use the ballot more directly. "If we would not use it then I really cannot see the harm of giving it to us, we would not hurt anybody with it and what an easy way for you men to get rid of us. No more suffrage meetings, never any nagging you again, no one could blame you for anything that went wrong with the town, if it did not run right, all you would have to say is you have the power, why don't you go ahead and clean up." Shaw then noted that the same woman had argued the awful results of suffrage, including the demise of the family and undesirable laws brought about by woman's votes. At the end of her pointing up of similar inconsistencies in all anti-suffragists' arguments, Shaw concluded with an effective summary, again accompanied by a humorous story and an acute observation of the irrelevancy of all such allegations:

> We will either vote as our husbands vote or we will not vote as our husbands vote. We either have time to vote or we don't have time to vote. We will either not vote or we will vote all the time. It reminds me of the story of the old Irish woman who had twin boys and they were so much alike that the neighbors could not tell them apart, so one of the neighbors said, 'Now Mrs. Mahoney, you have two of the finest twin boys I ever saw in all my life, but how do you know them apart?' "Oh,' she says, 'That's easy enough, anyone could tell them apart. When I want to know which is which I just put my finger in Patsey's mouth and if he bites it is Mikey.'
>
> Now what does it matter whether the women will vote as their husbands do or will not vote; whether they have time or have not; or whether they will vote for prohibition or not? What has that to do with the fundamental question of democracy, no one has yet discovered.(22)

Shaw's adeptness at such refutation and her effective ridicule of her opponents finally led the anti-suffragists to refuse to confront her on the platform.

While Shaw relied on concrete materials and scathing rebuttal to make her arguments both interesting and convincing, another important technique was less obvious, although pervasive. This was Shaw's appeal to key values in American society. For example, primary argument was based on democratic principles. Republics, she insisted, were governed by the consent of the citizens. Because women were citizens and because they lacked the vote, the United States did not merit the label of a democratic republic. This logical argument was, of course, grounded in American values of justice and freedom. The argument also appealed strongly to American's patriotism and their respect for the cornerstones of their government. These implicit appeals to patriotism and key values were an important, though subtle strategy in Shaw's speeches.

These characteristic strategies, of course, must be viewed in the light of other features of Shaw's rhetoric if we are to assess their impact. By relying so heavily on anecdotes and refutation and by subtly appealing to American values, Shaw built her credibility and enhanced the audience's identification with her. Moreover, because she was the premier spokesperson for her cause, she emerged as a representative of the type of women her movement embraced and encouraged. Her rhetorical strategies did much to create the image of the new woman as an attractive, dynamic force.

ASSESSMENT

Assessing the rhetorical effectiveness of Shaw is an extremely complex and difficult task for a variety of reasons. Because her work extended over such a long period of time and embraced so many activities, one cannot trace the impact of any single effort. Moreover, so many other persons were active in the suffrage movement that its status at any point or its ultimate success cannot be attributed to any one individual. Of course, too, suffragists were not working in a social or political vacuum and their cause was only one facet of a complex cultural scene. All these factors make facile judgments about Shaw and her work suspect.

Still, since one must begin somewhere, the final success of the suffrage movement seems a suitable point. Obviously, no one person produced the passage of the amendment; probably the political pressures exerted by groups led by women like Alice Paul had more immediate and direct impact than did Shaw's oratory. However, the political efforts of more activist groups did not occur *de novum*. The public support for the measure was the result of sustained efforts by others over a long period. In reality, workers like Shaw made Paul's activities both possible and productive.

In her presidential "Farewell" to the NAWSA Convention in 1915, Shaw in an untypical but effective metaphor somewhat unwittingly described her role exactly: "Political necessity has supplanted the reform epoch, the reapers of the harvest have replaced the ploughman and seed sower, each equally needed in the process of the cultivation and the development of an ideal as in the fruitage of the tree." Shaw then developed the contrast between the idealists necessary to create the movement in the early stages and the practical politicals essential to its final success, placing herself with the early visionaries. While Shaw was fond of labeling herself an idealist, which she was in a sense, her contribution to the suffrage movement was not as a visionary;

she was always a practical person. Her role in the movement was to plough and sow rather than to plan the garden or reap the harvest. If one views Shaw as a plougher and sower for suffrage, one can consider how well she performed the tasks of preparing the ground, how well she selected her seed, and, finally, how well she sowed that seed.

When Shaw entered the suffrage movement, some of the most glaring legal inequities and hardships of women had been at least partially removed. The primary arguments for suffrage had been articulated and refined. The tasks that confronted her were to disseminate those arguments, to refute allegations of the opposition, and, perhaps most important, to enhance the ethos and credibility of the movement. This final task was particularly daunting since the public often associated the movement with radical and therefore unacceptable women like Victoria Woodhull, who championed free love. Even Elizabeth Stanton's *Woman's Bible*, which critiqued the Old Testament passages derogatory to women, added fuel to the flames of the anti-suffragists who decried supporters as home breakers and fanatics. The movement itself had gone through a traumatic period of separation with two national organizations, which suggested to the public in-fighting and general turmoil. In modern parlance, the movement had an image problem and some members realized that its future success lay in becoming more in tune with social standards without abandoning its principles. As Flexner notes, the leaders of the movement in the last twenty years of the nineteenth century "were drawing the suffrage movement into the camp of decorum." Thus, Shaw's unstated and perhaps unconscious rhetorical problem was to project a more acceptable and attractive image of the suffrage movement as she advocated its ideas.(23)

As we have seen, Shaw was quite sensitive to the impact her physical appearance and demeanor had on audiences. Quite shrewdly she recognized that she must adapt her personal appearance to fit audience expectations. She could not risk alienation on such superficial grounds. While the incident about her short hair suggests her sensitivity to issues about appearances, an occurrence recorded in her autobiography confirms the wisdom of her attitude. At a private seaside cottage, Shaw and her nieces adopted unconventional dress: they wore knickerbockers and she "found vast contentment in short, heavy skirts over bloomers." Unfortunately, a woman reporter visited and wrote "a sensational full-page article for a Sunday paper with the heading "The Adamless Eden." Although Shaw deemed the article "almost libelous," she also recognized that even in her private retreat she must be careful of her dress and behavior. Thus, Shaw carefully crafted her physical appearance to conform to audience's standards of decorum.(24)

While Shaw controlled her appearance to appear conventional, other aspects of her behavior subtly undermined sexual stereotypes. She was dynamic and forceful as a speaker at a time when demureness was a primary female virtue. She was assertive and confrontational when passivity was the womanly norm. Moreover, on her lecture tours she endured hardships and forced challenges that belied her matronly appearance. Her carefully reasoned, humor-filled speeches undercut the image of suffragists as fanatic ideologists and radicals. In short, Shaw embodied the image of the suffragist as a woman who combined traditional elements and new ideas. From this perspective, Shaw did an excellent job of plowing the field for suffrage ideas.

The seed that she chose to sow among her audiences was also shrewdly chosen. Eschewing emotionalism and ornate language, Shaw offered reasoned arguments for her cause. Her devastating refutation exposed the irrationality and contradictions of her opponents. Largely basing her views in generally accepted political principles and arguing from definition, Shaw constructed an airtight case for suffrage. She forced her audience to confront the contradictions between their principles and their political actions. As she expressed it in her "Farewell": "Our protest is not against the vision or the ideals of the founders of our government, but against the false interpretation of these ideals and their application to a chosen group and not to the whole people." In constructing her arguments and refuting her opponents, Shaw included liberal doses of humor, often in the form of anecdotes. Even in her most dramatic rebuttals, she did not become vicious nor caustic. Nor was she condescending. Instead, she included her audience in the joke, laughing with them at the human foibles and inconsistencies of her opponents.(25)

This combination of reason and wit worked on two levels. Not only did it lay waste the arguments of her opponents, but also it enhanced her own credibility and improved the image of the movement. Press coverage of her, for example, almost always commended her reason and her raillery. Audiences, even if they disagreed with her ideas, found her an interesting speaker and an attractive individual. Gradually, these reactions coalesced into respect and esteem. Shaw emerged as a dignified, intelligent, dynamic woman. Her selection to head the Woman's Committee in World War I suggests that the public admired her. That regard for Shaw inevitably transferred, at least in part, to her cause.

With the emergence of the "new suffragists" typified by Alice Paul, Shaw continued to be an important image for the movement. These radical women frightened and disturbed many Americans. But Shaw and others like her had moved into respectability. While they remained stalwarts for the cause, they loomed large in the public mind as "acceptable" women, who preserved some traditional values. In this sense, Shaw served a very important leadership function even as the militants gained ascendancy. As Herbert Simons has observed of social movement leaders, "Militants are effective with 'power vulnerables'; moderates are effective with power invulnerables'; neither is effective with both." Thus, Shaw and similar women were winning general public support for suffrage, while militants effectively threatened elected officials.(26)

Shaw's ability to project such a favorable image is somewhat surprising because she was so untraditional in many ways. Her background as a minister and a doctor, her activities on the lecture circuit, the absence of a husband and a family, and even her status as a professional woman made her distinctly different from most American females. Part of the secret of her success lay in her acceptance and affirmation of key values that her audience endorsed. Shaw was religious, she affirmed the importance of the home and the role of wife and mother, she repeatedly emphasized her concern for children and education, and she was intensely patriotic. Indeed, her "radical" notions derived from her conservative values. She argued that both political principles and religious truth endorsed her views. Shaw was the person that the image of the new woman conveyed: she combined a respect for old values with a regard for new truths. In this sense, she was the perfect sower of the seeds of suffrage.

One could speculate whether Shaw selected the best available means of persuasion and one could assess the logical rigor of her arguments, which, incidentally would receive high marks; but to ask those questions is in a real sense to miss the point of Shaw's life. Shaw ploughed and sowed quite excellently. We may criticize her verbal style and be dismayed at some of her ethnic references. But overall she argued her cause on the basis of our finest political and religious principles. Moreover, she remained true to her cause; she did not compromise nor retreat. She had absolute integrity. In the final analysis, she was the new woman this nation needed to achieve greater justice and equality. Carrie Chapman Catt in her eulogy spoke of Shaw's contribution to the cause: "There are no words with which to measure the part which Dr. Shaw played in this monumental victory. She was of the suffrage struggle its greatest orator, its wit, its humor, its deathless spirit." *The New York Times* labeled her accurately: "A personage, a thinker, an orator, a thrice clever and all-around woman. Indeed, she is singular, without dual or plural." But perhaps Shaw chose her own best epithet when she labeled her autobiography simply "Story of a Pioneer." She was neither explorer nor colonist. Instead, she was a pioneer spirit who established and developed a foothold for those who followed.(27)

The world gives lashes to its pioneers
Until the goal is reached--then deafening cheers.(28)

II

COLLECTED
SPEECHES

The Heavenly Vision

Two versions of this speech are extant: one published by the *Report of the International Council of Women*, pp. 24-29, and the other by *The Woman's Tribune*, March 27, 1888. Both texts were made by stenographers. There is basic agreement between the two versions, except that a few passages and words, and even short paragraphs, are missing from the Council's *Report*. Additionally, the *Report* fails to record the last two or three pages of the address. The text that follows is from *The Woman's Tribune*, which appears to be an authentic and accurate recording of what Shaw said on the occasion.

The speech was given at a religious service held Sunday, March 25, 1888, in conjunction with a meeting of the International Council of Women, which had been assembled in Washington, D.C., by the National Woman Suffrage Association. The Albaugh Opera House was full and people crowded the aisles. The meeting was opened with an invocation, Rev. Ada C. Bowles read the 26th chapter of Acts, and the congregation sang "Nearer My God to Thee." Rev. Antoinette Brown Blackwell then offered a prayer, which was followed by Rev. Shaw's sermon. Shaw gave this sermon many times. It was listed on all her lecture brochures with "Sunday" placed in brackets before it. She very often delivered it on suffrage campaigns from some local pulpits on Sunday mornings.

The passage of Scripture to which we invite your attention this afternoon will be found in the 26th chapter of Acts and the 19th verse:

"Whereupon, O King Agrippa, I was not disobedient unto the heavenly vision."

In the midst of the beauty of his oriental home the Psalmist of the Lord caught the vision of the events in the midst of which you and I are living to-day. And though he wrought the vision into the wonderful prophecy of the 68th psalm, yet so new and strange were the thoughts to men that for thousands of years they failed to catch its spirit and understand its power. The vision which appeared to David was a world lost in sin, sunken in the mire of its degradation, weak in its false desires and blighted purposes. He heard its cry of deliverance, he saw its uplifted hands with no outstretched hand answering. Everywhere the eyes of good men were turned towards the skies for help. For ages had they striven against the forces of evil; they had sought by every device to turn back the flood-tide of base passion and avarice, but all to no purpose. It seemed as if all men were engulfed in one common ruin. Patiently, prone upon the earth, Sphinx-like, sat woman limited by sin, limited by social custom, limited by false theories, limited by narrow bigotry and by still narrower creeds, listening to the tramp of the weary millions as they passed on through the centuries, patiently listening, toiling and waiting, humbly bearing the pain and weariness which seemed to fall to her lot. Century after century came forth from the divine life but to pass into the great eternity; and still she toiled and still she waited. At last in the mute agony of despair she lifted her eyes above the earth to heaven and away from the jarring strifes which surrounded her and there that which dawned upon her gaze was so full of wonder and light that her soul burst its prison-house of bondage as she beheld the vision of the grandeur and dignity of womanhood.

The truth stood before her, and she knew it was not the purpose of the Divine that she should crouch beneath the bonds of selfishness and custom, that she should yield blindly to prejudice and ignorance. She learned that she was created not from the side of man, but rather by the side of man. The world had suffered that she had not kept her divinely-appointed place. Then she remembered the words of prophecy, that salvation was to come to the race not through the man but through the descendant of the woman.

Recognizing her divinely appointed mission she cried out: "Speak now, Lord, for thy servant heareth Thee." And the answer came: "The Lord giveth the word, and the women that publish the tidings are a great host."(1)

To-day the vision is a reality. From every land the voice of woman is heard proclaiming the word which is given to her, and the wondering world which for a moment stopped its busy wheel of life that it might smite and jeer her has at last learned that wherever the intuitions of the human mind are called into special exercise, wherever the art of persuasive eloquence is demanded, wherever heroic conduct is based upon duty, rather than impulse, wherever her efforts in opening the sacred doors for the benefit of truth can avail--in one and all of these respects woman greatly excels man; and the wisest and best people everywhere feel that if woman enters upon her tasks wielding her own effective armor, if her inspirations are pure and holy, the Spirit Omnipotent whose influence has held sway in all movements and reforms, whose voice has called into its service the great workmen of every age, shall in these last days fall especially upon woman, and if she venture to obey, what is man that he should attempt to abrogate her sacred and divine mission? And in the presence of what woman has already accomplished, who is compelled to say that a true woman, noble in her humility, strong in her gentleness, rising above all selfishness, gathering up the varied gifts and accomplishments to consecrate them to God and humanity--who shall say that such an one is not in a position to do that for which the world will no longer rank her other than among the first in the work of human redemption. Then influenced by lofty motives, with her own womanly nature in her, stimulated by the wail of humanity and the glory of God, woman may go forth and enter into any field of usefulness which God and the world opens up before her.

Yet there are those who still contend that men, and men only, are able to reason out the great problems of life.

We to-day do not grant this. But were it true, there are other avenues to truth than that which lies through the uncertain by-ways of reason. To assume that it were not so is to know why heads and not hearts were made.

Some of the deepest, profoundest truths that have ever come to the knowledge of the race, were felt, not reasoned out. "The world by wisdoms knew not God. The Divine Master and Son of God taught that a pure heart and upright life would quicken the intellect--not "Become learned and you shall know," but "Obey and you shall understand." Up through the universe the Lord himself has cast a highway by which we may arrive at spiritual and human freedom; not by knowledge, but by truth. And the deepest insights of truth are given not by the intellect, but by love.(2)

Who, then, but the mother-heart of the race shall be able to read to its deepest depths the mystery? She shall be able to unearth its profoundest secrets.

In the Scripture from which the text is taken we recognize a universal law which has been the experience of every one of us. Paul is telling the story of a vision which he saw, a vision which became the inspiration of his life, the turning point where his whole life became an entirely new and changed life, at the time when he caught a glimpse of what his life might become, when, in obedience to that vision, he put himself in relation to the power to which he belonged, and recognizing in that One which appeared to him on his way from Jerusalem to Damascus his Divine Master, he also recognized that the purpose of his life could be fulfilled only when in obedience to that Master he caught and assimilated to himself the nature of Him whose servant he was.

He had been recounting the story of this vision to the king and his court. He recalled how he had gone as a persecutor from Jerusalem to Damascus and how he had had manifested to him on his way the vision which changed the whole tone of his life. There was the one point from which his life became something different and new, the point where a new inspiration had come to him. A voice, claiming him as His disciple, spoke unto a soul and spoke the word which turned him from his old prejudices and purposes into a new channel and a new life. He who had been Saul of Tarsus, the persecutor of the disciples of the Lord, became Paul, the prisoner of the Lord Jesus Christ. Permit me to use this vision, which is so familiar to us all, as a type of that which must appear to every one of us who is able to do anything for God and humanity.(3)

Every reformer the world has ever seen has had a similar experience. Every truth which has been taught to humanity has passed through a like channel. No one of God's human children has ever gone forth to the world who has not had first revealed to him his mission in a vision.

To this Jew, bound by the prejudices of past generations, weighted down by the bigotry of human creeds, educated in the schools of an effete philosophy, living amid the bleaching bones of the dead past, down through the darkness and gloom which surrounded him, when as a persecutor he sought to annihilate the disciples of a new faith, there came this vision into his life, there dawned the electric light of a great truth, which, found beneath the hatred and pride and passion which filled his life and heart, the divine germ which is implanted in the soul of each one of God's human children. The divine within the man recognized the light and the voice of the divine without the man, and answered to the voice which spoke from without, "Speak, Lord, who art Thou?" and the Truth spoke unto him, "I am Jesus, whom thou persecutest."

Then came crowding through his mind new queries: Can it be that my fathers were wrong, and that their philosophy and religion does not contain all there is of truth? Can it be that outside of all we have known there lies a great unexplored universe of truth to which the mind of man can yet attain? Can it be that my past has been wrong? And filled with the Divine purpose he opened his heart to receive the new truth which came to him from the vision which God revealed to his soul.

All down through the centuries God has been revealing in visions the great truths which have lifted the race step by step, until to-day womanhood, in this sunset hour of the Nineteenth Century, is gathered here from the East and the West, and the North and South, women of every land, of every race, of all religious beliefs, with diverse theories and plans. But diverse and varied as are our races, diverse and varied as are our theories, diverse as are our religious beliefs, yet we come together here and now with one harmonious purpose-that of lifting humanity, both men and women, into a higher, purer, truer life.

And to-day leaning over the battlements of the Kingdom of God, the angels of the Lord witness what they have never seen before in all the ages of the past--a great body of women, each one filled with the great purpose of her own peculiar life's vision, and yet each one making her own mission subservient to the one great purpose for which we have all gathered together.

To one has come the vision of political freedom; she saw how the avarice and ambition of one class with power made him forget the rights of another. She saw how power made him forget the rights of another. She saw how the unjust law embittered both, those who made them and those upon whom the injustice rested; she recognized the great principles of universal equality and right, and seeing this thing that all alike must be free; not that men, not that black men and white men, but that mankind, humanity everywhere, must be lifted up out of the subjection into the free and full air of divine liberty.

To another was revealed the vision of social freedom. She saw that sin, which crushed and blackened the lives of one class, rested lightly on the lives of the other. She saw its blighting effect on both, and she lifted up her voice and demanded that there be recognized no sex in sin. Another has come hither, who, gazing about her, saw men brutalized by the rum fiend, the very life of a nation threatened, and the power of the liquor traffic, with its hand on the helm of state, guiding her with sails full spread straight upon the rocks of dire destruction. Then looking away from earth, she beheld a vision of what the race and our nation might become with all its possibility of wealth, with its possibility of power, if freed from the rum fiend, and forth upon her mission of deliverance she sped her way.

Another beheld a vision of what it is to be learned, to explore the great fields of knowledge the Infinite has spread out before the world. And this vision has driven her out from the seclusion of her own quiet life that she may give this great truth to the world, to womanhood everywhere.

By the shores of the Ganges sat a young girl upon whom a great vision had dawned, of deliverance to thousands of her own kind, and breaking away from the bondage of the customs of centuries, she is revealing to the world the vision that dawned upon her there, of what India might become when her child widows are free to carry the gospel of liberty to her secluded millions.

And so we come, each bearing her torch of living truth, casting over the world the light of the vision that dawned upon her own soul.

These are the visions that pertain to men, which when wrought out into living truths will transform this world, bringing humanity into harmonious relations with itself and infusing justice into citizenship, honesty into business, purity into social relations, and the spirit of the golden rule over all life.

But there is still another and higher vision which reaches above earth, beyond time; a vision which has dawned upon so

many of God's children that they are here not to do their own
work but the will of Him who sent them. Before their gaze there
has dawned the great eternity of truth.   Before them lies the
great eternity when the earth and the fashion of it shall have
passed away.   And the woman who recognizes the still higher
truth recognizes the great power to which she belongs and what
her life and the lives of all of God's children may become, when
in submission to that Master she takes upon herself the nature of
Him whom she serves; and while she sees the sin and injustice
and suffering, and while she hears the groaning agony about her,
and while she bears the blows of oppression and scorn, yet
around and about and through her life is a peace so deep, so full
that the hand which rests in the hand of a Divine Master moves
with no quiver of fear.   The child of God puts her hand in the
hand of her Father and knows that where He leads her He gives
her His own support of peace, and she gives out her vision to the
world in the spirit of the life of Him whom she serves and loves.

These, then, are the visions which come to us, but God does
not let us rest in visions.

Never has there dawned upon the life of any of God's children
a vision but there was a purpose in that vision. Therefore we will
notice in the second place the purpose of all these visions which
have come to us.

Paul was not permitted to dwell on the vision of truth which
came to him. God had a purpose in its manifestation, and that
purpose is revealed when God said to the wonder-stricken
servant, "Arise! For I have appeared unto thee for this purpose,
not that thou behold the truth for thyself, but to make thee a
minister and a witness both of the truth which thou hast already
seen and of other truths which I shall reveal unto thee. Go unto
the Gentiles. Give them the truth which thou shalt receive that
their eyes may be opened, and that they may be turned from
darkness to light and from the power of Satan unto God; that
they too may receive a like inheritance with thyself. Take to
them this truth that the power of the truth over their lives may
make them free." This we believe to be the inner purpose of
every truth which the Divine has made manifest to his workmen
and women in all ages.(4)

Not that they to whom the vision comes may study its effect
upon men, if it were revealed to them, not that they may
speculate upon the expediency of its practical operation over
human lives, not that God lets those to whom he reveals the
truth decide as to whether the rest shall receive it or not, not
that they are to be the favored repositories into which the Divine
shall pour His sacred secrets; but that they to whom the truth is
revealed may carry it to a waiting race, that their eyes may be
opened and that they may be turned from darkness unto light
and from the power of Satan unto God. This then is God's lesson
to the reformers, God's lesson to you and to me.

He opens before our eyes the vision of a great truth, and for a moment He permits our wondering gaze to rest upon it; then He bids us go forth. Jacob of old saw the vision of God's messengers going forth up and down the world, up and down the mount of visions, ascending and descending, but none of them were standing still.(5)

This is the greatest age the world has ever seen. Vision after vision appears to God's children in such quick succession that we cannot comprehend them; and what is needed is someone to bring the truth and the race together, to bring God's thought to the minds of God's children.

Herein, then, lies the secret of the success of the reformer. First the vision, then the purpose of the vision. "I was not disobedient unto the heavenly vision." This is the manly and noble confession of one of the world's greatest reformers, and in it we catch a glimpse of the secrets of the success of his divinely appointed mission. The difference between the Saul of Tarsus and Paul the Prisoner of the Lord, was measured by his obedience. This, too, is a universal law, true of the life of every great reformer, who, having had revealed to him a vision of the great truth, has in obedience to that vision carried it to men standing midway with the world of truth on the one hand and the world of men on the other, and he becomes the medium through which these two find each other. Though at first he holds the truth to himself, and longs to be lifted up by its power, he soon learns that there is a giving forth of that which one possesses which enriches the giver, and more, he learns that the more he gives out of his vision to men the richer and larger and fuller it becomes, and the clearer and brighter it grows, until it enriches his whole life and illuminates all his pathway. This was the experience of Paul, and though we saw him this afternoon in our Scripture lesson bound with fetters, on trial for his life, yet his words are the words of a conqueror, and they ring forth with such a triumphant tone, as for a moment to make us forget that they are the utterances of a prisoner, and not of one who has become a conqueror over all his foes.

Yet his life was not an idle dream; it was a constant struggle against the very people whom he tried to save; his greatest foes were those to whom he was sent. He had learned the lesson all reformers must sooner or later learn; that the world never welcomes its deliverers save with the dungeon, or the fagot, or the cross. No man or woman has ever sought to lead his fellows to a higher and better mode of life without learning the strength and power of the world's ingratitude, and though at times popularity may follow in the wake of a reformer, yet the reformer knows popularity is not love. The world will support you when you have compelled it to do so by manifestations of power and you have favors to bestow, but it will shrink from you as soon as the power and greatness are no longer on your side.

This is the penalty paid by strong and good people who sacrifice themselves for others. They must live without sympathy; their feelings will be misunderstood; their efforts will be uncomprehended. Like Paul, they will be betrayed by friends. Like the Lord Christ in agony of Gethsemane, they must bear their struggle alone; they must be content to live and die like the Divine Master, betrayed and forsaken.(6)

It is true posterity will judge them and esteem them, but that is poor consolation while they are braving the foe. Our reverence for the reformers of the past is posterity's judgment of them. But to them what is that now? They have passed into the shadows where neither our voice of praise or blame disturbs the repose of truth's martyrs. What avails the admiration or reverence of posterity to the heart that ached in all its aloneness then?

This is the hardest lesson the reformer has to learn. When with the soul aglow with the light of a great truth he or she is obedience to the vision turns to take it to the needy one, and instead of finding a world ready to welcome her, instead of finding a world ready to rise up and receive her, she finds a world wrapped in the swaddling clothes of error eagerly seeking to win others to their condition of slavery. She longs to make them free; she listens to their jarring, conflicting views and creeds and longs to save them from the misery they bring. She knows that there is no form of slavery more bitter or arrogant or brutal than error, and that truth and truth alone can make man free, and she longs to bring the heart of the world and the heart of truth together that the truth may exercise its transforming power over the life of the world. And the greatest test of the reformer's courage comes when, with a warm earnest longing for humanity, she breaks for it the bread of truth which God has put into her hand and the world turns from this life-giving power and asks instead of bread a stone. It crucifies its Savior while it demands to have delivered unto it a robber.(7)

It is just here that so many of God's workmen fail and themselves need to turn back to the vision as it has appeared to them, and to gather fresh courage and new inspiration for the future.

This, my sisters, we all must do if we would succeed. The secret of success is in earnestness. The reformer may be inconsistent, he may be stern or even impatient, but if the world feels that the reformer is in earnest he cannot fail. Let the truth which he desires to take to me first take possession of himself. Every woman who to-day goes out into the world with a truth, who has not herself become possessed of that truth, had better stay at home.

But let the truth first take possession of her and let all doubt be driven out of the mind, and then let the soul be aglow with its divine purpose, and there is no power on earth or in hell that can long keep the truth from the lives of men and from working its miracles of light.

Apparent failure is oft times the grandest success. Christ commended the widow, you remember, when she gave her mite to an apparently failing cause. Jesus climbed the hill of Cavalry step by step, spit upon, reviled, derided, and yet erect, knowing that at its top was to be erected His cross. But He climbed, and you and I to-day get our inspiration from the cross. Apparent failure is then oft times the grandest success. Let us cleave to our hope despite what appearances may bring to us.(8)

Who would have dreamed, when at that great meeting in London some years ago the arrogance and pride of men excluded from its body the women whom God had moved to lift up their voices in behalf of the baby that was sold by the pound, who would have dreamed that that very exclusion was the keynote of woman's freedom? That out of the prejudice and bigotry of that hour God should be able to flash upon the crushed hearts of those excluded the grand vision which we see manifested here to-day? That out of a longing for liberty of a portion of the race God should be able to show to women the still larger, grander vision of the freedom of all human kind? Thus is even the wrath of men made to become the agent of the Divine will!(9)

Grand as is this vision which meets us to-day, it is but the dawning of a new day; and as the first beams of morning light give promise of the radiance which shall envelope the earth when the sun shall have arisen in all its splendor, so there comes to us to-day a prophecy of that glorious day when the vision which we are all now beholding, which is beaming in the soul of one, shall enter the hearts and transfigure the lives of all God's people.

In our eagerness and earnestness two things are necessary for us if we succeed.

The true reformer must be possessed of two things--infinite hope and infinite love; but out of the gloom and discouragement, out from the error and bigotry that opposes the work, he must look up in hope, hoping even against hope and with his eye following the eye of the Divine Master, he must see man, fallen it is true, but magnificent in his ruin. He must catch the thought which burned in the soul of Christ; that, beneath the vilest outside, there is within a human soul capable of endless growth. Christ saw this, hence He treated all with respect, not because they were titled Rabbis, not because they were rich Pharisees, but because they were men, men out of whose lives the truth is able to work its miracle of glorious humanity.

Infinite love! This must baptize the reformer. She must be bathed in it and walk in its light. The true reformer recognizes truth in the vision which has come to others. As the magnet draws to itself the needle, so love draws to itself love.

This, however, is where we are most apt to fail in our desire
to advance our peculiar truths. We fail to recognize the truth in
others; especially are we apt to look upon the conditions we
have outgrown with contempt; and too often we despise the
past, forgetting that the things which are to be must develop
from what is now, as the things which now are the enlargement
and development of that which was. As looking upon the
building spring-time we ask the earth for a flower, she answers
back to us, "I cannot give you a flower unless you give me
something to begin with," we go back to the dark hard remnant
of a past life and bring her a seed, and the mother earth wraps it
in her warm embrace, sending the life current through its being,
then there grows for us a new body, more beautiful even than
that life from which it sprang. So when we look back upon the
past and see how prejudice and ignorance, how bigotry and the
creeds and narrow views of men have stayed the progress of
truth, we must not forget that the growth of truth, like the
growth of a flower, is progressive. So of the creeds and dogmas
of the past, which men have called Christian and which you and I
know in this brighter, fuller, clearer life of the noontide of glory
which shines upon us to-day were not Christian.

Still these are not to be despised, for when Jesus wished to
bring us Christianity he went to Judaism which had some truth
in it, though mixed with much that was not truth and though it
was very meagre and insufficient, he took what truth he did find,
and brought Christianity out of it--so much we lead and teach to-
day the truths we do find. We must bring them into clearer
light, we must not despise them, for out of them we are to build
a greater, newer and broader truth than that which the world
has heretofore known. If God has led us to see truths which we
once did not see, and to regard as error what once we thought
was true, we are not to despise the way through which we have
come, nor the narrower forms which gave us the promise of a
higher life. We will receive more light only as the knowledge we
have within us glows and burns into a brighter flame and reveals
to us more and more of the the truths which are to be known.

But by all you hold sacred, let me in the name of my Master
say to the young women who are here to-day if you have a bit of
truth hold fast to that which God has given you; let no power, no
injustice, no obstacle, no scorn, no opposition, let nothing
extinguish this flame. Hold it high, and if the world lags behind,
and calls upon you to go back to it, hold it still higher. Bid the
world come up to your truth, never take your truth down to the
world's level.

The life which God intends us to live is not one long dream of
truth and of its power. He calls us to lift ourselves upon our feet,
and, in the dignity of a truer, nobler womanhood than we have
ever heretofore known, to stand face to face with truth and open

up a way for it to enter into our soul, and there to bloom into the eternal flower of constant purpose and of a new life.

Open the windows of your souls, let the sunshine of God's love rush down into them, and as the world becomes a new world when the sun has risen, so let your poor human lives become new and transformed lives as the sun of God's spirit enters into them. Out of the vision of truth which is within you He is able, by the influence of His spirit upon your life, to work a miracle and bring the truth therein to other lives.

This, then, shall be the heavenly vision. Not that which we behold to-day, but when every man and woman into whose soul the light of truth has burned goes forth in the name and in the spirit of his Master to give this truth to the world that the world by it may be lifted out of its bigotry and sin, out of its false life into the fullness of a truer and broader living. When every man and woman shall have caught the vision which Paul caught, the vision of Jesus Christ as his master, and whose own life is transformed and fulfilled in its purpose as the spirit of that Master works upon him, and there is wrought upon his life the miracle of divine truth and of a divine resurrection.

Paul standing in the light of that vision beheld the glory of what a true man might become. He saw all the possibilities that were before him when he took upon himself the service of Him to whom he belonged, and what Paul saw every child of God has seen who has stood in the light of truth, and has seen the possibilities that are his if he will only open his heart and let the truth come in there and illuminate his whole life until he is filled with all the fullness of God. So the child of God, beholding in him the Glory of the Father, shall be changed into the same image from glory to glory as by the spirit of the Lord. Then when this light shall have rested upon us all, and we are filled with his spirit we shall be ready to give ourselves to the world, and then will the world receive us in the name of Him through whom we come, whose name is love--God.

Our Father, who art in heaven, we thank Thee for all the infinite possibilities that are opened to Thy children; we thank Thee, O God, for the truths which have dawned upon our lives; we thank Thee that when one of Thy children holds fast to any part of Thy great truth, all truth is possible to him. O, God, we pray unto Thee that Thou wilt bless with Thy spirit the truth which each one of us holds to-day; that we may go forth in Thy name and in Thy spirit to do Thy will. Hear our prayer our God; bless Thou the heart of each one of us as it is lifted towards Thee for guidance and help. We pray thee that the time may come when that heavenly vision shall be the inspiration of all lives, when all men shall know God and the power of His love over human hearts and lives. Lift us up, we beseech Thee, O God, into the radiance of Thy divine spirit and help us in the spirit of

truth to go forth in His name who is able to overcome all things.
In His name we ask it. Amen.

The New Man

The source of this text is a typewritten manuscript in box 22, folder 491, Shaw papers. Because of the brevity, the manuscript may not be the complete text of Shaw's lecture. In all probability it is the essence of the lecture and Shaw made various local adaptations each time she delivered it. According to notations in her diary, she delivered this address most frequently during the late nineties. Her 1898 diary, for example, lists it forty times. The New Man was easily one of her most popular lectures.

The world is perfectly familiar with the new woman. She has been preached about and at. She has been written about and at, until we know everything about her, except the truth. She has been misrepresented, misunderstood and maligned until the distorted image we behold as she is held up to public ridicule is neither human nor possible. Her dress is the one subject which the Old Man never wearies of discussing, as he fears she may invade his prerogatives in dress. This is a useless fear, as the real new woman will always want to look as well as she can, and no human being could look well in men's clothes, and the new woman will not wear them for that reason if for no other. But there is a new woman, and, taking her all in all, we rather like her, for she is the same old woman, with a few modern improvements. The new woman should be an improvement on the old, when we realize all the advantages of education and culture, all the opportunities for acquiring trades and professions, all the open avenues by which she may come in contact with the larger life of the world which has made her what she is--more broad-minded and better developed than in any previous period in the world's history. The problem for the new woman to solve is how to blend the broader, larger culture of the present with the devotion to duty, the loyalty to family, and the best service of life, which were the pride and glory of the women of the past. And I have so much faith in the new woman that I believe the result will be a woman in which head and heart will be so perfectly balanced that the woman to be will be an ideal human woman.

But since there is a new woman, there must be a new man. What manner of man shall he be who shall be a fit mate for the new woman?

The first demand made upon the new man is that he shall be a perfectly developed physical organism.

Statistics compiled in our higher institutions of learning tell us that our young women are better physically developed than their mothers of twenty-five and thirty years ago, but that young men are continually deteriorating physically. These statistics are not confined to our Higher Institutions of Learning, but from the recruiting stations during the Spanish War the reports were made that the young men who offered themselves for enlistment did not attain to the stature of those who enlisted during the Civil War.

Not only do statistics tell us of decreased stature of men in this country, but from England, France, Germany and other lands. The reasons given by those who have studied the subject are insufficient nourishment in childhood among the poor, and the excessive use of tobacco and liquor among the growing youth of all classes.

What we claim for the new man, if he wishes to have the new woman look up to him, as it is said, the old woman did to the old man, is this: that he will no more form a habit which interferes with his physical development than he would deliberately form one which interfered with his intellectual growth.

The second demand upon the new man is that he must be intellectually developed to be the fit mate for the new woman. Statistics compiled by men tell us that we are graduating in our High and Grammar Schools nearly two girls to one boy, that the increase in the percent of young women in our secondary schools and colleges are greatly in excess of men, and that at the same rate of increase they will soon outnumber men as college graduates.

Since in the world's market of labor the value of life has changed from brawn to brain, the ungraduated man is at a disadvantage when pitted against a graduated woman, and he is handicapped at the very beginning of his career. The only remedy that some people are able to suggest is to prevent the young women from graduating, instead of insisting that the young man must graduate and properly fit himself for life's service.

The evil is due to our false social ideal, which places material wealth above character, which sees no other form of success than material prosperity, until our boys feel that to be out in the world's market of struggle is of more importance than to be an educated man. That a silver dollar in his pocket is of more importance than the value of that silver in gray matter in his head. Our boys are all right, the fault lies in the false social ideals of our age which lead them into wrong estimates of values. We must change our ideals, and teach them that character is of infinitely greater value than material wealth, that intelligence is of more importance than a bank account. The new man must have the higher ideals of labor and service which women are holding to-day. The time has gone by when any man or woman can claim the world owes them a living. This world has never owed anyone a living, and never will; all it owes to any of us is an opportunity to *earn* a living. We have, each one of us, a right to the opportunity; then, given the opportunity, we have a right to the living after we have earned it--earned it in toil of brain, or brawn, or heart, in the home or out of it, wherever duty and the needs of the world call us.

The new man will not spend his time in holding conventions to discuss and argue and settle by his vote what God meant women to do, or rather not to do; he will know that the only way you can find out what either men or women were intended to do is to let them alone until they have solved the problem for themselves.

They will not talk of women crowding men out of lucrative positions until they examine the facts, and learn that instead of women taking men's work from them it is men who have come into our homes, and by inventive energy and changed economical conditions have taken out of the home and from women all the old time industries by which women earned a livelihood within the home. There are more men doing the work which women formerly did than there are women doing the work which men formerly did; all the carding, weaving and spinning, all the churning, cooking and table waiting, the washing, the knitting, the preserving and baking, the dressmaking and mil-linery, every industry of the home men have taken to the factories and shops of the country, and when women start out to find their grandmothers' work, ten to one, they find a man doing it. It is not that men object to women working, for they have always worked--ceaseless, grinding toil has been their lot, and no one complained until they set a price upon their labor and demanded payment for their service. We have never been denied work, it is only the pay to which objection is made.

The great folly is to try to cheapen women's labor. The injustice is as great to men as to women, for men can no more compete with cheaply paid woman labor than they can with cheaply paid Chinese or Japanese labor. There is but one remedy, and that is a universal demand for equal pay for equal quality and quantity of work.

The new man must be a moral man. There have been two standards of moral living in this world for men and women, both of which have been erected by men. We women ought to be forever gratified that when men erected moral standards for us they erected the highest they knew. The great evil was that they failed to erect the same standards for themselves, and that they allowed the world to accept lower ideals for men than for women. The new man and woman must stand upon the same moral plane, and it must be the one which men have erected for women. The reason men and not women have erected moral standards in the past is because, as Alexander Hamilton said: "The man who controls my physical substance controls my moral nature." In the past men controlled the physical substance of the world, and could dictate to women the terms on which they could share it, and the terms dictated by men women must accept. In the future women will control their physical substance, but they will, instead of lowering their own, compel men to elevate their standards of moral living.

Then the new man will be just, and will refuse to accept for himself either political or other privileges which he denies to women. Equality and Justice will be terms which men will apply to women as they do to each other, and in the new time no one sex will deprive the other sex of their citizen's right to vote, and a government will be recognized as a Republic only when it derives its power from the consent of the governed women as well as governed men.

God's Women

"God's Women" was one of Shaw's standard lectures. She gave it many times and chose to deliver it at a meeting of the National Council of Women of the United States held in Washington, D.C., February 22-25, 1891. The address was one of Shaw's most entertaining lectures, and it was enthusiastically received by the National Council of Women. In a letter to Clara Osburn dated March 7, 1891, Shaw wrote:

> Never in my life did I make the success I did there at the Council on my Speech "God's Women." The audience cheered, stood up waved their hankerchiefs and then broke out singing "Praise God from Whom all Blessings Flow." It was a perfect oration. I wish Father and Mother had been there. I thought of them all the time and thought how glad they would be.

The text is taken from the *National Council of Women of the United States 1891*, edited by Rachel Foster Avery, Corresponding Secretary, (J. B. Lippincott, Company, Philadelphia, 1891), pp. 242-249. The text reflects Shaw's extemporaneous style, and is probably a slightly polished stenographic report.

The subject, God's Women, was suggested to me by reading an article in a Chicago newspaper, in which a gentleman defined God's Women. It has always seemed to me very remarkable how clear the definitions of men are in regard to women, their duties, their privileges, their responsibilities, their relations to each other, to men, to government, and now to God; and while they have been elucidating them for years, we have been patiently listening.

The woman of the nineteenth century has taken to definition, and she has come to the conclusion that it may be quite possible for a woman as well as a man to comprehend the relations of women to each other, to their homes, to the Church, to the State, and listen for the voice of God themselves, to know what the relation of women to the Divine is; and, believing this, no divine, whether he bears the name of Elder, Deacon, Priest,

Bishop, or Pope, shall define for the woman of the twentieth century her right to be and to become all God makes it possible for her to be. (Applause.)

Every reform must pass through three stages of struggle. Ours has passed through the first, and we have gotten clear beyond it. We are just at the end of the second stage, and in the dawn of the next century will come the third stage upon us.

The first stage, through which every reform must pass, is that of the assertion that it is impossible, it is impracticable, it is ridiculous, it is unthinkable; and they who begin in the beginnings of reform, and bring the question before the people, must stand and bear all the scorn, all the loneliness, all the "aloneness" of great reformers in great questions, and, like the Lord Jesus Christ, they must learn to tread the wine-press alone. Womanhood has had its leaders, who have taken the stand and borne the scorn of it; and now you and I to-day are able to walk in a smooth path, to be welcomed by thousands, to be cheered for the sentiments for which they were scorned, and to be paid for doing that which they paid for the privilege of doing. (Applause.)

We have passed that stage. The second stage of every reform is the religious phase of it, the stage in which it must meet all the obstacles reared by religionists, by theologians, and by a class of people who are always afraid that religion born of God, emanating from God, the soul and life of the world, will be overthrown by a few of God's simple human children; and these people fearing that God--I speak reverently--shall not be able to hold His own against a few, think they must stand up in defense of God and the great principle and soul-life of His Being, and of our being. We have been passing through this stage for some time. We have proved by the Bible that when God created man in the beginning in his own image, He created man, male and female man, and called their name Adam, and to this male and female man, who he called Adam, He gave all things, and bade this man Adam, male and female, to subdue all things, even the world, to themselves.

The race has believed all this time that Adam was Mr. Adam, and not Mrs. Adam at all. (Laughter.) Eve was not Mrs. Adam because she was the wife of Mr. Adam. She was no more Mrs. Adam because she was the wife of Mr. Adam than Adam was Mr. Adam because he was the husband of Mrs. Adam; not a bit. (Laughter.) They were each Adam, and neither of them alone was Adam. They were Adam together. (Applause and laughter.) You can never have a male Adam or a female Adam. You must have a male and female Adam, and you have manhood and womanhood,--humanity.

The great divine who originated this subject for me was lecturing before an Institute of Sacred Theology in the city of Chicago. Before him was a class of students, male and female, and he was defining to the male students what they, the males, might permit the females to do. He says, "There are some things which women may be permitted to do." Now, we like that, don't we? Something that we may be permitted to do. "They may be permitted to dispense certain charities; they may be permitted to speak in prayer and class-meetings; they may be permitted to do certain lines of church-work. There are other things which women may not be permitted to do. Among the things which they may not be permitted to do is to hold high official relation to the Church, to become its ministers and to dispense its sacraments. These things women may not be permitted to do."

In referring to the relation of woman to the Church, he spoke of the argument, raised by many women, that it was the design of God that woman should be eligible to any position she could occupy. The women go to the Bible to prove their position, and the one woman upon whom we have all laid our claim and our boast, is that grand old woman who was able to cry out, in looking over Israel in its hours of peace, "There was trouble, there was dissension, there was unrest in Israel until I, Deborah, a mother in Israel, rose," and we point to the fact that the judges of Israel were always understood by those people to be divinely selected for their position; and, being thus divinely selected, we cannot assume that any human being could have taken this position who was not recognized by the people at least to have been chosen by God, and, even with the authority of the Bishop back of it, we cannot assume that God did not know what He was doing when He chose Deborah to be a judge in Israel.(1)

If the Bishop thinks God made a mistake, he will have to wait forever to correct it, for it is done, and we cannot go back of the record. This woman found a country greatly disturbed, a country where the judges had been taking bribes, a country where the people were utterly demoralized, where they dared not walk on their highways because of thieves and robbers, but were compelled to go secretly through cross-lots in order to get from city to city. During the forty years of her reign as judge of Israel the whole condition of things was revolutionized. We are told that she judged all the people in righteousness, and the people had peace for forty years. Just think of forty years of peace! We have never known such a period since that day. (Applause.) Now, then, this woman was not, we are told by the Bishop, God's woman. If, then she was not God's woman, whose woman was she? (Laughter.) And if God is not able to recognize His own, what will become of us at the last? We believe that this judge in Israel was divinely ordained for the work, because otherwise she could not have done her work so well.

This same divine tells us that Miriam was not God's woman either; that this woman was a sort of a something interpolated for the times of war and distress. All great souls are interpolated

for great occasions when they are needed. (Applause.) And
when God wants a certain thing done that he knows needs a
woman to do it, he generally raises a woman and not a man for
the position. (Laughter and applause.) The world needed a
woman.(2)

Here was the boy Moses, under the reign of a man by whom
he would have been put to death in his babyhood, but that the
loving heart of his mother said, "He shall not die"; and she hid
him away.(3)

We are told that women have no reasoning powers. They are
not able to arrive at logical conclusions. When I was studying
theology a young man in my class in the same college who was
arrayed, as they always are the first year, with a coat buttoned up
high around the neck, and all that, said he thought it was his
duty to warn me in the beginning. He said, "You are making a
great mistake; God never intended woman to preach the gospel.
God has so constructed the brain of a woman that she cannot
give a correct and continuous exegesis of Scripture." Doesn't
that sound like a first-year student? (Laughter.) "It may be," I
said, "that God has constructed our brain so that we cannot give
a correct and continuous exegesis of Scripture. But he has, at
least, constructed our brain so that somewhere He found a place
in it in which He has bestowed a large amount of gumption.
Now, if we have not the power of exegetical ability, we have
gumption enough, if we undertake to preach and preach our
church empty, to get out of the pulpit and go into the pew."
(Laughter and applause.) What a grand thing it would be for the
church at large if the other sex had some of that kind of
gumption! (Laughter and applause.)

There might not be so many Bishops, either. (Laughter.)

Now this woman, Miriam, we are told, is not God's woman.
But see this little woman's gumption, how she gets around the
young princess, and the mother-heart of the young princess goes
out towards the baby! She was a woman, though she was a
princess. See how shrewdly this little girl planned it so that the
child's mother should become his nurse, and how, under the
guidance and care of his mother, Moses was reared to become
the leader of the people of Israel! You see that in all that
transaction God did not need a man, and He did need a number
of women; and He found women enough of the kind He wanted
to do just the work that He wanted done. What is more natural
than that when Moses, years after, led the people out from
Egypt, there went by the side of the great leader his sister
Miriam, and that they, with their other brother, became the
united leaders of the children of Israel out from their bondage?

If God chose a woman to act in these cases, when the world
needed a clear brain, a tender, affectionate, loving, motherly
heart, a firm and determined will, and chose the woman to do it,
and if when the people needed a leader to guide them out of

bondage to freedom He chose a woman to be among the leading instruments of that great undertaking, who shall dare to say, be he layman or priest, that such a woman is not God's woman?

The Bishop says there are certain classes of women who are God's women. We want to know who they are, because then we can range ourselves on the right side. God's women, according to the Bishop, are "the Ruths, the Rachels, and the Marys."(4)

Ruth was certainly a remarkable young woman, because she was absolutely devoted to her mother-in-law (great laughter and applause), and that takes a great woman. I shall never rise to say that a woman devoted to her mother-in-law is not God's woman. But then, Ruth had some peculiar ways of getting along in this world. I hardly think the Bishop would like to have some of us who are unmarried follow Ruth's method of securing a husband. I hardly think he would like us to follow her line of courtship; yet the only two things for which she is admired are a devotion to her mother-in-law and a peculiar method of obtaining a husband. These are perhaps two very good things in themselves, but we should hardly think they were of such importance to the race that such a woman should be specially held up as a type of God's woman.

Then there was Rachel. We know two or three things about Rachel. One is that she had a high sense of the subserviency of woman to man that, while the lazy shepherds lay about, gazing at each other, and at the skies, and perhaps at her, she left them gazing while she went to the well and drew the water to water the flocks. That might be the Bishop's idea of God's woman, but it is hardly my idea of the proper division of labor between the sexes. I should prefer to let the Bishop draw the water while I gazed. There is another thing we know about Rachel--that she was a very handsome woman. Every man and every woman likes to see a handsome woman; but I have heard it said that women are always jealous of each other's beauty, and always angry if anybody says anything about the beauty of another woman.

This gathering of women is certainly an exception to the rule, for we have been the proudest set of women you ever saw, because in the providence of God there has been gathered here with us in this Council such a magnificent band of beautiful young women of whom we are all proud, and we glory in their beauty. Those of us who have passed out youth look at these young girls, not with envy, but with a little bit of pain in our hearts, and say, "If God had only made us that way, we would have been glad." We do rejoice in each other, and we are glad of a good looking young woman. Rachel was so good looking that Jacob wanted to marry her, and he worked seven years for her. She must have been a very desirable woman for Jacob to give seven years' hard labor for her. Nowadays if a man courts for a few evenings he thinks it is plenty of time to spend on it. Jacob waited seven years and then got cheated out of the woman he wanted, and had to marry her oldest sister. Rachel, however, was a courageous woman, and he was a faithful man, so he waited seven years more. The only other thing I know about Rachel is that the Bible says she wept for her children because they were not. The inference is that you men may go on behaving, as you say you do, improperly in politics; that you may make the politics of this nation dark, damaging, and unclean; that at last you may have an unrighteous war, and then take our children and kill them on the battle-field, and all we have to do about it is to stay at home and weep for our children because they are not! We are to have nothing to say as to whether you shall kill them or not. All we are to have to do about it is to cry about it. Would it not be infinitely better for the race if, instead of weeping for their children slain in battle or by the unrighteousness of cruel and wicked laws, women would rise in the dignity of their motherhood and demand that wars shall cease, and children shall be protected by law?

Then the Bishop tells us Mary was one of God's women. There are a number of Marys, and the Bishop does not designate which of them it was. If he means the Mary out of whom the seven devils were cast, I should agree with him, for when seven devils have been cast out of a woman she must be something of a saint. If it was the Mary who washed the feet of Christ and wiped them with the hairs of her head, in token of penitence, I again agree with him, for that kind of penitence shows us she had been lifted up very close to the Divine life.(5)

There was the Mary who sat at the feet of the Lord learning theology of Him; and the only reproof the Lord ever gave a woman was not given to Mary, the theological student, but to Martha, the woman who worried about her house-work, and wanted Mary to give up theology and go into the kitchen and cook the dinner.(6)

Then there was another Mary, and she is the Mary whom I have taken as my example in my profession. This was the Mary who stood by the tomb of the Lord, and there at the mouth of the open tomb she received the first divine commission from the Divine One Himself to go out into the world and preach the gospel of a risen Lord.(7)

If it was the Mary who was his mother, the Bishop has brought forward the wrong Mary to prove his case. What does the Bible tell us? In the fullness of time God needed for the world a Redeemer. How should He give the Redeemer to the world? He gave the Redeemer to the world by choosing out of the world a woman to become the mother of the Savior of the race. God and a woman gave to the world its Redeemer.(8)

Here are the Marys, two of whom were sinners. One was a woman who was a theological student learning at the feet of the Master. The other was the first divinely-commissioned preacher of the resurrection. One was the mother of the Lord, doing the greatest public work for the race that has ever been done in the world. I am glad the Bishop holds that women theological students are God's women; that women ministers are God's women; and that the woman who was the mother of the Saviour of the world was also God's woman. I believe they were; I believe that the Miriams and the Deborahs and the Vashtis were God's women too.

When I was a girl I read the Bible through in order to select from it the two people who were to be my hero and heroine through life. My hero was Caleb, my heroine Vashti. Vashti disobeyed her husband, and was driven from her palace because of it.(9)

I selected Vashti from among them all because she did disobey her husband--a woman away back in the centuries, who recognized the dictates of her own self-respect; a woman who refused to become the puppet of a king and of his drunken courtiers; a woman ready to give up a throne, a husband, and a kingdom rather than do an ignominious thing; such a woman is God's woman, husband or no husband. I wish the world were full of Vashtis to-day, standing by the right of their individual self-respect.

The concluding remarks of the Bishop were in relation to motherhood. He referred to that passage of Scripture which we have heard so much about in this discussion: "She shall be saved in childbirth." Most of us regard this passage of the Scripture as meaning that she shall be saved by the coming of the Child--shall be saved by the birth of Jesus Christ. She shall be saved because Jesus Christ came into the world to save not man alone, but women also. Women shall be saved because of the coming of Him who is the Emancipator of the race, women included. Believing this, we think the discussion which has been raised upon this line is a mere makeshift; it has nothing to stand upon.(10)

There are two things to be considered in relation to motherhood. We have heard that motherhood is the greatest crown of glory which a woman can wear. We answer, No; motherhood is not the greatest crown of glory which a woman can wear. Motherhood may even not be a crown of glory at all. It may become a crown of shame. It requires that there shall be a something back of motherhood to define what motherhood shall be, and in this something back of motherhood lies that which may make it a crown of glory. The highest crown of glory which a woman can wear is not motherhood, it is *womanhood*--true, noble, strong, healthy, spiritual womanhood; the daughter of the King, the child of God, equal with the Bishop or any man in the world. If the woman is first of all a woman, all things shall be to her a crown of glory, whether it be motherhood or spinsterhood. The mother-heart of woman, the mother-heart that reaches out to the race and finds a wrong and rights it, finds a broken heart and heals it, finds a bruised life ready to be broken and sustains it--a woman instinct with mother-love, which is the expression of the Divine love; a woman who, finding any wrong, any weakness, any pain, any sorrow, anywhere in the world, reaches out her hand to right the wrong, to heal the pain, to comfort the suffering--such a woman is God's woman. It matters not where she may be--where she was born, under what skies she has lived, she is God's woman, and at the last she shall find her God. (Great applause.)

The Fate of Republics

This was Shaw's most famous lecture. It was one of the first lectures on woman suffrage she composed, and she delivered it hundreds of times over the course of several decades. She chose to deliver this address at the first National Woman Suffrage Association Convention she attended in 1889. The text here is taken from *The Congress of Women, World's Columbian Exposition*, Chicago, Illinois, U.S.A., edited by Mary Kavannaugh Oldham Eagle, chairman of the Committee on Congresses, E. H. Gregg & Co., Kansas City, Mo. 1894, pp. 152-156. A typewritten manuscript of this speech can be found in the Shaw papers (box 22, folder 499). The original manuscript seems to be an earlier version of the address and is somewhat more primitive than the address delivered at the Congress of Women in 1894. The Congress of Women text obviously underwent some editorial polish. The ideas and the language of the two texts correspond closely. Since this speech was given many times, always extemporaneously, it is difficult to argue that one text is more authentic than the other. In all probability the Congress of Women text is a stenographic transcription slightly polished.

The study of the rise and fall of great republics shows a remarkable correspondence in them all. They all had like beginnings, having been established by a body of people whose views were in advance of the age and the people among whom they dwelt; who were driven forth from their native country or became voluntary exiles, wandering into new lands, establishing a new system of government, the central idea of which was civil and religious liberty. About this central idea, by industry, perseverance, indomitable courage and patriotism, republics have grown more rapidly and attained to their period of glory in much shorter time than any other form of government. They have also decayed and come to their ruin more rapidly than other equally great nations, until statesmen are beginning to ask, Is it possible for a republic to become a permanent form of government? Republics have also grown along like lines, and have come to their ruin from similar causes. The lines of growth correspond with those elements in human nature where men are superior to women. Point out a line of strength which is peculiarly masculine, and you will find a corresponding line of marked progress in all great republics--business enterprise, and inventive genius, the aggressive spirit and warlike nature, are the lines of strength in all of the great republics of the world.

On the other hand, republics have decayed along the lines of our human nature in which men are inferior to women. Those of morality and purity, temperance and obedience to law, of loyalty to the teachings of religion and a love of peace. No republic, ancient or modern, ever died from the lack of material prosperity. Rome, Greece, Carthage, the Dutch Republic, all manifested evidences of decay while rich and powerful. Vice followed in the wake of great wealth, corruption close following on vice, then barbarism, the final fate of all. When we find a uniform result in any system of government, it is the part of wisdom to seek for the cause, and if the result is disastrous to the best interests of the nation, it is then the duty of patriots to remove the cause, regardless of prejudice or precedent.

It is an axiom in political economy "that in a republic, the class which votes affects the government in the long run along the lines of its nature." Following this law, it will readily be seen why republics into whose structure men have built their own nature, have manifested in all their lines of growth the strength of the masculine character; and on the other hand, since women have been excluded from all participation in governmental affairs, the peculiar characteristics of their nature have never been developed in the nation's life, therefore republics have always become weak and have ultimately come to their death through the decay of the moral and spiritual side of their life.

The question before us then is this: Is there anything in the nature of woman, differing from the nature of man in such a manner, that if women were permitted to vote it would enable them to affect the government differently from the way in which men affect it? In a speech made in Kansas some time since a United States senator said, "The nature of woman is as different from the nature of man, as the East is from the West." From which fact, he drew the conclusion that women ought to be disfranchised. He further states that, "If women were permitted to vote, the result would not be changed, as they would affect the government just as men affect it." In his speech the senator made a strong plea for the superiority of his sex on the ground of their reasoning and logical powers, and said: "Women cannot reason, but arrive at their conclusions intuitively." On reading the senator's speech one is led to inquire what woman's head he borrowed to enable him to arrive at his conclusions from the premises with which he started. If in a republic every class that votes affects the government in the long run along the line of its nature, and the nature of woman differs from the nature of man

as the East differs from the West, how can any reasoning or
logical mind conclude that the votes of women would affect the
government exactly as those of men? Reason, or intuition, or by
whatever mental process women reach their conclusions, they
would claim the result of woman's voting to be as different from
that of men as the East is from the West.

We need no argument to prove that the liquor class is able to
affect the government, and that it influences it because of its
power in the caucus, at the ballot box and in halls of legislation.
Recent laws in many states show us how men interested in many
forms of gambling and vice are able to affect the government
through the power of the ballot. In one of my old parishes in
Massachusetts, a body of men interested in cranberry culture
were equally successful in defeating another body of men
engaged in the fishing industry, because the cranberry men
elected their candidate to the legislature, who through his ability
to exchange votes, secured the passage of a bill in the interests
of his constituents. Had women owned the property, in whose
behalf legislation was secured, they could have done nothing but
watch the shiny herring swim up and down the stream which
was dammed by legislative enactment, until the last rump had
sounded; because, not having votes, they could have sent no
representative to the legislature to look after their special
interests. If in a republic liquor men, gambling men and
cranberry men having votes are able to affect the government,
and to affect it along the line of their nature, then women, if
they have votes, could affect it along the line of their nature; and
if women differ from men, as the East does from the West, then
the effect of their participation in government would differ less
from that of men in like manner.

Wherein does the nature of women differ from that of men in
such a way that if they voted they would be able to affect the
government? It is universally admitted that women are more
moral than men. The great moral factor of the world is its
womanhood. Men recognize this fact even more than women,
as, in all their arguments against the extension of suffrage to
women, they claim it would degrade them to the level of men.
In the congressional debate over the admission of Wyoming
territory into the Union as a state, every gentleman who opposed
it based his argument upon the woman suffrage plank in its
constitution, urging that women are "too good and pure to vote."
For the first time in history goodness and virtue were made the
basis of disfranchisement. In response to this sentiment Mr.
Carey, the United States delegate from Wyoming, declared this
very characteristic of womanhood had compelled both great
political parties in that territory to nominate their best men in
the caucuses, since the women defeated the immoral men at the
polls. Said a woman in Wyoming: "We are not particular to hold
offices ourselves, but we are very particular who do hold office."

Women are more temperate than men; yet when the state has a temperance question to settle, the ballot is placed in the hands of every distiller, every brewer, every saloonkeeper, every bartender and every male drunkard, and is kept out of the hands of the women, the great temperance factor of the world, which, to our intuitive natures, is a mark of very poor statesmanship. Women are also more religious than men; nearly three-fourths of the church members are women, and nine-tenths of the spiritual and philanthropic work of the world is done by them. Yet when it comes to building up the life of a republic this spiritual factor is counted out. And this men call statesmanship. It is charged that women, if possessed of political power, would seek to unite church and state. This statement is wholly without foundation; knowing as we do that such a union would be disastrous to both church and state, women would oppose it even more than men. Yet we answer the gentleman who claimed that "there is no place in the politics of this country for the decalogue and the golden rule," that if it be true, then there is no place in God's universe for the politics of this country. He has no place for the politics of any country in which there is no room for the decalogue or the golden rule. What we need more than the settlement of any of the problems which are at present agitating the political mind is an infusion of the golden rule into politics, and of the decalogue into the laws of the land. This cannot be accomplished either by putting the name of Deity into the Constitution, or by the union of church and state, but by bringing to bear upon the government the influence of that class of people who are the spiritual strength of the church.(1)

Again, women are more peace-loving than men. This has led some to say that women ought not to vote because they cannot bear arms. This claim is usually made by men who, in the hour of their country's need, sent substitutes to the army, or fled to Canada; or else, by the young men who have been born since the close of the war. The class who never make the statement that the ballot and the bayonet go together, are the heroes maimed in battle or broken in health, and prematurely old because of exposure and suffering in their country's behalf. They know the value of women in war time, and that women do go to war. Had it not been for the forty thousand women who went to the hospitals, visited the camps and battle-fields to care for our wounded heroes, there are thousands of us today who would never have seen home or friends again, but who would be sleeping in unknown graves. These heroes remember not only the services of the women in the field, but the great sanitary commission, sending its millions of dollars' worth of those things which were made for health and comfort, to hospital and fields during those terrible years of suffering. But, best of all, they remember the Grand Army of the Republic that stayed at home, who, when the citizen soldiers laid down the implements of peace, to take up the weapons of war, took those implements of peace and went to the workshop, the factory, the counting-room, the store and the farm, filling the places of men and earning the livelihood for the family, when prices were such as had never been known in the history of our time; and when the news came flashing over the wire that they who had gone forth would never more return, the broken-hearted wives, forgetting the agony of their own loss, gathered their children about their knees, and asked God that they might be both father and mother to their fatherless little ones; and alone and single-handed all over the land women have reared to manhood and womanhood the children left by their dead heroes as their only legacy. Then some man who never struck a blow in behalf of his country exclaims: "Women must not vote, because they cannot fight." In the face of the loyalty of America's Womanhood the darkest stain on the escutcheon of our country is its utter forgetfulness of their services. From the beginning of its history to the present hour, by no act of Congress or of any state legislature has there ever been any public recognition of the services of its women. By no monument of granite, or marble, or bronze has it ever commemorated the memory of their patriotism. They are as utterly forgotten as if they had never lived, suffered or died for their country.

When a committee appealed to Congress, asking that when the Negroes were enfranchised the loyal women might share their freedom, Congress answered: "It is the negro's hour, women must wait." The Negro's hour struck, again women asked for liberty, and were again assured that Congress had weightier measures to consume its time and attention--it had the South to reconstruct, and the North to bring back to a sound business basis. The severest form of punishment it could devise for the crime of treason was disfranchisement, reducing traitors to the level of loyal women, who had given all they had for their country, and this is the only recognition that Congress has ever granted them. I have traveled in many countries, and in every one, save in these United States, I have seen stately monuments erected in grateful memory of the patriotic services of women. We had a faint hope of at least a part in one, when we learned that a national monument to the Pilgrims was to be unveiled at Plymouth, Massachusetts. On the great day, scores of women gathered to witness the ceremonies. We were told that this government had taught the nations of the world the great principle that "taxation without representation is tyranny." We sighed as we remembered the taxes we had paid, and yet were still refused representation. We were also told that in this country under God the people rule, and yet the constitution of every state in the Union, at that time, declared it was the males, and not the people, who rule. The orator again assured us that the powers of this government were just, since governments derive their just powers from the consent of the governed; but they recently hung a woman, in one of these just states, who had never given her consent to the law under which she was executed, nor had the consent of women, her peers, ever been asked regarding it. Then we were told that as the voice of the people is the voice of God, and this was repeated both in Latin and in English, that there might be no doubt in regard to it, that the laws of our land were the crystallized voice of Deity. The speaker, forgetting that in the compass of the people's voice there is a soprano as well as a bass, and that if the voice of the people is the voice of God, we will never know what His voice is until the bass and soprano unite in harmonious sound, the resultant of which will be the voice of God. After many other statements of a similar character, which are true in spirit, but had never been practiced by any nation, the monument was unveiled, and our hearts sank with intense disappointment when we read the inscription, "Erected by a grateful country in honor of the Pilgrim Fathers." We had again witnessed the evidence of a country's easy forgetfulness of its debt to women. We felt just as we do when we gaze on that picture so familiar to you all; a ship in the background, between it and the shore is a man carrying what seems to be a woman in his arms, on the beach kneel a company of people, and farther up the beach stand another group with uplifted hands, thanking God for their deliverance. They look like men and women. You wonder what company of people it is, and read the inscription beneath the picture to learn, that it is not a company of men and women at all, but is a representation of "The Landing of the Forefathers." You instinctively exclaim how kind the forefathers were to carry each other ashore, and how much some of them resemble mothers, but they were not mothers, they were all fathers, every mother of them.

There never was another country which had so many parents as we have had, but they have all been fathers--pilgrim fathers, Plymouth fathers, forefathers, revolutionary fathers, city fathers and church fathers, fathers of every description--but, like Topsy, we have never had a mother. In this lies the weakness of all republics. They have been fathered to death. The great need of our country today is a little mothering to undo the evils of too much fathering. Like Israel of old, when the people were reduced to their utmost extremity, in order to save the nation, there was needed a ruler who was at once a statesman, a commander-in-chief of the armies and a righteous judge, who would render justice and be impervious to bribes. God called a woman to rule, and Deborah tells us in her wonderful ode that the great need of the nation in this hour of its extremity was motherhood applied to government, when she exclaims, "Behold the condition of Israel when I, Deborah, a mother in Israel, arose." "Then was there peace in Israel" and prosperity and success, as "Deborah ruled the people in righteousness for forty years."(2)

Women are more law-abiding than men. It is universally accepted that the class of people who best obey the laws are best fitted to make them. It is also stated that everything in a republic depends upon the obedience of the citizens to law. I visited the penitentiary of a state whose senator made this statement, and asked the warden how many prisoners he had. He replied, "Eight hundred and eighty-nine, of whom eight hundred and eighty are men and nine are women," so that in the State of Kansas the women are a hundred times more law-abiding than the men. In the United States the same year there were sixty-eight thousand and five prisoners, of whom fifty-three thousand were men and only five thousand and five were women, showing that in the whole United States there were ten times as many men criminals as women.

It has been claimed that the small number of women prisoners is due to the fact that women have no part in politics, for in the thought of some people politics and prisons are synonymous terms. If, however, this statement were true of women, then where they are most in politics they would be most in prison. We have but one state to which we can turn for statistics. At the close of the census in 1890 Mrs. Clara Bewick Colby, of Washington, consulted the statistics of crime, and learned to our great satisfaction that the only state in the Union in which there was not a woman criminal in jail or penitentiary was Wyoming, the state where women had voted for twenty-one years.

It has also been charged that on account of her emotional nature woman's mental condition would be unsettled if she engaged in anything so exciting as public affairs. But Mrs. Colby also learned from the same source that the only state in which there was not an insane woman in public or private asylum was the State of Wyoming, where women have been voting for twenty-one years. She also learned that Wyoming was the only state in which but few men were insane--only three--and concludes that the exercise of suffrage makes women so peaceable to live with that very few men go insane. The same authority points to the fact that Wyoming is the only state in which during the last two decades the percent of marriage has increased over the percent of divorce.

If, then, in a republic the class which votes affects the government in the long run along the line of its nature, and women are more moral, more temperate, more religious, more peace-loving and more law-abiding than men, then if they were permitted to vote they would affect the government along these lines. It needs but a glance at the world's history to show that these are the lines of weakness in republics, and that they have all died because of their immorality, licentiousness, intemperance, their disregard of their own laws, the violation of the statutes of God and by their warlike nature, and they can only become strong by the incoming of that class of people who are strong where they are weak. Then shall the voice of the people become the voice of God, and for the first time in history the voice of God shall be crystallized into the laws of a republic.

The Fundamental Principle of a Republic

Shaw delivered this speech during the 1915 New York State equal suffrage campaign at a fully packed City Opera House in Ogdenburg on the evening of June 21. The original source of the text is *The Ogdenburg Advance and St. Lawrence Weekly Democrat*, July 1, 1915. A clipping from the newspaper bearing Shaw's speech is found in the Shaw papers, box 20. This text seems to be a highly authentic stenographic recording of Shaw's address because it reflects her style exceptionally well. Because the entire speech as printed in the newspaper has only three paragraphs, we are using the paragraphing of the speech provided by Wilmer A. Linkugel, *The Speeches of Anna Howard Shaw*, Ph.D. dissertation, University of Wisconsin, 1960, pp. 258-292.

When I came into your hall tonight, I thought of the last time I was in your city. Twenty-one years ago I came here with Susan B. Anthony, and we came for exactly the same purpose as that for which we are here tonight. Boys have been born since that time and have become voters, and the women are still trying to persuade American men to believe in the fundamental principles of democracy, and I never quite feel as if it was a fair field to argue this question with men, because in doing it you have to assume that a man who professes to believe in a Republican form of government does not believe in a Republican form of government, for the only thing that woman's enfranchisement means at all is that a government which claims to be a Republic should be a Republic, and not an aristocracy. The difficulty with discussing this question with those who oppose us is that they make any number of arguments but none of them have anything to do with Woman's Suffrage; they always have something to do with something else, therefore the arguments which we have to make rarely ever have anything to do with the subject, because we have to answer our opponents who always escape the subject as far as possible in order to have any sort of reason in connection with what they say.

Now one of two things is true: either a Republic is a desirable form of government, or else it is not. If it is, then we should have it, if it is not then we ought not to pretend that we have it. We ought at least to be true to our ideals, and the men of New York have, for the first time in their lives, the rare opportunity, on the second day of next November, of making the state truly a part of a Republic. It is the greatest opportunity which has ever come to the men of the state. They have never had so serious a problem to solve before, they will never have a more serious problem to solve in any future year of our Nation's life, and the thing that disturbs me more than anything else in connection with it is that so few people realize what a profound problem they have to solve on November 2. It is not merely a trifling matter; it is not a little thing that does not concern the state, it is the most vital problem that we could have, and any man who goes to the polls on the second day of next November without thoroughly informing himself in regard to this subject is unworthy to be a citizen of this state, and unfit to cast a ballot.

If Woman's Suffrage is wrong, it is a great wrong; if it is right, it is a profound and fundamental principle, and we all know, if we know what a Republic is, that it is the fundamental principle upon which a Republic must rise. Let us see where we are as a people; how we act here and what we think we are. The difficulty with the men of this country is that they are so consistent in their inconsistency that they are not aware of having been inconsistent; because their consistency has been so continuous and their inconsistency so consecutive that it has never been broken, from the beginning of our Nation's life to the present time. If we trace our history back we will find that from the very dawn of our existence as a people, men have been imbued with a spirit and a vision more lofty than they have been able to live; they have been led by visions of the sublimest truth, both in regard to religion and in regard to government that ever inspired the souls of men from the time the Puritans left the old world to come to this country, led by the Divine ideal which is the sublimest and supremest ideal in religious freedom which men have ever known, the theory that a man has a right to worship God according to the dictates of his own conscience, without the intervention of any other man or any other group of men. And it was this theory, this vision of the right of the human soul which led men first to the shores of this country.

Now, nobody can deny that they are sincere, honest and earnest men. No one can deny that the Puritans were men of profound conviction, and yet these men who gave up everything in behalf of an ideal, hardly established their communities in this new country before they began to practice exactly the same sort of persecutions on other men which had been practiced upon them. They settled in their communities on the New England shores and when they formed their compacts by which they governed their local societies, they permitted no man to have a voice in the affairs unless he was a member of the church, and not a member of any church, but a member of the particular church which dominated the particular community in which he happened to be. In Massachusetts they drove the Baptists down to Rhode Island; in Connecticut they drove the Presbyterians over to New Jersey; they burned the Quakers in Massachusetts and ducked the witches, and no colony, either Catholic or Protestant allowed a Jew to have a voice. And so a man must worship God according to the conscience of the particular community in which he was located, and yet they called that religious freedom, they were not able to live the ideal of religious liberty, and from that time to this the men of this government have been following along the same line of inconsistency, while they too have been following a vision of equal grandeur and power.

Never in the history of the world did it dawn upon the human mind as it dawned upon your ancestors, what it would mean for men to be free. They got the vision of a government in which the people would be the supreme power, and so inspired by this vision men wrote such documents as were sent from the Massachusetts legislature, from the New York legislature and from the Pennsylvania group over to the Parliament of Great Britain, which rang with the profoundest measures of freedom and justice. They did not equivocate in a single word when they wrote the Declaration of Independence; no one can dream that these men had not got the sublimest ideal of democracy which had ever dawned upon the souls of men. But as soon as the war was over and our government was formed, instead of asking the question, who shall be the governing force in this great new Republic, when they brought those thirteen little territories together, they began to eliminate instead of include the men who should be the great governing forces, and they said, who shall have the voice in this great new Republic, and you would have supposed that such men as fought the Revolutionary War would have been able to answer that every man who has fought, every one who has given up all he has and all he has been able to accumulate shall be free, it never entered their minds. These excellent ancestors of yours had not been away from the old world long enough to realize that man is of more value than his purse, so they said every man who has an estate in the government shall have a voice; and they said what shall that estate be? And they answered that a man who had property valued at two hundred and fifty dollars will be able to cast a vote, and so they sang "The land of the free and the home of the brave." And they wrote into their Constitution, "All males who pay taxes on $250 shall cast a vote," and they called themselves a Republic, and we call ourselves a Republic, and they were not quite so much of a Republic that we should be called a Republic yet. We might call ourselves angels, but that wouldn't make us angels, you have got to be an angel before you are an angel, and you have got to be a Republic before you are a Republic. Now what did we do? Before the word "male" in the local compacts they wrote the word "Church-members"; and they wrote in the word "taxpayer." Then there arose a great Democrat, Thomas Jefferson, who looked down into the day when you and I are living and saw that the rapidly accumulated wealth in the hands of a few men would endanger the liberties of the people, and he knew what you and I know, that no power under heaven or among men is known in a Republic by which men can defend their liberties except by the power of the ballot, and so the Democratic party took another step in the evolution of a Republic out of a monarchy and they rubbed out the word "tax-payer" and wrote in the word "white," and then the Democrats thought the millennium had come, and they sang "The land of the free and the home of the brave" as lustily as the Republicans had sung it before them and spoke of the divine right of motherhood with the same thrill in their voices and at the same time they were selling mother's babies by the pound on the auction block-and mothers apart from their babies. Another arose who said a man is not a good citizen because he is white, he is a good citizen because he is a man, and the Republican party took out that progressive evolutionary eraser and rubbed out the word "white" from before the word "male" and could not think of another word to put in there-they were all in, black and white, rich and poor, wise and otherwise, drunk and sober; not a man left out to be put in, and so the Republicans could not write anything before the word "male," and they had to let that little word "male" stay alone by itself.

And God said in the beginning, "It is not good for man to stand alone." That is why we are here tonight, and that is all that woman's suffrage means; just to repeat again and again that first declaration of the Divine, "It is not good for man to stand alone," and so the women of this state are asking that the word "male" shall be stricken out of the Constitution altogether and that the Constitution stand as it ought to have stood in the beginning and as it must before this state is any part of a Republic. Every citizen possessing the necessary qualifications shall be entitled to cast one vote at every election, and have that vote counted. We are not asking, as our Anti-Suffrage friends think we are, for any of awful things that we hear will happen if we are allowed to vote; we are simply asking that that government which professes to be a Republic shall be a Republic and not pretend to be what it is not.(1)

Now what is a Republic? Take your dictionary, encyclopedia, lexicon or anything else you like and look up the definition and you will find that a Republic is a form of government in which the laws are enacted by representatives elected by the people.

Now when did the people of New York ever elect their representatives? Never in the world. The men of New York have, and I grant you that men are people, admirable people, as far as they go, but they only go half way. There is still another half of the people who have not elected representatives, and you never read a definition of a Republic in which half of the people elect representatives to govern the whole of the people. That is an aristocracy and that is just what we are. We have been many kinds of aristocracies. We have been a hierarchy of church members, than an oligarchy of sex.

There are two old theories which are dying today. Dying hard but dying. One of them is dying on the plains of Flanders and the Mountains of Galicia and Austria, and that is the theory of the divine right of kings. The other is dying here in the state of New York and Massachusetts and New Jersey and Pennsylvania and that is the divine right of sex. Neither of them had a foundation in reason, or justice or common sense.

Now I want to make this proposition, and I believe every man will accept it. Of course he will if he is intelligent. Whenever a Republic prescribes the qualifications as applying equally to all the citizens of the Republic, when the Republic says in order to vote, a citizen must be twenty-one years of age, it applies to all alike, there is no discrimination against any race or sex. When the government says that a citizen must be a native-born citizen or a naturalized citizen, that applies to all; we are either born or naturalized, somehow or other we are here. Whenever the government says that a citizen, in order to vote, must be a resident of a community a certain length of time, and of the state a certain length of time and of the nation a certain length of time, that applies to all equally. There is no discrimination. We might go further and we might say that in order to vote the citizen must be able to read his ballot. We have not gone that far yet. We have been very careful of male ignorance in these United States. I was much interested, as perhaps many of you, in reading the Congressional Record this last winter over the debate over the immigration bill, and when that illiteracy clause was introduced into the immigration bill, what fear there was in the souls of men for fear we would do injustice to some of the people who might want to come to our shores, and I was much interested in the language in which the President vetoed the bill, when he declared that by inserting the clause we would keep out of our shores a large body of very excellent people. I could not help wondering then how it happens that male ignorance is so much less ignorant than female ignorance. When I hear people say that if women were permitted to vote a large body of ignorant people would vote, and therefore because an ignorant woman would vote, no intelligent women should be allowed to vote, I wonder why we have made it so easy for male ignorance and so hard for female ignorance.(2)

When I was a girl, years ago, I lived in the back woods and there the number of votes cast at each election depended entirely upon the size of the ballot-box. We had what was known as the old tissue ballots and the man who got the most tissue in was the man elected. Now the best part of our community was very much disturbed by this method, and they did not know what to do in order to get a ballot both safe and secret; but they heard that over in Australia, where the women voted, they had a ballot which was both safe and secret, so we went over there and we got the Australian ballot and brought it here. But when we got it over we found it was not adapted to this country, because in Australia they have to be able to read their ballot. Now the question was how could we adapt it to our conditions? Someone discovered that if you should put a symbol at the head of each column, like a rooster, or an eagle, or a hand holding a hammer, that if a man has intelligence to know the difference between a rooster and an eagle he will know which political party to vote for, and when the ballot was adapted it was a very beautiful ballot, it looked like a page from *Life*.

Now almost any American woman could vote that ballot, or if she had not that intelligence to know the difference between an eagle and a rooster, we could take the eagle out and put in the hen. Now when we take so much pains to adapt the ballot to the male intelligence of the United States, we should be very humble when we talk about female ignorance. Now if we should take a vote and the men had to read their ballot in order to vote it, more women could vote than men. But when the government says not only that you must be twenty-one years of age, a resident of the community and native born or naturalized, those are qualifications, but when it says that an elector must be a male, that is not a qualification for citizenship; that is an insurmountable barrier between one half of the people and the other half of the citizens and their rights as citizens. No such nation can call itself a Republic. It is only an aristocracy. That barrier must be removed before that government can become a Republic, and that is exactly what we are asking now, that the last step in this evolutionary process shall be taken on November 2d, and that this great state of New York shall become in fact, as it is in theory, a part of a government of the people, by the people and for the people.

Men know the inconsistencies themselves; they realize it in one way while they do not realize it in another, because you never heard a man make a political speech when he did not speak of this country as a whole as though the thing existed which does not exist and that is that the people were equally free, because you hear them declare over and over again on the Fourth of July "Under God, the people rule." They know it is not true but they say it with a great hurrah, and they repeat over and over again that clause from the Declaration of Independence,

"Governments derive their just powers from the consent of the governed," and then they see how they can prevent half of us from giving our consent to anything, and then they give it to us on the Fourth of July in two languages, so if it is not true in one it will be in the other, "vox populi, vox Dei." "The voice of the people is the voice of God," and the orator forgets that in the people's voice there is a soprano as well as a bass. If the voice of the people is the voice of God, how are we ever going to know what God's voice is when we are content to listen to a bass solo? Now if it is true that the voice of the people is the voice of God, we will never know what the Diety's voice in government is until the bass and soprano are mingled together, the result of which will be the divine harmony. Take any of the magnificent appeals for freedom which men make, and rob them of their universal application and you take the very life and soul out of them.

Where is the difficulty? Just in one thing and one thing only, that men are so sentimental. We used to believe that women were the sentimental sex, but they cannot hold a tallow candle compared with the arc light of the men. Men are so sentimental in their attitude about women that they cannot reason about them. Now men are usually very fair to each other. I think the average man recognizes that he has no more right to anything at the hands of the government than has every other man. He has no right at all to anything to which every other man has not an equal right with himself. He says why have I a right to certain things in the government; why have I a right to life and liberty; why have I a right to this or this? Does he say because I am a man? Not at all, because I am human, and being human I have a right to everything which belongs to humanity, and every right which any other human being has, I have. And then he says of his neighbor, and my neighbor he also is human, therefore every right which belongs to me as a human being, belongs to him as a human being, and I have no right to anything under the government to which he is not equally entitled. And then up comes a woman, and then they say now she's a woman; she is not quite human, but she is my wife, or my sister, or my daughter or an aunt, or my cousin. She is not quite human, she is only related to a human, and being related to a human a human will take care of her. So we have had that care-taking human being to look after us and they have not recognized that women too are equally human with men. Now if men could forget for a minute--I believe the anti-suffragists say that we want men to forget that we are related to them, they don't know me-- if for a minute they could forget our relationship and remember that we are equally human with themselves, then they would say--yes, and this human being, not because she is a woman, but because she is human is entitled to every privilege and every right under the government which I, as a human being am entitled to. The only reason men do not see as fairly in regard to women as they do in regard to each other is because they have looked upon us from an altogether different plane than what they have looked at men; that is because women have been the homemakers while men have been the so-called protectors, in the period of the world's civilization when people needed to be protected. I know that they say that men protect us now and when we ask them what they are protecting us from the only answer they can give is from themselves. I do not think that men need any very great credit for protecting us from themselves. They are not protecting us from any special thing from which we could not protect ourselves except themselves. Now this old time idea of protection was all right when the world needed this protection, but today the protection in civilization comes from within and not from without.

What are the arguments which our good Anti-friends give us? We know that lately they have stopped to argue and call suffragists all sorts of creatures. If there is anything we believe that we do not believe, we have not heard about them, so the cry goes out of this; the cry of the infant's mind; the cry of a little child. The anti-suffragists' cries are all the cries of little children who are afraid of the unborn and are forever crying, "The goblins will catch you if you don't watch out." So that anything that has not been should not be and all that is is right, when as a matter of fact if the world believed that we would be in a statical condition and never move, except back like a crab. And so the cries go on.(3)

When suffragists are feminists, and when I ask what that is no one is able to tell me. I would give anything to know what a feminist is. They say, would you like to be a feminist? If I could find out I would, you either have to be masculine or feminine and I prefer feminine. Then they cry that we are socialists, and anarchists. Just how a human can be both at the same time, I really do not know. If I know what socialism means it means absolute government and anarchism means no government at all. So we are feminists, socialists, anarchists and mormons or spinsters. Now that is about the list. I have not heard the last speech. Now as a matter of fact, as a unit we are nothing, as individuals we are like all other individuals.

We have our theories, our beliefs, but as suffragists we have but one belief, but one principle, but one theory and that is the right of a human being to have a voice in the government under which he or she lives, on that we agree, if on nothing else. Whether we agree or not on religion or politics we are not concerned. A clergyman asked me the other day, "By the way, what church does your official board belong to?" I said I don't know. He said, "Don't you know what religion your official board believes?" I said, "Really it never occurred to me, but I will hunt them up and see, they are not elected to my board because they believe in any particular church. We had no concern either as to what we believe as religionists or as to what we believe as women in regard to theories of government, except that one fundamental theory in the right of democracy. We do not believe in this fad or the other, but whenever any question is to be settled in any community, then the people of that community shall settle that question, the women people equally with the men people. That is all there is to it, and yet when it comes to arguing our case they bring up all sorts of arguments, and the beauty of it is they always answer all their own arguments. They never make an argument but they answer it. When I was asked to answer one of their debates I said, "What is the use? Divide up their literature and let them destroy themselves."

I was followed up last year by a young married woman from New Jersey. She left her husband home for three months to tell the women that their place was at home, and that they could not leave home long enough to go to the ballot box, and she brought all her arguments out in pairs and backed them up by statistics. The anti-suffragist can gather more statistics than any other person I ever saw, and there is nothing so sweet and calm as when they say, "You cannot deny this, because here are the figures, and figures never lie." Well they don't but some liars figure.

When they start out they always begin the same. She started by proving that it was no use to give the women the ballot because if they did have it they would not use it, and she had statistics to prove it. If we would not use it then I really cannot see the harm of giving it to us, we would not hurt anybody with it and what an easy way for you men to get rid of us. No more suffrage meetings, never any nagging you again, no one could blame you for anything that went wrong with the town, if it did not run right, all you would have to say is, you have the power, why don't you go ahead and clean up.

Then the young lady, unfortunately for her first argument, proved by statistics, of which she had many, the awful results which happened where women did have the ballot; what awful laws have been brought about by women's vote; the conditions that prevail in the homes and how deeply women get interested in politics, because women are hysterical, and we cannot think of anything else, we just forget our families, cease to care for our children, cease to love our husbands and just go to the polls and vote and keep on voting for ten hours a day 365 days in the year, never let up, if we ever get to the polls once you will never get us home, so that the women will not vote at all, and they will not do anything but vote. Now these are two very strong anti-suffrage arguments and they can prove them by figures.

Then they will tell you that if women are permitted to vote it will be a great expense and no use because wives will vote just as their husbands do; even if we have no husbands, that would not affect the result because we would vote just as our husbands would vote if we had one. How I wish the anti-suffragists could make the men believe that; if they could make men believe that the women would vote just as they wanted them to do you think we would ever have to make another speech or hold another meeting, we would have to vote whether we wanted to or not.

And then the very one who will tell you that women will vote just as their husbands do will tell you in five minutes that they will not vote as their husbands will and then the discord in the homes, and the divorce. Why, they have discovered that in Colorado there are more divorces than there were before women began to vote, but they have forgotten to tell you that there are four times as many people in Colorado today as there were when women began to vote, and that may have some effect, particularly as these people went from the East. Then they will tell you all the trouble that happens in the home. A gentleman told me that in California--and when he was talking I had a wonderful thing pass through my mind, because he said he and his wife had lived together for twenty years and never had a difference in opinion in the whole twenty years and he was afraid if women began to vote that his wife would vote differently from him and then that beautiful harmony which they had had for twenty years would be broken, and all the time he was talking I could not help wondering which was the idiot--because I knew that no intelligent human beings could live together for twenty years and not have differences of opinion. All the time he was talking I looked at that splendid type of manhood and thought, how would a man feel being tagged up by a little woman for twenty years saying, "Me too, me too." I would not want to live in a house with a human being for twenty years who agreed with everything I said. The stagnation of a frog pond would be hilarious compared to that. What a reflection is that on men. If we should say that about men we would never hear the last of it. Now it may be that the kind of men being that the anti-suffragists live with is that kind, but they are not the kind we live with and we could not do it. Great big overgrown babies! Cannot be disputed without having a row! While we do not believe that men are saints, by any means, we do believe that the average American man is a fairly good sort of a fellow.

In fact my theory of the whole matter is exactly opposite, because instead of believing that men and women will quarrel, I think just the opposite thing will happen. I think just about six weeks before election a sort of honeymoon will start and it will continue until they will think they are again hanging over the gate, all in order to get each other's votes. When men want each other's votes they do not go up and knock them down; they are very solicitous of each other, if they are thirsty or need a smoke, or--well we don't worry about home. The husband and wife who are quarreling after the vote are quarreling now.

Then the other belief that the women would not vote if they had a vote and would not do anything else; and would vote just as their husbands vote, and would not vote like their husbands; that women have so many burdens that they cannot bear another burden, and that women are the leisure class.

I remember hearing Rev. Dr. Abbott speak before the anti-suffrage meeting in Brooklyn and he stated that if women were permitted to vote we would not have so much time for charity and philanthropy, and I would like to say, "Thank God, there will not be so much need of charity and philanthropy." The end and aim of the suffrage is not to furnish an opportunity for excellent old ladies to be charitable. There are two words that we ought to be able to get along without, and they are charity and philanthropy. They are not needed in a Republic. If we put in the word "opportunity" instead, that is what Republics stand for. Our doctrine is not to extend the length of our bread lines or the size of our soup kitchens, what we need is the opportunity for men to buy their own bread and eat their own soup. We women have used up our lives and strength in fool charities, and we have made more paupers than we have ever helped by the folly of our charities and philanthropies; the unorganized methods by which we deal with the conditions of society, and instead of giving people charity we must learn to give them an opportunity to develop and make themselves capable of earning the bread; no human being has the right to live without toil; toil of some kind, and that old theory that we used to hear "The world owes a man a living" never was true and never will be true. This world does not owe anybody a living, what it does owe to every human being is the opportunity to earn a living. We have a right to the opportunity and then the right to the living thereafter. We want it. No woman, any more than a man, has the right to live an idle life in this world, we must learn to give back something for the space occupied and we must do our duty wherever duty calls, and the woman herself must decide where her duty calls, just as a man does.(4)

Now they tell us we should not vote because we have not the time, we are so burdened that we should not have any more burdens. Then, if that is so, I think we ought to allow the women to vote instead of the men, since we pay a man anywhere from a third to a half more than we do women it would be better to use up the cheap time of the women instead of the dear time of the men. And talking about time you would think it took about a week to vote.

A dear, good friend of mine in Omaha said, "Now Miss Shaw," and she held up her child in her arms, "is not this my job." I said it certainly is, and then she said, "How can I go to the polls and vote and neglect my baby?" I said, "Has your husband a job?" and she said, "Why, you know he has." I did know it, he was a banker and a very busy one. I said, "Yet your husband said he was going to leave his bank and go down to the polls and vote," and she said, "Oh yes, he is so very interested in election." Then I said, "What an advantage you have over your husband, he has to leave his job and you can take your job with you and you do not need to neglect your job." Is it not strange that the only time a woman might neglect her baby is on election day, and then the dear old Antis hold up their hands and say, "You have neglected your baby." A woman can belong to a whist club and go once a week and play whist, she cannot take her baby to the whist club, she has to keep whist herself without trying to keep a baby whist. She can go to the theatre, to church or a picnic and no one is worrying about the baby, but to vote and everyone cries out about the neglect. You would think on election day that a woman grabbed up her baby and started out and just dropped it somewhere and paid no attention to it. It used to be asked when we had the question-box, "Who will take care of the babies?" I didn't know what person could be got to take care of all the babies, so I thought I would go out West and find out. I went to Denver and I found that they took care of their babies just the same on election day as they did on every other day; they took their baby along with them, when they went to put a letter in a box they took their baby along and when they went to put their ballot in the box they took their baby along. If the mother had to stand in line and the baby got restless she would joggle the go-cart--most everyone had a go-cart--and when she went in to vote a neighbor would joggle the go-cart and if there was no neighbor there was the candidate and he would joggle the cart. That is one day in the year when you could get a hundred people to take care of any number of babies. I have never worried about the babies on election day since that time.

Then the people will tell you that women are so burdened with their duties that they cannot vote, and they will tell you that women are the leisure class and the men are worked to death; but the funniest argument of the lady who followed me about in the West: Out there they were great in the temperance question, and she declared that we were not prohibition, or she declared that we were. Now in North Dakota which is one of the first prohibition states, and they are dry because they want to be dry. In that state she wanted to prove to them that if women were allowed to vote they would vote North Dakota wet and she had her figures; that women had not voted San Francisco dry, or Portland dry or Chicago dry. Of course we had not voted on the question in Chicago, but that did not matter. Then we went to Montana, which is wet. They have it wet there because they want it wet, so that any argument that she could bring to bear upon them to prove that we would make North Dakota wet and keep it wet would have given us the state, but that would not work, so she brought out the figures out of her pocket to prove to the men of Montana that if women were allowed to vote in

Montana they would vote Montana dry. She proved that in two years in Illinois they had voted ninety-six towns dry, and that at that rate we would soon get over Montana and have it dry. Then I went to Nebraska and as soon as I reached there a reporter came and asked me the question, "How are the women going to vote on the prohibition question?" I said, "I really don't know. I know how we will vote in North Dakota, we will vote wet in North Dakota; in Montana we will vote dry, but how we will vote in Nebraska, I don't know, but I will let you know just as soon as the lady from New Jersey comes."

We will either vote as our husbands vote or we will not vote as our husbands vote. We either have time to vote or we don't have time to vote. We will either not vote at all or we will have time to vote. We will either not vote at all or we will vote all the time. It reminds me of the story of the old Irish woman who had twin boys and they were so much alike that the neighbors could not tell them apart, so one of the neighbors said, "Now Mrs. Mahoney, you have two of the finest twin boys I ever saw in all my life, but how do you know them apart." "Oh," she says, "That's easy enough, anyone could tell them apart. When I want to know which is which I just put my finger in Patsey's mouth and if he bites it is Mikey."

Now what does it matter whether the women will vote as their husbands do or will not vote; whether they have time or have not; or whether they will vote for prohibition or not. What has that to do with the fundamental question of democracy, no one has yet discovered. But they cannot argue on that; they cannot argue on the fundamental basis of our existence so that they have to get off on all these side tricks to get anything approaching an argument. So they tell you that democracy is a form of government. It is not. It was before governments were; it will prevail when governments cease to be; it is more than a form of government; it is a great spiritual force emanating from the heart of the Infinite, transforming human character until some day, some day in the distant future, man by the power of the spirit of democracy, will be able to look back into the face of the Infinite and answer, as man cannot answer today, "One is our Father, even God, and all we people are the children of one family." And when democracy has taken possession of human lives no man will ask for him to grant to his neighbor, whether that neighbor be a man or a woman; no man will then be willing to allow another man to rise to power on his shoulders, nor will he be willing to rise to power on the shoulders of another prostrate human being. But that has not yet taken possession of us, but some day we will be free, and we are getting nearer and nearer to it all the time; and never in the history of our country had the men and women of this nation a better right to approach it than they have today; never in the history of the nation did it stand out so splendidly as it stands today, and never ought we men and women to be more grateful for anything than that there presides in the White House today a man of peace.(5)

As so our good friends go on with one thing after another and they say if women should vote they will have to sit on the jury and they ask whether we will like to see a woman sitting on a jury. I have seen some juries that ought to be sat on and I have seen some women that would be glad to sit on anything. When a woman stands up all day behind a counter, or when she stands all day doing a washing she is glad enough to sit; and when she stands for seventy-five cents she would like to sit for two dollars a day. But don't you think we need some women on juries in this country? You read your paper and you read that one day last week or the week before or the week before a little girl went out to school and never came back; another little girl was sent on an errand and never came back; another little girl was left in charge of a little sister and her mother went out to work and when she returned the little girl was not there, and you read it over and over again, and the horror of it strikes you. You read that in these United States five thousand young girls go out and never come back, don't you think that the men and women, the vampires of our country who fatten and grow rich on the ignorance and innocence of children would rather face Satan himself than a jury of mothers. I would like to see some juries of mothers. I lived in the slums of Boston for three years and I know the need of juries of mothers.

Then they tell us that if women were permitted to vote that they would take office, and you would suppose that we just took office in this country. There is a difference of getting an office in this country and in Europe. In England a man stands for Parliament and in this country he runs for Congress, and so long as it is a question of running for office I don't think women have much chance, especially with our present hobbles. There are some women who want to hold office and I may as well own up, I am one of them. I have been wanting to hold office for more than thirty-five years. Thirty-five years ago I lived in the slums of Boston and ever since then I have wanted to hold office. I have applied to the major to be made an officer; I wanted to be the greatest office holder in the world, I wanted the position of the man I think is to be the most envied, as far as ability to do good is concerned, and that is a policeman. I have always wanted to be a policeman and I have applied to be appointed policeman and the very first question that was asked me was, "Could you knock a man down and take him to jail?" That is some people's idea of the highest service that a policeman can render a community. Knock somebody down and take him to jail. My idea is not so much to arrest criminals as it is to prevent crime. That is what is needed in the police force of every community. When I lived for three years in the back alleys of Boston, I saw there that it was needed to prevent crime and from that day to this I believe there is no great public gathering of any sort whatever where we do not need women on the police force; we need them at every moving picture show, every dance house, every restaurant, every hotel and every great store with a great bargain counter and every park and every resort where the vampires who fatten on the crimes and vices of men and women gather. We need women on the police force and we will have them there some day.

If women vote will they go to war? They are great on having us fight. They tell you that the government rests on force, but there are a great many kinds of force in this world, and never in the history of man were the words of the Scriptures proved to the extent that they are today, that the men of the nation that lives by the sword shall die by the sword. When I was speaking in North Dakota from an automobile with a great crowd and a great number of men gathered around a man who had been sitting in front of a store whittling a stick called out to another man and asked if women get the vote will they go over to Germany and fight the Germans? I said, "Why no, why should we go over to Germany and fight Germans?" "If Germans come over here would you fight?" I said, "Why should we women fight men, but if Germany should send an army of women over here, then we would show you what we would do. We would go down and meet them and say, "Come on, let's go up to the opera house and talk this matter over." It might grow wearisome but it would not be death.(6)

Would it not be better if the heads of the governments in Europe had talked things over? What might have happened to the world if a dozen men had gotten together in Europe and settled the awful controversy which is today discriminating the nations of Europe? We women got together over there last year, over in Rome, the delegates from twenty-eight different nations of women, and for two weeks we discussed problems which had like interests to us all. They were all kinds of Protestants, both kinds of Catholics, Roman and Greek, three were Jews and Mohamedans, but we were not there to discuss our different religious beliefs, but we were there to discuss the things that were of vital importance to us all, and at the end of the two weeks, after the discussions were over we passed a great number of resolutions. We discussed white slavery, the immigration laws, we discussed the spread of contagious and infectious diseases; we discussed various forms of education, and various forms of juvenile criminals, every question which every nation has to meet, and at the end of two weeks we passed many resolutions, but two of them were passed unanimously. One was presented by myself as Chairman on the Committee on Suffrage and on that resolution we called upon all civilizations of the world to give to women equal rights with men and there was not a dissenting vote.(7)

The other resolution was on peace. We believed then and many of us believe today, notwithstanding all the discussion that is going on, we believe and we will continue to believe that preparedness for war is an incentive to war, and the only hope of permanent peace is the systematic and scientific disarmament of all the nations of the world, and we passed a resolution and passed it unanimously to that effect. A few days afterward I attended a large reception given by the American ambassador, and there was an Italian diplomat there and he spoke rather superciliously and said, "You women think you have been having a very remarkable convention, and I understand that a resolution on peace was offered by the Germans, the French women seconded it, and the British presiding officer presented it and it was carried unanimously." We none of us dreamed what was taking place at that time, but he knew and we learned it before we arrived home, that awful, awful thing that was about to sweep over the nations of the world. The American ambassador replied to the Italian diplomat and said, "Yes Prince, it was a remarkable convention, and it is a remarkable thing that the only people who can get together internationally and discuss their various problems without acrimony and without a sword at their side are the women of the world, but we men, even when we go to the Hague to discuss peace, we go with a sword dangling at our side." It is remarkable that even at this age men cannot discuss international problems and discuss them in peace.(8)

When I turned away from that place up in North Dakota that man in the crowd called out again, just as we were leaving, and said, "Well, what does a woman know about war anyway?" I had read my paper that morning and I knew what the awful headline was, and I saw a gentleman standing in the crowd with a paper in his pocket, and I said, "Will that gentleman hold the paper up," and he held it up, and the headline read, "250,000 Men Killed Since the War Began." I said, "You ask me what a woman knows about war? No woman can read that line and comprehend the awful horror; no woman knows the significance of 250,000 dead men, but you tell me that one man lay dead and I might be able to tell you something of its awful meaning to one woman. I would know that years before a woman whose heart beat in unison with her love and her desire for motherhood walked day by day with her face to an open grave, with courage, which no man has ever surpassed, and if she did not fill that grave, if she lived and if there was laid in her arms a tiny little bit of helpless humanity, I would know that there went out from her soul such a cry of thankfulness as none save a mother could know. And then I would know, what men have not yet learned, that women are human; that they have human hopes and human passions, aspirations and desires as men have, and I would know that that mother had laid aside all those hopes and aspirations for herself, laid them aside for her boy, and if after years had passed by she forgot her nights of sleeplessness and her days of fatiguing toil in her care of her growing boy, and when at last he became a man and she stood looking up into his eyes and beheld him, bone of her bone and flesh of her flesh, for out of her woman's life she had carved twenty beautiful years that went into the making of a man; and there he stands, the most wonderful thing in all the world; for in all the Universe of God there is nothing more sublimely wonderful than a strong limbed clean hearted, keen brained, aggressive young man, standing as he does on the border line of life, ready to reach out and grapple with its problems. O, how wonderful he is, and he is hers. She gave her life for him, and in an hour this country calls him out and in an hour he lies dead; that wonderful, wonderful thing lies dead; and sitting by his side, that mother looking into the dark years to come knows that when her son died her life's hope died with him, and in the face of that wretched motherhood, what man dare ask what a woman knows of war. And that is not all. Read your papers, you cannot read it because it is not printable; you cannot tell it because it is not speakable, you cannot even think it because it is not thinkable, the horrible crimes perpetrated against women by the blood drunken men of the war.

You read your paper again and the second headlines read, "It Costs Twenty Millions of Dollars a Day," for what? To buy the material to slaughter the splendid results of civilization of the centuries. Men whom it has taken centuries to build up and make into great scientific forces of brain, the flower of the manhood of the great nations of Europe, and we spend twenty millions of dollars a day to blot out all the results of civilization of hundreds and hundreds of years. And what do we do? We lay a mortgage on every unborn child for a hundred and more years to come. Mortgage his brain, his brawn, every pulse of his heart in order to pay the debt, to buy the material to slaughter the men of our country. And that is not all, the greatest crime of war is the crime against the unborn. Read what they are doing. They are calling out every man, every young man, every virile man from seventeen to forty-five or fifty years old, they are calling them out. All the splendid scientific force and energy of the splendid virile manhood are being called out to be food for the cannon, and they are leaving behind the degenerate, defective imbecile, the unfit, the criminals, the diseased to be the fathers of the children yet to be born. The crime of crimes of the war is the crime against the unborn children, and in the face of the fact that women are driven out of the home shall men ask if women shall fight if they are permitted to vote.

No we women do not want the ballot in order that we may fight, but we do want the ballot in order that we may help men to keep from fighting, whether it is in the home or in the state, just as the home is not without the man, so the state is not without the woman, and you can no more build up homes without men than you can build up the state without women. We are needed everywhere where human life is. We are needed everywhere where human problems are to be solved. Men and women must go through this world together from the cradle to the grave, it is God's way and it is the fundamental principle of a Republican form of government.

The Other Half of Humanity

This speech was stenographically recorded and then printed as a pamphlet. Both the manuscript and the published copy are found in box 22, folder 540, of the Shaw papers.

There are two classes of people here this afternoon--saints and sinners; the sinners are the people who do not agree with us, and the saints are the people who do. We want the sinners to be seated. I am a Methodist, and having been a Methodist for years, I know that, if you want to convert a man, he must be physically comfortable while you are attempting it, so, if any sinner here is uncomfortable, let him come and take my seat.

In the old Methodist meetings, the old-fashioned Methodist always began his speech with, "I am glad to be here." I want to say that this afternoon, for I remember that when I was here years ago, I was forbidden to speak on woman suffrage; today I should be forbidden to speak on anything else. Yet today one man is politically still worth one thousand women; two years hence, when Alabama's women are free, one woman will be politically equal to one.

I am very glad that I am speaking on Sunday. I am glad to speak on the day of the week when men and women have leisure to listen to the problems which concern their lives; and I know of no better service for Sunday afternoon than for men and women to discuss the fundamental principles of the government under which they live. No man is fitted to become a citizen of the Kingdom of Heaven who is not a good citizen on this earth. No man who thinks this earth and its problems unworthy of consideration understands the moving of the Divine Spirit; and anyone who thinks that women suffrage is not a proper subject for discussion on Sunday afternoon, does not comprehend the profound, sublime and divine principles of democracy.

Democracy is not merely a form of government; it is a great spiritual force emanating from the heart of the Infinite, permeating the universe and transforming the lives of men until the day comes when it shall take possession of them, and shall govern their lives. Then will men be fitted to lift their faces to the Source from whence the spirit of democracy flows, and answer back in the spirit, in their recognition of that fundamental principle of democracy: "One is our father, even God, and we are members one of another." And as soon as the spirit of democracy takes possession of us, we shall not quibble as to whether it is male or female, bond or free, Jew or Greek; we shall recognize only that every child has an equal right with every other human child of God, in the things that belong to God.   Liberty, justice, freedom, belong alike to God's human children.(1)

The fundamental reason for the prejudice that the average man brings to the discussion of woman suffrage to-day is not that he is living unchaste, or that he does not want to be fair towards women; it is that he has not yet grasped the fact that women are human. Men are usually very fair to other men. The average man will say of himself: "Being a human being, I have a right to everything which in any way benefits me as a human being; and the government is under obligation to confer upon me such political powers as shall enable me to control and regulate the conditions under which I live and labor"; and then he looks into the face of his brother-man and says: "Whatever is fair and just for me, is fair and just for him." The average man is perfectly just in considering this problem in regard to other men; it is when he is considering women, instead of men, that the average man becomes so sentimental that he immediately forgets the fundamental principles of justice and righteousness and freedom, and flies off at a tangent with: "My wife! My mother! My sister! My daughter!" He does not think of women as human, but merely as related to human beings. We *are* related to human beings. We do not want to be anything else, but we are also human. Every political right conferred upon man belongs to him not because he is male but because he is human, and to women not because she is female but because she too is human. If a man has no right to self-government because he is a man and has a right to self-government because he is human, the woman also has no right to self-government because she is a woman, but she has, today, a right to self-government because she is human. It is this fundamental principle of democracy which underlies the whole woman suffrage movement.

Men recognize this fact--that humanity is the only real basis of democracy, in their political writings and declarations, and in the sentiments which they utter. Read the utterances of men about democracy; how splendid, how thrilling they are! Should they not apply to all alike when they declare that, "under God,

the people rule"? Yet the men who declare this prevent one-half
of the people from having anything to do with ruling! Men will
extol the Declaration of Independence with its fundamental
principle of democracy which declares that "governments derive
their just powers from the consent of the governed," and will
then proceed to govern women without giving them any chance
of consenting to any law which men compel them to obey. On
the Fourth of July and other great patriotic occasions, orators
declare that the voice of the people is the voice of God, yet
forget that, in the compass of the human voice there is a soprano
as well as a bass. If the voice of the people is the voice of God,
we shall never hear the voice of God in government until the
soprano and bass mingle together, the result of which may be
divine harmony. That time will never come so long as we are
content to listen to a bass solo!

In our Methodist Love Feast we always give our experiences. I
want to give my experiences this afternoon and tell you--not why
I am a suffragist, that is because, thank Heaven, I was born with
intelligence!--but why I gave up everything else in the world to
work for woman suffrage.(2) When I was a young girl, I had, as
you all have had, my ideal of the kind of human being I should
like to become; the noblest character in the world; and I had no
faith in the usual allotment to women of certain particularly
virtuous characteristics and the reservation to men alone of
certain other honorable qualities. I believed that the most
perfect human being in the world is the one who possesses
those characteristics which we call the most desirable in
women, blended with the characteristics which we call most
desirable in men. When I was a young preacher on Cape Cod, I
delivered a series of sermons, and, among others, a sermon on
"Jesus Christ, the ideal man," and the next Sunday another on
"Jesus Christ, the ideal wo-man"; and I said that all desirable
womanly traits could be found in him, and all desirable manly
traits were also found in Him. In Him, the Man, were blended
perfectly the ideal characteristics of man and woman. In my
youth, He was too exalted an ideal for me; therefore, I selected
from the Scriptures two characters who, to my mind, stood as
the highest type of man and the highest type of woman, and I
thought that the blending of these two would make a perfect
character, an ideal character, if one dared aspire to it. For the
woman, I took one about whom I had never heard a minister
preach, Vashti, one of the noblest characters in all history; a
woman who so respected herself and the dignity of her
birthright as the daughter of a king--who held her virtue in such
high honor--that, rather than debase herself before her
husband's drunken guests, she was ready to leave home and
throne and husband and country, to give up everything for the
dignity of her womanhood. And the man I selected was Caleb.
The Bible does not say much of him; it has no need to. You may

have to read sixteen or eighteen volumes to find out who George
Washington was, but the Bible does not need eighteen or twenty
volumes to set forth the characteristics of a man. In the few
sentences it devotes to Caleb its readers may see the man as he
was--so he stands out to this day. Caleb did not say much. He
was sent out as an emissary through the promised land, just as
we suffragists are sent out. He came back with the other spies
and told exactly the same story as they, but to a different end.
The others said: "We are not able to go up against the people to
occupy the land, for they are stronger than we; the cities are
walled and very great." "All the people that we saw in the land
are men of great stature, and there we saw the giants, and were
in our own sight as grasshoppers and so we were in their sight."
"We cannot go up and take the land." But Caleb said: "Let us go
up at once and possess it, for we are well able to overcome it."
"In the strength of Jehovah, we will go forth, notwithstanding
that the cities are vast and the walls high and the men giants. In
the strength of Jehovah we can go up and possess the land."
Reading of Vashti and Caleb I said to myself: "Here are dignity of
character, courage and womanly virtue on the one hand, and
undaunted faith and courage on the other. The blending of these
will make an ideal character. Such a combination of qualities, I
thought, is exactly what all reformers need, for theirs is a most
difficult task--a task which especially confronts the women who
stand for the movement represented by this audience today."
Could there be anything more discouraging, more full of
despairing anguish than the task of the women who inaugurated
this great movement? Yet their faith, their undaunted courage,
their perseverance, and their belief in the dignity of womanhood
and in the eternal triumph of justice, led them and still leads
them on today.(3)

When I started out in life, having before me the ideals of
which I have told you, I made up my mind that I would become a
missionary and would go to the women who, more than others,
need friends and yet suffer the greatest abuses. So I studied
theology and, when I graduated, thinking I knew something
about what I had undertaken, I attempted to help the homeless
and the forsaken and the betrayed women of that community. In
a little while I found out that I had nothing to give that
community. In a little while I found out that I had nothing to
give that they wanted, and I also found out that, although I knew
some things about theology, I knew very little about human
beings; and I learned something there that I had not learned at
any school. I learned to understand why the Master taught us to
say: "Give us this day our daily bread" before He said: "Forgive us
our sins"; for I learned that it is useless to talk virtue to a
starving girl. The cry of this human body of ours is so much
louder, so much more gross, so much more exacting in its
demand than is the cry of the soul, that we cannot hear the still

small voice until after the other voice is silenced.   I looked around to see what was needed and found that I could do practically little. "But," I thought, "there is one woman who does do something, and that is a doctor; for a woman-doctor can go to these women when they are sick and suffering, and minister to them and bring them some sort of relief and comfort." So I went back to school and studied medicine and took my degree, and again went down into the by-ways to live and to work and unceasingly tried to do something to be helpful. At the end of three years I gave it up in utter despair. The same desperate problems that had faced all other workers in such lines faced me also. I felt like one waiting with an ambulance at the foot of a precipice for the certain fall of a living body over the brink; waiting merely to take up the remains and give them a decent burial, instead of being at the top of the precipice to prevent the unwary from falling over. And I said, "This is no place for me. What is needed first of all for these poor girls is some rational satisfaction for their human nature; what they need is employment under conditions which shall not crush out and strophy all their natural human demands; what is needed is a fair chance for each--a fair day's wage for a fair day's work." It was not that I did not believe in women's working; I believe so much in women's working, that I think no woman has a right to occupy space in the world who does not give valuable service in return for the space she occupies. Something, either of brain, of brawn, or of heart, something the world needs, something a woman must give, either inside the home or outside the home, wherever duty calls her; and she is to be the judge of her call to duty. I believed, then, in work, but under conditions that left the worker human after the day's toil was done, in work which, instead of crushing out the vital energies of a young woman and leaving her with stooped shoulders, atrophied heart and downcast eyes, would leave her capable of feeling in her soul the joy of living, of lifting her eyes to the sky and knowing that the blue was for her, the flowers of the field and the sun of comfort were for her, the laughter of little children, the love of husband and home and the joys of comradeship were for her. I believed that working women should have in life this human satisfaction, which we all need, of friendship, love, home and comradeship. That is why, then as now, I wanted to do my share to see that other toilers got an equal day's pay for an equal day's work regardless of whether they were men or women. But, lo! I found that women are a branded sex--and no matter whether of a branded sex or a branded race, no group of people who bear the seal of inferiority ever have a fair and equal chance anywhere in this world!--and I saw that, so long as women are branded as the inferior sex, and men are distinguished as the superior sex, there is no hope in the market of the world of an equal day's pay for an equal day's work; there is no hope of a fair chance of opportunity for rising; there is even no hope that, under the government, the one who can pass the examination will get the government position; there is no fair chance anywhere, until that stigma is removed which declares women an inferior sex in the business of life.

It is no use to deny that women *are* branded as the inferior sex; it is no use any longer to talk poetry to us. That was all very well in the time of Elizabeth before women began to read.(4) It is no use to talk chivalry; it is no use to talk anything but common sense, to women today, to know whether women are reckoned an inferior sex or not, we have to but listen to the conversation of men and women about us. What do you say if you want to touch a man to the quick with the most contemptuous name? If he is an elderly man you call him an "old woman"; if he is a young man, of the namby pamby good-for-nothing sort, you call him a "sissy", or "Miss Nancy." If you ask a little boy to do the task which is ordinarily done by his sister, he says that it is "girls work"--an inferior job! Not long ago a gentleman introduced me to an audience, and, after having said a great many pleasant things about me, most of which were not true, he said, wishing to conclude with the most flattering thing possible: "I now have the pleasure of introducing to you a woman with the brains of a man!" What more could a man say of a woman? He thought that he had heaped upon me the highest possible praise-" a woman with the brains of a man!" I never answer back when people say things about me personally, but when they say things about my sex, it becomes my business to answer them, so, when I got over my surprise, I said, "I really don't know how to take my introduction, whether to take it as a reflection upon my sex or as a compliment to my intelligence. If the gentleman intends it as a compliment to my intelligence to say that I have the brains of a man, before I feel duly proud over it--I should like to see the man whose brains I have got! There is a lot of difference in brains among men as well as among women." Are we to be censured when we ask why we are branded as inferior? We are indeed not men, but is it not astonishing that men so superior should have such inferior mothers? We are, of all God's creation, the only species in which an inferior mother can produce a superior son. I do not pretend that women know more than men. I know that men know a great deal more than women about many things; but I also know that women know a great deal more than men about many other things; and I know that men and women together know all there is to know about everything!

Such knowledge is what we want at the ballot box--the fullness of all the knowledge there is needed for the government of the people; and we shall never get it in this government until men and women vote it there together. It is absurd to make sex-distinctions in government. Of all the foolish things in the world, nothing was ever more foolish than is the assumption of sex-superiority. Over in the old world they are fighting to the death a fetish which has possessed the old world for centuries. It is the assumption of the divine right of kings. And it will receive its death blow before this fierce struggle is over. The time will come when men will refuse to die at the behest of a king! While men in Europe are fighting to the death the ancient fetish of the divine right of kings, women, all over the United States, are fighting to the death a similar fetish, and that is the divine right of sex. Years ago, when the Emperor William ascended the throne of Germany he claimed that he ruled Germany by divine right, and I remember how the assumption of this young man was ridiculed; but I could not understand why it was any more absurd for the Emperor William to assume that he ruled Germany by divine right, than it is for men in this country to assume that they rule women by divine right.(5)

Men, what have you been doing? Read your own history and see what your consistent course has been! One remarkable characteristic of men in their consistency is their inconsistency; from the beginning of our life as a people on this continent to the present hour, this consistency in inconsistency has been marked. From the beginning, we have called ours a great, free country, we have called it the land of the free and the home of the brave; and we have never really believed this! We have called ourselves a Republic and yet we are not a Republic today. We get into the habit of repeating things one after another like magpies; and so we speak of this great Republic of the United States, whereas, in reality, the United States has never been a Republic. Take your lexicon and read the definition of a "Republic!" You will find that a Republic is a form of government in which the laws are enacted by representatives elected by the people. When have the people in this country, save in States where women are enfranchised, ever elected their representatives? Never in our whole history! *Men* have elected their representatives, and men are indeed people, excellent people so far as they go, but they are only half the people, there is still another half of the people who have *not* elected their representatives. Yet who ever read a definition of a Republic as a government in which one half the people elected representatives to govern the whole of the people! That is not a Republic, that is aristocracy. In this country we have an aristocracy of sex! We are, however, trying to evolve a Republic; that is all we have been doing from the beginning of our life as a nation. We have been seeking to evolve a Republic out of a Monarchy but we are not yet fully evolved.

You should read the history of your country. Men have not always ruled in this country because they were men; they have ruled because they were some particular kind of men. The first men who voted in this country, after the Pilgrims had settled here, were church-members; a man did not then vote because he was a male, he voted because he was a particular kind of male. He had to be a member of some church. After the Revolutionary War, when the State Constitutions were framed, the word "taxpayer" was written before the word "male" so that, if a man were not a church-member he could yet vote, provided that he had some property and paid taxes. And the evolutionary process continued until that great Democrat appeared who saw that rapidly increasing wealth in the hands of a few people would endanger the liberty of the masses, unless the working man had the power to protect themselves by the only weapon known to a republican form of government--the ballot. And under the leadership of that great statesman, Thomas Jefferson, the right of suffrage was extended to the laboring men of the country, and the word "taxpayer" was stricken out of the Constitution, but the word "white" was still written in, and they sang of "the land of the free and the home of the brave," and talked beautifully of motherhood, while at the same time they sold mother's babies by the pound on the auction block. Then another political party arose and said: "A man is not a good citizen because he is white: he is a good citizen because he is a man." So they rubbed out the word "white", and they left that little word "male" standing alone, by itself. They could not think of another qualifying word to write before it. There was no man left out, they were all in-- black and white, rich and poor, wise and otherwise, drunk and sober, all men were in, and for the first time the little word "male" stood all alone. And yet God said in the beginning: "It is not good for man to stand alone!"

Now, all that is meant by the woman-suffrage movement lies in that first divine utterance to man: "It is not good for man to stand alone"--either in the home, or the state, or even in the Garden of Eden.(6) Therefore, we women are asking that the word "male" be stricken out of our State and National Constitutions, and that these shall read as they ought to have read in the beginning: Every citizen twenty-one years of age, possessing the necessary qualifications may cast one vote at every election and have that vote counted. That is all suffragists are asking. And yet, by the opposition with which we are met and the horror of anti-suffragists, one might suppose that we were seeking to up-root the foundations of the government, that we were asking that women should leave their homes and forsake their children, should cease to love their husbands, and should become so absorbed in politics that they would never again think of anything else in the world; whereas all we are asking of men is to be true to the fundamental principles of democracy, and to take, in their day, the step that belongs to their time, as their ancestors in their day took the steps which belonged to their time, in the evolution of a republic out of a monarchy. We are not yet fully evolved; there is one step still to be taken; and no State as a part nor the United States as a whole can become a republic until the word "male" is stricken out of their respective constitutions and the word "citizen" incorporated; until all citizens are alike free.

Whenever a government, calling itself a republic, prescribes qualifications for voters, these qualifications must be such as apply equally to all citizens of the republic. When the government says that the citizen, in order to vote, shall be twenty-one years of age, that could apply to men and women alike. When it says that the voter must have been a resident of the State for a certain length of time, that too applies to both alike. When, again, the government might even go further and say that, in order to vote, a citizen must be able to read the ballot and know for whom he or she is voting, and that also might apply fairly to all. Nor would women object to such a qualification, for there are more women than men in the United States who could read their votes. The government, however, has never imposed upon its citizens a hardship so great as that; the government has been very careful to protect male ignorance. What exciting debate there was in Congress when they tried to pass the Immigration Bill! What remarkable speeches were made against the literacy test! Yet the bill was carried; it was sent to the President, and the President then vetoed it. I was especially interested in the language used by our President in vetoing the bill on account of its literacy clause. That clause, he said, would keep out of our country "a large body of very desirable people." I wondered why we make it so easy for male ignorance to enter our country or to gain political power, and are so fearful at the very thought of injecting a little female ignorance into our electorate that we withhold the ballot from the large body of intelligent American women. I fail to understand why female ignorance is so much more deadly than the male ignorance which has been imposed upon us in this country.(7)

When I was a girl we occasionally had elections in the community in which I lived. We never knew just how these were coming out, because we had the old-fashioned tissue ballots, and the number of ballots cast depended upon the size of the ballot-box and had little relation to the number of electors. Men were desirous of finding a ballot that would be both safe and secret but could not devise one. At last they heard of the ballot used in Australia (a country where women vote) and our Statesmen sent for the Australian ballot. They found it safe and secret, but not adapted to our electors, because in Australia voters must be able to read the ballot. But how could we impose a hardship of that kind on male citizens? However politicians hit upon the plan of putting at the head of the column of each political party a symbol, like a rooster, or an eagle, or a star, or a man with a hammer in his hand, to stand for the different political parties, so that, if a man has intelligence enough to know the difference between a rooster and an eagle, he knows which party to vote for. The people who do not want women to vote for fear of their ignorance so arrange our ballots in the United States to adapt them to male illiteracy! I think women could vote a ballot carefully prepared like that, especially if the eagle were taken out and a hen put in! I am quite sure we could vote the ticket! When men make it so easy to bring to the polls all the male ignorance of the country, it ill becomes them to say that women may not vote because they are not intelligent. But we are outgrowing these symbols now. Where women vote, as they do in Colorado and in Washington, and some other states, they are pleading that the symbols may be removed, so as to make it necessary for the American citizen to be able to read his vote. In Wyoming, the first state to enfranchise women, they never used them.

When the government says that, in order to vote, a citizen shall be a male, that is not a qualification, that is an insuperable barrier between one half of the people and their rights as citizens. And no government calling itself a republic may erect an insuperable barrier between one half its citizens and their rights and privileges, and remain a republic. A government which does that is not a republic; it is an aristocracy, and the poorest kind of aristocracy on earth, an aristocracy of sex.

However, in our country, all men are not allowed to vote. I listened this winter to the debate upon woman suffrage in Congress. For forty-three years suffragists have had a bill in Congress asking for a National Constitutional Amendment enfranchising women citizens. We never got that bill out of committee in all the forty-three years until this winter; but nothing was more amusing than the reasons men gave for not wishing women to vote. Those opposed to suffrage were also opposed to dragging women from the pedestal men had put them on down into the dirty pool of politics. It always impresses me greatly that men should be so willing to remain in that dirty pool themselves. How chivalrous they are and how proud of not wanting us to get our skirts soiled in the pool which they know they themselves made so unfit! If they made the pool so undesirable that we cannot go near it, it is about time that, for the health of the nation, women should help men to clean it up. While these congressmen were giving their reasons for disenfranchising women, among others man's high regard for women, I wondered if that was the reason they disenfranchise certain classes of men--because of their high regard for them. When they spoke of women as being on a pedestal, and of not wanting them to come down, I wondered if they had in mind the other people of their own sex who are up on that pedestal of disenfranchisement with women. All the male idiots, insane men, male criminals (those inside the penitentiary), all the male children and all aliens. They talk about our honored position on that pedestal; if there is any woman who wishes to stand on a pedestal with that group, she ought to do so--she belongs there; but I for my part do not! I want to come down; I want to get into the place where opinions are crystallized into laws which are made to govern me and to govern the lives of other women who are out in the world fighting life's battle; I want to stand beside the men who are warring today against the forces of evil and vice and ignorance and poverty; to strike such blows as can be struck by free men and women only against the injustices which are dragging us downward as a Nation! I want to be in this fight with men and women worthy to fight such battles; and the pedestal is no place for a warrior until after he is dead. I am going to say something which some of you men may not like to hear; but by tomorrow, after going home and thinking about it, you will know that I told the truth. In no other nation in the world--I am going to say it slowly--in no other nation in the world have the women of that nation been reduced to the humiliating political position occupied by the women of the United States today. In Germany, German women are governed by German men; it may not be fair, but one takes a certain pride in one's own countrymen, one may not feel it a degradation to live under the laws of one's native countrymen; at least the men of one's own blood and one's own country have more right to govern than the men of some other race. In France, Frenchwomen are governed by Frenchmen; British women in Great Britain by British men; but, in these United States, American women are governed by every kind of man under the light of the sun. There is not a color from black to white, from red to yellow, there is not a race, there is not a nation, which has not contributed men to be our sovereign rulers. Read the history of the world, and you will see that no nation has ever made its women the subjects of their former slaves save this our nation where we sing of the Land of the Free and the Home of the Brave. And so I say that the most humiliating political position that the women of any nation have ever occupied is that which American women occupy today. If any man thinks it is not, I should like to ask him how he would like it himself. No man shall talk "poetry" or "pedestals" to me, while American women are governed by every and any class of men under the sun! I was in New York, not long ago, while foreigners were being made full-fledged citizens in order to vote at the last election, and men were there who had been primed day after day by their own political parties with a view to answer a few questions; and one even of these did not know that Charles Murphy, the head of Tammany Hall, was not the President of the United States! Yet these men govern New York women. New York native-born women who have given everything for their country; and I claim that this is a form of degradation which burns into the heart of any patriotic woman--which burns into the heart of any self-respecting woman, and that no woman with self-respect can timidly sit under such conditions when she realizes them.

It is time that American men should think where American women stand politically; it is time that American men should begin to think what American women are becoming industrially. It is time for us all to think that, if we are to save America's womanhood, if we do not wish to see it overwhelmed by external forces, we must give American women the power to save themselves. I am not opposed to foreigners, I am one myself; I do not object to enfranchising any man under the light of the sun who is an alleged citizen, with the qualifications necessary for citizenship. I do not object that a man happens not to be born here, when he comes her to live and build his home, and rear his children and educate them in our public schools, and start them out in life with our public school ideals. I do not know why, if he gives his brawn and brain to the development of the country, he should be denied a voice in his children's education because he happens not to be born here. It is right that he should have just the same rights as if he had been born here. What women object to is that men who are not Americans, who are not of our race, should have the power to deprive American women of their right to a voice in their own government.

And what objections confront such an appeal as this? They may be expressed in beautiful poetical phrases about "the sturdy oak, and the clinging vine"; but we know that they who observe more closely the sturdy oak about which the ivy clings, find it dead at the top. The truth is that there has been too much of the clinging vine and too much of the sturdy oak theory in the world.

And are there no sensible anti-suffrage arguments? Well! the other arguments, such as they are, generally come in pairs. The anti-suffragists have the happy faculty of answering their own arguments. I do not know what we should have done for argument if it had not been for our opponents since they positively refuse to meet us on fundamental principles. When women tell me that there is no anti-suffrage organization in their State, I reply: "You are to be pitied; the only States that are really happy are those that have anti-suffragists, for without them there is no argument." One may assert that two and two make four, but to argue the point there must be objections to answer. When I was in the campaigns last year, I was followed from place to place by an anti-suffrage speaker from New Jersey. She was a very agreeable young woman who had left her husband and home and gone forth to tell women that their place is at home, that they have not time to vote, and that they must not go out in public because it is unwomanly! One of her arguments was that it is useless to give women the ballot, because if they had it they would not use it. If women would not use it, what harm could there be in giving it to them? In that case, you men need only give women the vote to be completely rid of them. They could never blame you for anything which goes wrong politically; you could sit back and say: "We told you so, we told you so!" No! I do not see why you should not grant suffrage if women would not use it! But to return to the young anti-suffragist: "What," she asked, "will become of the home if you give women the ballot?" Women will neglect their homes; they will forsake their children, they will cease to love their husbands. Women are hysterical, and if they should once get into politics, they would become so enamored of the life that once at the polls men could never get them home again. They would want to do nothing at all but vote.

On the other hand, anti-suffragists say that it would be useless to give women the vote as they would vote exactly as their husbands do, and it would only double the vote. Is a man so ashamed of his vote that he would not like his wife to vote in the same way as himself? I only wish that the anti-suffragists could make men believe that women would vote as they wish them to. They could give women the ballot at once. Do you suppose that, if men believed this, women would have to hold another suffrage meeting? No! They would *have* to vote, whether they wished to do so or not. And, of course, spinsters would be as welcome to the ballot as married women, because any woman who had no husband would probably vote as he would if she had one! But suppose that two persons should vote alike. Has nothing been done but to double the number of votes in the ballot box? Does it not imply that two persons have been reading, two have been thinking, two have been discussing, and two have deposited the result of all this in their ballots which crystallize their will into law? Does it not mean that two persons have been bound by their ballots to the interests of the community, instead of one being so bound while the other remains an irresponsible citizen who cannot be held by the country responsible for the influence she exerts, although the country must endure its results? If there were a hundred people who all voted alike, it would be better for the community and better for the people themselves that each should vote than that one should cast the vote for all.

Our opponents, however, who urge that wives will vote as their husbands do, will, nevertheless declare on other occasions that they will not vote as they are directed to, and they draw a most woeful picture of the discord, the quarrels, the disorganization of the family, the divorce, that will ensue, until one shudders to think of it! A man told me once that he and his wife had lived together for twenty years without a difference in opinion in all those years. He was going to vote against woman suffrage he said, for fear that he and his wife might differ. And, while he talked, I could not help wondering which of the two was the greater idiot; for I know very well that no two intelligent minds could think on parallel line for twenty years. I wondered as I looked at that great big man, how a man like that could stand being followed about by a little woman all these twenty years, saying: "Me, too! Me too! Me too!" I should not want to live in the house even twenty hours with another human being who agreed to everything I said. The stagnation of a frog pond would be hilarious in comparison. Think of the absurdity of it; think what a libel it is on men! Anti-suffragists say that suffragists hate men. It is they who have a poor opinion of men, and not we. We think that the average American man is an agreeable sort of human being and that it would be quite possible to live in the house with him even without always agreeing with him.

Again they tell us that if we women should vote, we should have to mingle at the polls with horrid men--the same horrid men with whom we live the rest of the year. In my precinct, the men who vote in the polling booth where I would vote are my neighbors who come to my home; men who sit by me or by whom I stand in the street cars. I do not know why men so decent that women would not like to live without their society for three hundred and sixty-four days of the year should, on the three hundred and sixty-fifth day, be such ruffians that women cannot go near them without contamination. Even if men are, as our opponents claim, dangerously unworthy, the securest possible place for a woman would be at the polls, since the law forbids any interference with an elector within fifty or, in some states, one hundred feet of the voting booth. The polls, compared to a New York subway, for example, is the safest place imaginable.

We hear, again, that women have no time and are burdened with too many responsibilities and cares to vote. One might suppose that it took all day or even a week to vote! They tell us that women would have to neglect their children because they would be occupied by politics. A lady in one of the campaign States whose guest I was, held up her baby and said: "Is this not my job?" "It certainly is," I replied, "and any woman who has that kind of a job has a job that she ought to attend to." Then she exclaimed: "How can I go to the polls and vote?" I said: "Your husband who is the president of a bank also has a job that requires his closest attention, yet he told me that he intended to vote for this amendment." "Oh yes," she cried, "he is very keen about it." Then I said: "See what an advantage you have over your husband. He has to leave *his* job to go and vote, while you may take your job with you." It is a strange thing that nobody worries about a woman's baby except on election day! They know that, if a woman who has a baby goes to church, she probably either takes it with her or finds someone to take care of it; that if she spends one afternoon of every week of the season at a bridge-whist party, she probably provides somebody to take care of the baby; that if she goes to the opera or to a dance, or to a play, she sees that somebody takes care of the baby. The only time they think that a woman has not enough interest to take care of a baby is on election day! I have often wondered why, if voting is a mere question of using up time, we do not, since men are paid a third to a half more for their time than are women, use the cheap time of women rather than the dear time of men for that purpose. That, an argument against woman's suffrage! And again the very women who tell you that women have not the time to vote will also tell you that women form the leisure class.

The most amusing argument against suffrage is in regard to prohibition. Last year, when we were campaigning in the West, which, as you know, is divided on the prohibition question, our anti-suffrage opponents declared, according to circumstances, either that suffragists were not for prohibition or that they were. In North Dakota, which is one of the strong prohibition States, in which they are "dry" because they want to be "dry," the anti-suffrage speakers naturally tried to prove that, if women were allowed to vote, they would vote North Dakota "wet." They produced statistics to show it. Women, they asserted, had not voted Los Angeles "dry," nor San Francisco "dry," nor Portland "dry," nor Chicago "dry." (As a matter of fact, women had not voted on the question in Chicago, but that did not affect anti-suffrage statistics.) Therefore, they would vote North Dakota "wet." In Montana, on the other hand, which is "wet" and very "wet," any argument that could prove that women, if enfranchised, would keep Montana "wet" would not serve their purpose, so they got out their other set of statistics to prove that if women were allowed to vote in Montana they would vote Montana "dry." They showed that, in less than two years, women had in Illinois voted ninety-six towns dry. How long, at that rate, they asked, would it take to vote Montana dry? Afterwards, I went to Nebraska and, as soon as I arrived, a reporter asked me: "How will women vote on the prohibition question in this State?" I said, "I really don't know. I know how they will vote in North Dakota, they will vote wet; and I know how they will vote in Montana, they will vote "dry," but how they will vote in Nebraska I cannot tell, but I will let you know just as soon as the anti-suffrage lady from New Jersey arrives." And so the temperance forces are against woman suffrage for fear women will vote "wet," and the liquor interest for fear they will vote "dry." They grind us between the upper and the nether mill stone.

There is another argument urged by some men and women, namely, that it would not be ladylike to vote. Some women who belong to the Federation of Clubs think that. They do not think it would be ladylike to go to the polls and cast their ballot to elect a man to the Legislature who will do the things that ought to be done for the community in which they live; but they do think it perfectly ladylike to go to the Legislature themselves and lobby, to send their cards to members and to buttonhole and way-lay them until they hate the sight of women, trying to persuade them to vote for the things that they were elected not to vote for. Of all the unladylike things that a lady ever did, the most unladylike is to go to the Legislature and lobby. We have done it over and over again. It is the only way that is left to women to secure favorable legislation--and then we usually can't get it! How much more ladylike it would be to go to the polls and deposit a ballot to elect a man who desires to do the things women want to have done. Why, in comparison to lobbying, voting is so ladylike that I almost wonder a man is willing to do it!

Then, again, there are the sentimental arguments. Men are so sentimental about women! I once heard one say: "I am opposed to woman suffrage, and so are all men;" and the reason he gave for the opposition is that "men fear the loss of woman's subtle charm, of that bloom of womanhood which is one of her greatest treasures and which has made man her slave through all centuries." "If you rub the bloom from the cheek of the peach, no power in the world can restore it. It is the loss of the bloom we fear." And then he sat down and I got up and said: "I am glad to be here; it has always been the joy of women to be the comforters of men, and I am glad to be able to assure the gentleman that, if it is true that if you rub the bloom from the cheek of the peach no power can ever restore it, then, there is a difference between the peach and the woman; for, give the woman five minutes and the opportunity, and the bloom will be restored just as it was before." The bloom that rubs off so easily is as easily restored. But there is a bloom of womanhood which will enable a woman to go anywhere, to do anything circumstances demand; which will glow with a beauty more wonderful as the years go by. It is not the bloom that rubs off from without, it is the bloom which glows forth from within. It is the power of character which enables a woman to give help in the world's great need. Yes, I would trust the mothers of men with the power to protect their children. I am not afraid of the fadeless bloom of womanhood. God has not done his work so badly, nor have women done their work in the world so badly, that we need fear that women will ever forget their womanhood!

I will deal with one further so-called objection. "If women vote they must go to war." In the last campaign I was speaking in North Dakota to a great group of men, gathered out of doors. One of them, who sat on a day-goods box whittling a stick in defense of his country all the time I was talking, said, when I had finished: "Well, if we give women the vote, will they go to Germany and fight the Germans?" "No sir," I replied, "why should we?" Then he said: "If the Germans came over here would the women fight?" I said, "No sir, why should we? If

German *men* come over here to fight, *men* must fight them, but if Germany should send an army of women to fight, then we will show you what we will do. We will go to New York Harbor and meet them, and we will say: "Come on, lets go to the Metropolitan Opera House and talk this thing over." Nobody would be killed; it might be wearisome, but it would not be fatal!

Women did that very thing last summer in regard to war. In the International Council of Women we settled this whole war question without any slaughter. For two weeks the women delegates from twenty-eight nations were assembled in the city of Rome, discussing great international problems. There were women of all forms of the Protestant faith and of both the Greek and Roman Catholic faith. There were Jews and women of many other religious beliefs; there were women differing politically: conservatives, radicals, democrats, republicans, socialists, prohibitionists, all were there. They discussed problems which were international, of equal interest to every Nation. The discussions were conducted with great forbearance. Many resolutions were passed, two of them unanimously. One was presented by myself, as chairman of the Committee on Suffrage and Rights of Citizenship, calling upon all civilized nations of the world to grant to women-citizens equal political rights with men; the resolution was passed without a single dissenting vote from any men; the resolution was passed without a single dissenting vote from any of the nations. The other was a resolution on behalf of peace. Most women believed then, as they do now, that preparation for war is an incentive to war, and that war will never cease until the nations of the world cease to prepare for war. We passed unanimously the resolution calling upon the nations of the world systematically and gradually to disarm, both on land and sea, in order that there might be no incentive for nations to fight. A few days afterwards, we attended a reception given by the American Ambassador, and, among others whom I met, was a prominent Italian Diplomat, who, with a little touch of sarcasm, said: "I understand that you have been having a most profitable convention; that the German Delegation presented a resolution on peace, that the French women seconded it, and that a British woman put it to the body, and that it was carried unanimously." I said, "No, that was not exactly the process, but the conclusion is correct; we carried it unanimously." And he said, "Remarkable, very remarkable." And our Ambassador remarked later, "It is very remarkable that the only body of people of different religious faiths and organized for different objects, who can come together internationally and discuss different problems for two weeks without a drawn sword in their hands, are the women of the world, while men, even when they come together at the Hague to talk of peace, come with a sword buckled at their side." As we read of the deeds perpetrated by men today, of the slaughter of men, women and children under the direction of Christian Rulers, instigated by their hatred and fear of each other and their greed for gain, we too wonder why men cannot discuss their problems without hatred and war.(8)

But, to return to the man in North Dakota--as I was about to leave he called out again: "Well, what does a woman know about war anyhow?" I had read the paper that morning. I knew what the headlines were and, seeing a man with a paper in his pocket, I said to him: "I wish you would hold up that paper." The glaring headline read: "250,000 men killed since the war began." (Alas, what would it be today?) I said: "Two hundred and fifty thousand dead men! No woman can comprehend the meaning of such horrible slaughter! The horror of it alone would drive her mad. It means that two hundred and fifty thousand strong splendid men lie dead; there are miles of dead men, choking the rivers with their dead bodies, filling the trenches with the dead and dying; their blood mingling with the waters of rivers turning them to crimson. I for one cannot comprehend the horror of such slaughter. But, if you were to tell me that one man lay dead, and if I were to look into the upturned face of one dead soldier and see its pallor, I should know what one woman knows about war. I should know that years before, a woman, whose heart beat in sympathy with her love and her desire for motherhood, had walked day by day with her face to an open grave with a courage which no man has ever surpassed, that she might become the mother of a child. And I should know that if she did not fill the grave as thousands upon thousands do, if she lived, and a tiny little bit of helpless humanity was laid in her arms, there went out from that woman's heart a cry so deep, so sacred, so full of hope, that it laid hold on the Infinite Himself. I should know that that cry was not for herself, but for the tiny helpless being that lay in her arms, that her boy might be worthy, and that she might know as the years went on, that he would live a life of usefulness. She did what all mothers must do, and what men have failed to understand as the real significance and price of motherhood. Men have failed to realize that women are human, that they have the same human ambitions and hopes and aspirations and desires as have men, that they desire to reach out and grasp the problems of life and solve them as do men, that they long for intellectual development and power as men do. Men have not yet learned that women are human, hence they as yet do not realize that the mother lays all these ambitions aside for herself, but she never lays them aside for her boy. In her joy of motherhood, she forgets her nights of sleeplessness and her days of fatiguing toil year after year until at last he has grown to be a man, and she looking up into his eyes, beholds him bone of her bone, and flesh of her flesh, and life of her life, for she has carved out twenty years and more of her life and built them into the making of a man. In him she beholds

the most marvelous work of God, for in all the universe there is
nothing more wonderful than a noble human being, clean of
brain, and clean of heart, strong of limb, ambitious in his
purpose to lay hold of life and to master it. How wonderful he
is!--but it took the life, toil and joyous sacrifice of a woman to
develop him. And then his country calls him, and in an hour
that wonderful being lies dead--dead. And in his death there
died the life, toil, and hope of the mother who gave him birth.
Looking out into the darkness of the lonely and desolate years,
she knows that a woman died too, for merely to breathe is not
life. Multiply that mother's loss by hundreds of thousands and
even God pity them! Millions, and, I ask, what does a man know
about war in face of the tragedy of motherhood? Did you read in
your paper that letter from Russia?   Did you read what the
women of Russia know about war? Did you read what the women
of Galicia, the women of Poland and all those mountainous
countries, know about war? Did you read the price that women
are paying? But no! you could not read it, for they dare not print
it. You cannot tell it, for it is unspeakable! You cannot even
think of it, for it is unthinkable! While the world lasts let no one
ever again ask: "What do women know about war?"

Or again, read what war costs--thirty million dollars a day, for
what?   To buy the material to slaughter the manhood of the
world. Did you read about the one hundred and twenty men that
belonged to no country, though born in Germany?--for when God
sends forth a great scientist into the world he belongs to no one
nation.   More than one hundred and twenty of those men lie
dead already since the war began, and the whole world is robbed
of God's rich gift of men who had given their life to the study of
saving and prolonging the life of the race. This is not the loss of
Germany alone but of the whole world. Thirty million dollars a
day, paid for the material to destroy the brains, the learning and
the manhood of the world, putting a mortgage on the unborn, on
every thought of their brain, on every effort of their brawn, on
every throb of their heart, to pay the debt Europe is today
making for the sake of slaughtering the civilization of the world.
And that is not the worst; the worst of war is crime against the
unborn.   The warring nations are calling their men from
seventeen to fifty years of age and upward, the very flower of
their people, to be food for cannon! And they are leaving behind
the defective, the diseased, the degenerate, the criminal, the
unfit, to become the fathers of the children of the future. The
crime of crimes in war is the crime against unborn children, in
robbing them of virile fathers, and against women in robbing
them of fit mates to be the fathers of their children; yet you ask
what women know about war! They are learning more every day,
and what they learn leads them to demand the ballot, not that
they may fight, but that they may help men to keep from
fighting.

Oh men! Forget your sentimentality and think of women as human; as human factors in the world's progress. Think of their devotion to you and to their families, and then never again say that a woman should have no voice in the things that so vitally concern herself, her family and her country. Whether in war or in peace, the man is not complete without the woman; and as it is impossible to conceive of an ideal home without the man, so it is equally impossible to conceive of an ideal Republic without the woman.

Select Your Principle of Life

Shaw delivered this speech at a student convocation at Temple University at a time when she was chairman of the Woman's Committee of the Council of National Defense. Since she was asked by the university to speak on her life's experiences, she reminisced considerably about her youth. From her personal experiences she drew two conclusions that make life's struggle worthwhile and used them as the basis for her message. Other speeches, such as Women's War Service delivered in Baltimore, Maryland, January 4, 1918, give a more detailed explanation of the activities of the Woman's Committee. However, the Temple University address is of special interest because of the biographical narrative Shaw presents prior to discussing women's wartime activities. The source of the Temple University text is box 23, folder 546 of the Shaw papers. The first page of the manuscript has been lost. The text reprinted here begins with the first full sentence at the top of page two of the manuscript. The manuscript is otherwise in good condition and seems most authentic.

Youth, its light-heartedness, freedom from care, and joy in simply living, is a beautiful thing; and in the time to come, let us hope that under the right conditions it will be the portion of every child. That time is not yet. As I look over this vast body of students, who are equipped to enter the great university of the world, where they will be compelled to face it without the fostering care of the noble body of men and women who compose the faculty of Temple University, I am glad to feel that most of you do not go forth blindly without some previous knowledge of its difficulties, and, better still, a knowledge and a will to overcome them.

It is the habit of youth to look back for the heroic events and crises in the world's history, when opportunities were presented for men and women to become great. But when you have reached my age, you will say, and I so often say, "Oh if I were but 21, what might I not do with my life!"

I feel that today as I look into your faces. If I were but 21 and this world crisis were before me in which to take my place and do my part, what might I not do.

There never was a time in the memory of man when such vast possibilities and opportunities for world service were open to women of vision as your day brings.

I was asked to talk to you of my own personal experiences and early struggles for an education and the opportunity to serve. But at this time, for in the short time, so rapidly do events move these days since the request came to me, it hardly seems best to take your time for an hour for that purpose. Still I will give you the result of my observations in the hope that it may be helpful to some of you who are facing like problems.

When I decided that I would not pattern my life upon the same plan laid down for all women in my girlhood, I was but thirteen years old. Even the women's position in the plan of human development seemed so meager and undesirable and without either self-respect or the respect of others.

To be bound by outworn customs and traditions, and to be hampered by every known obstacle which could be put in one's path, and then to have the world calmly look on and tell you it was no use it was the divine will, was growing too absurd to be longer tolerated with dignity or accepted with self-respect.

The soul within me refused to beat out its life against barred doors, and I rebelled. I would not submit to the untrained life of an ignorant girl of the old-time farm. I knew in my soul that the world and all the things in it were my heritage and I had a right to share in their power to build me up and make me worthy to be a part of the world's fighting force for better things which I believe even then God had for His children.

So in the midst of a dense forest, by the side of a swift-rushing stream, I spent a day making up my mind whether or not I should defy all conventions and declare my purpose to have something of an education. I knew for me there would be no such thing as yielding if I once fully made up my mind. So that it must not be a half-way decision which could be changed if either inclination or opposition stood in my way. So I faced the vastness of the great calm of a dense forest, and faced myself as I looked at my little anxious face in the waters of the brook, and waited all day long. When night came the decision was reached, and it was I WILL.

Then there swept over me the reaction, and a great fear took possession of me. The vastness of everything, the great unknown world, the prejudices of the people, my own family and its ridicule, for brothers and sisters are very sensitive and intolerant of eccentricities in one's family.

At last I went home, weary and overcome, with a desire for comfort and understanding on the part of those dearest to me. I wanted to feel the human sympathy we all crave when a reaction follows a mental or spiritual struggle.

Instead I was met by reproaches for having spent the day in idleness. Idleness--it was the hardest day's work I have ever done in my life, and left me, as did the struggle in Gethsemane of my Master, heart hungry for human sympathy.(1)

Perhaps sympathy at that time would have been my undoing, but the reproach filled me with the heroic fire for martyrdom, and I flamed forth with my purpose. That I would not be a failure--that I would go to college--and that some day they would be as proud of me as they were then ashamed of me.

That night sealed my determination. I would go to college. I would live my life--not the life which had been urged as the destiny of all women, but the life which, face to face with my divine creator, I believed was my right and His will.

Then the struggle began. I cannot describe it; and for you, with the changed attitude of public opinion and the larger opportunities which the past half century has brought to women, it would hardly be possible to accept the accuracy of the story.

A lifetime seems short at best, but what may not take place in a lifetime!

I remember when I was but eight years of age, I went one Sunday night to a gathering in the Garden St. Methodist church in Lawrence, Massachusetts, where a service was being held in honor of a company of immigrants who were going to test their fortunes so far away that we never expected to see them again. They were going to the Territory of Kansas to lay the foundation of the city of Lawrence, Kansas. Twenty years ago, on a visit to California, a young girl in response to a statement from me on the beauty of California said: "Oh, yes, it is beautiful, but I spent last winter in the East, and did enjoy the change." On being asked where in the East, she replied, "Lawrence, Kansas." This in a short lifetime, pioneers leave the Atlantic coast to penetrate so far into the Western wilderness that one never expects to hear from them again, and in forty years after residents of the Pacific coast come to the spot which these pioneers settled to spend a winter in the "East."

So rapidly has this great nation become a homogeneous people from Atlantic to Pacific that there is no longer any frontier.

But rapidly as this vast territory has changed from the haunts of wild beasts and fierce men, the attitude of mind of the people and their ideals have changed still more rapidly. The wild man is now a sovereign citizen, who with his ballot instead of his tomahawk assists in the formation of the Government and shapes the destiny of the nation.

I had put my hand to the plow, and I would not turn back. There was no college or even a common school within many miles of our forest home. We had few books, but the few we had were good books, and believing that the place to begin was where an opportunity offered itself, I began over again, reading with great care every one of the books we had. They were largely historical and biographical, with Uncle Tom's Cabin, Dread and a few other radical anti-slavery works, but they gave me a foundation for the love I still have for history and the struggle of the making of civilization. I got enough of history so that when I entered college I passed the history examination, modern and ancient, for the whole college course without having really studied history a day.

It is interesting to note how when your mind is fully set upon a purpose so many things seem to point toward it, and every way you turn you find leads toward it.

From the hour I had set my heart on a college education, a thousand things pointed in that direction which had hitherto been unnoticed. I saw it before my mind everywhere. I heard the sound of it in the song of birds, in the music of the brook and the sighing of the wind through the branches of the trees just as much as in the roaring of the hurricanes and fierce storms which used to sweep over the great prairies and through the wonderful forests.

My eyes and ears and mind, as well as my heart, were open to receive, and everything helped toward my desire.

I taught school for such a pittance. I saved and gave up the things young girls love, until when my family felt I was determined to carry out my plan to go to college if it took a lifetime to do it and decided to help me. I had one year of High School, and then was ready to go. All the rest of such education as I had had been absorbed from every possible source but with no system.(2)

Then came the change, and I was led to give myself to the ministry. It was such a shock to everyone and created such a sensation that my people who had decided upon sending me to Michigan University refused to do so unless I gave them my pledge never to preach. This I could not do, so I again faced what seemed likc defeat.

After the twenty-four hours given me in which to decide, I determined to go to a smaller and cheaper college and trust to what might come. With eighteen dollars I started for Albion College. Then began a series of economics and labor--at times hunger and cold seemed about to conquer.

My clothes must have been grotesque, and my life was very hard. I shall not recount my experiences. They were similar to what many others endured in those hard days for women. But I lived and grew strong--and so the years have passed. Changes many and great have come, and as today I stand looking back over my seventy years of life, I would begin them all over again and make the same kind of fight.

I have seen much of the world--have been in many lands many times--have endured hardships which make me faint to recall-- but I would not give up the lessons I have learned-the friendships I have made--the knowledge of the value of life. It has all been worth more than it cost, and I have been repaid a thousandfold.

The great lesson of life came when I was brought to the place where I knew that it was a simple heart-throb between this life and the life beyond. And as I looked both worlds in the face and summed up the things worth while, I came to this conclusion.

There are two things in life which make its struggle, its pain, its losses, its joys and its victories worth while. They are, first, to be so possessed by a fundamental principle of right that it becomes consuming fire. The other is to have a heart filled with a great love for humanity.

Possessed by these two passions, no struggle can become too severe, no waiting too wearisome, no life useless. In the midst of a multitude or alone with God, at home or abroad, with friends or with enemies, life is worthwhile.

This does not mean the narrowing of your mental vision to one reform or to one line of service. It opens the soul to all reforms and realizes that in the success of one, your own and all others are by that much nearer to the good.

It brings you into the knowledge that all progress is one. That a reform no more than an individual can live to itself. That truth, all truth, is the atmosphere of the Infinite Mind, and is in its source and aim one with God.

My advice is, select your ideal reform. Get hold of the principle of life, which to you is worth living and fighting for, and if need be, dying for. Not because life is not infinitely sacred and should be guarded and never yielded lightly, but because there are some things worth more than life, for which the loss of all else, life itself, would be gain, if happily by the losing you might get nearer to the source from which the light came.

There always have been and always will be eager runners who bear the torch of life's ideal ahead of the multitude, but that which inspires and leads them on comes from a great love for humanity, a love which nothing can quench. Which can endure all things and still trust with such an abiding faith that it saves, if not others, at least oneself.

I speak out of the fullness of a life's experience, forty years of which I have given to one great cause, for one purpose. The cause is called woman's enfranchisement, but it is much greater than that. If that were all, it would be narrow, selfish, and not part of a great whole. It is not that women may vote, but that the human in mankind may triumph. That civilization may conquer barbarism, may triumph over autocracy. That every child of God may have a fair chance to be and to become all that it is possible for it to attain. That democracy, which is not merely a form of government but the divine law of life emanating from the heart of the Infinite entering into the souls of men and transforming human character until some day it will respond in like spirit to the source from whence it springs. And when it does, we shall know that in Him there is neither male nor female, but all are alike one.

It is in this faith and from this spirit, I believe, that we are entering into this war, to make the "world a fit place for that democracy."

In his most admirable address last week, Rabbi Wise dwelt upon democracy and war, and spoke of the need of the enfranchisement of women as a war measure. With that sentiment I am in the fullest accord, not alone because of its justice and reasonableness, because one of the two greatest needs of the hour is more manpower.(3)

There are two million members of the suffrage associations of the United States. What would it not mean if by one just act of Congress these two million women could be set free to serve the Government with singleness of purpose and undivided allegiance, and, fired by a spirit of gratitude and loyalty, they should turn all their splendidly organized force, their initiative and ability for propaganda, into service to maintain the army in the field and to preserve the existing moral and spiritual as well as industrial forces in the State.

That modern war calls upon women to respond to the call in many lines of war service, is one of the most telling lessons of the experience in Europe.

One of the members of the National Council of Defense said to me this week: "If the world only knew it, it is the French women who saved the day in the beginning of the war. When the German hosts came pouring into unprepared France, the French women furnished the munitions which enabled the men at that crisis to stay the tide at the Battle of the Marne. French women are among the world's great heroes." And, he added, "If the women of this country will only rise to their opportunity, they will make victory for the Allies possible."

I replied "Mr. Secretary, they will rise just as soon as the country appeals to them in a large patriotic manner; not as adjuncts, not as a by-product, but as an integral part of the national citizen power."(4)

It was the recognition of the need of woman power, cooperating with man power to win the war that led the Council of National Defense to create the Woman's Committee, authorizing them to become a clearing house to coordinate and make efficient the woman war work of the whole country.

Acting upon this instruction, we proceeded to appoint a temporary chairman in each State, whose duty it was to call together State women's organizations, and without creating any new machinery of organization, to coordinate the work of all State societies, to prevent duplication and overlapping, and to create a channel through which the demands of the Government and the requests of the various governmental departments should be able in the most direct and the quickest way to reach the individual women. Nearly all the States have perfected their organization and are ready to give immediate attention to any new demands the Government may make upon them.

The Woman's Committee has devised a plan of work which includes various departments. At the head of each is placed an expert, who, in cooperation with the national departments of the Government will be the connecting link between the national government through the State divisions to the individual woman.

We believe that there will be a civilian army of women as well organized that through their efforts, thrift and economy will become the habit of this country as it is of France.

Let the appeal be made to the loyalty and patriotism of women in America, as it has to the warring nations of Europe, and their response will be as generous.

To fight is not more noble than to inspire. (Lead up to flag.)

What the War Meant to Women

The source of this text is a pamphlet, *What the War Meant to Women*, by Dr. Anna Howard Shaw, chairman, Woman's Committee, Council of National Defense. The pamphlet can be found in many libraries. The Foreword of the pamphlet states: "The correction of the manuscript of this address, received at the office of the League to Enforce Peace the day before Dr. Shaw's death, was her last public service. The address has been delivered in a series of conventions held in May, and ordinarily followed an analysis of the Paris Covenant by ex-President Taft or President Lowell of Harvard University."

What are we women to do in this matter of a League of Nations? What part are we to play in it?

The time was when women were not considered as having any part in the concerns of Government. When I was a little girl a woman could not make a will, she could not make a deed or transact any legal business without the consent of somebody else; that is, if she were married.

In Philadelphia, the Woman's New Century Club decided to build a club house and, after they secured the plans and had everything all ready and they undertook to make a contract with the builders, they were informed that they could not contract with them because they were married women and could not contract. But, as these disabilities were removed and they were enabled to contract, women arose to their sovereignty. It may not be a super-sovereignty, such as our Senate seeks to guard us from, but it is a kind of sovereignty which is very comfortable when you want to make a contract.

Because of this newly found power women, more than men, understand the dignity that comes to a great nation when it has the power to use its will in deciding what it will and what it will not do, and the ability under that will to make such contracts with other peoples that it will bind itself to recognize in them the same obligations and the same rights which it claims for itself.

Women never had such an opportunity in the world's affairs before as we had during the war just closed. At the beginning of the war very little attention was paid to the women but gradually, as the man power began to leave for the front, and as the greater need for munitions and other necessary equipment of war demanded larger bodies of people in the service of the Government, more and larger demands were made upon women, until it came to such a pass that it is declared by every nation which has been at war that the war could never have been won if it had not been for the work of the women.

WOMEN'S WAR WORK

And so through this cooperative service of the men and women we have been able to reach this peace which now is so very near and which we trust the Senate of the United States will not retard, as no other nation save Germany has any desire to do so.

During the war women were called upon to serve and the response was universal. We women in America neither sacrificed nor served as did the women of the other countries. We were not called upon to do it; but as far as the country needed our services, as far as it made demands upon us for any particular line of work, we were ready to do what our government asked.

We have been able to count the men who died in the field. We are told that five million men in this war died in battle and that two million more died from wounds received in battle and that two million more died of disease in the hospitals, making a great total of nine million men who died. But when we speak of the cost of life in this war we enumerate only the men who died. We have made no enumeration of the women. We have made no enumeration of the children. We do not know the vast bodies of women and children who have been slaughtered, women who have been outraged and who today are filling the mad-houses of France and Belgium and Serbia and all the other nations which have been overrun by the armies. We know nothing about the horrible results which have come to the lives of women or of the cost of this war in women as well as its cost in men.

While we were called upon to serve during the war, what was it for? Why was it that women responded as they did respond? Why was it that as one woman we came together and said to the Government, "What shall we do?"

ORGANIZATION, NOT ENTHUSIASM, NEEDED

When I was appointed by the President of the United States and the Council of National Defense as Chairman of the Woman's Committee of the Council of National Defense, it was not because the women needed to be urged to do patriotic service, it was because women from all over the United States, in organized groups and individually, came with such a demand asking that they might serve that the Government was swamped by this desire; and the Government found it necessary to organize a group of women to direct the war work of women--not because they lacked patriotism but because of their patriotism; they all wanted to serve but they did not know in what way they could best render that service or what the country desired of them.

The Government called the women who organized the Woman's Committee together and they made us the medium in directing all the war work of the women of the United States.

What was the one cry that brought women together? What was the one impulse which drew them, as one woman? It was this!

You remember that when Mr. Wilson was re-elected President of the United States they said it was because of the pacifists and women; that the women of the West elected Mr. Wilson because he had kept us out of the war--that was the cry during the campaign. "He has kept us out of the war," and therefore many people said women were pacifists; and yet, if they had used their intelligence as they should have used it, they would have known that from the beginning of the war, long before our Government entered into it, the women of this nation began to organize. The society to which I belonged went to Washington in February prior to our entrance into the war with Germany. We called the women of our whole national organization together; they came by hundreds and we formulated a plan of service. We saw the war was coming and we wanted to be prepared. And after we had made our preparation, deciding what lines of work, as a society, we would undertake, we offered ourselves, our two million women, to the Government and declared that whenever the Government called us we were ready to respond.

That was in February and war was declared in April, and when the Government did call upon us we were ready. I asked the Secretary of War what it was that he expected the woman's committee to do. He said, "We want you to coordinate the women's work of the United States, all the war work of the women, so that they will not duplicate, they will not overlap and they will cooperate in carrying out every requirement of the Government."(1)

COUNCIL OF NATIONAL DEFENSE

That was a tremendous task, because women have been educated through the centuries not to have world vision, not to have a country vision, not to have even a community vision. We have been trained and educated to consider persons first and then little groups of persons afterwards--first, myself and my family--and then it comes "my church," then "my society" and "my set"--and so it has always been the personal relationship which has been developed in women until they were not able to forget their own narrow interests. But on the first call sent out by our Committee to the women of the country seventy-five presidents of the largest organizations in the United States came to Washington and we formed a group called the Advisory Committee of the Woman's Committee, Council of National Defense, all of these seventy-five societies agreeing to give up their individual, identical work, their individual service, as they had been expecting to perform it, and to come together and to unite to carry out any plan of united service which the Government might demand, while still retaining their identity.

What led those women to do this? What led them to forget the training of the past, and combine for one solid purpose?

When the Secretary of War told me that he wanted us not only to get the women to cooperate and prevent overlapping, etc., he said, "We want them to cooperate," and when the Secretary said that he smiled. I knew what was in the back of his head. He thought it would be impossible to get women to cooperate, and, being always ready to defend women--not, as it has been said, right or wrong, but being ready to defend them because I believed them to be in the right, I said to him, "Mr. Secretary, you seem to think that the women will not cooperate; that is because you have been dealing with men. If you will give them an object big enough and put back of them an incentive strong enough you will find that the women of this country will cooperate, Mr. Secretary." Now I frankly confess I did not quite believe what I said. I was bluffing a little bit but I was not going to have the Secretary think we could not cooperate, no matter what I thought about it.

To the honor of the women of this Nation, let it be said that from the beginning of the war to the end of it they maintained their pledge of cooperation.

"WAR TO END WAR"

Men told us that, if we made a conquered peace, if we subdued militarism and the militarist spirit which Germany was inciting not only in its own country, but in the countries of the world, it would be conquered forever. "This is the war to end war."

It was that thought which brought women together, "This is a war to end war," and women must play their part in helping to end war forever.

We know that men are ready to die in war; but there are a great many things harder than to die. Everybody must die sometime and it does not make so much difference perhaps as to the number of days we live as it does to the manner in which we live the days we *do* live. There are some things that are worth a great deal more than life, and one thing which was worth more than life to the men who went out and laid down their lives for their countries was not to leave a dishonored nation, a nation unworthy of the civilization of our time, a nation which had no heart to feel and no understanding to realize the conditions of intimate association between nation and nation and the obligation which one nation has to care for and sympathize with another.

Having grasped this idea of democracy, this idea of the oneness of the human family, we declared that we would give everything that we had and sacrifice everything that we had in the interests of ending war forever. So our women toiled and sacrificed and saved and toiled again, until the war ended.

NOT ENDED ON FIELD OF BATTLE

Now, whether we agree with every part of that Peace Treaty or not, no matter whether we agree with everything there is in the League of Nations or not, the question remains that now with the Germans, our opponents, defeated on the field of battle, is that the way to end war forever, merely to defeat them on the field of battle? Is there not something to be done afterwards? Every one knows that no war is ended on the battlefield. The last word in any war is not spoken on the battlefield. The last word in war is spoken in the halls where the people meet together to decide what shall be the result of the war, what shall be the penalties of the war, and how peace shall be made.

If President Wilson were to stand before us today and tell us even a part of what he knows that we do not know, we would be the most astonished people in all the world. The Peace Commission with all the facts before them know; and out of their knowledge, out of what they understand of the relation of nations to each other, they have given us this League of Nations, as the best solution they could produce to bring about a just and lasting peace. That is what we women have been working for from the beginning of the war. In a conversation with President Wilson just before he went to Paris, he said, "The most difficult task I have had since the war began, in dealing with foreign nations, has been to convince them that we do not want any material advantage out of this war. They cannot understand it. Never before did any great nation go into war such as this, with our men and our treasure, and then ask nothing in return. I could hardly make them believe that we were perfectly willing to come out with empty hands; and yet," he said, "they are beginning to understand that, because our men over there on the battlefield have shown them their disinterestedness, and they are able to feel that if we can send men to die in this disinterested way, those of us who are at home have perhaps the same spirit, and so they are beginning to trust us a little more than they did in the beginning."

WHAT WOMEN WANT OUT OF WAR

While Mr. Wilson said we want nothing out of the war, I said in my own heart--It may be we want nothing material out of the war, but oh, we want the biggest thing out of this war that has ever come to the world. We want Peace now and Peace forever.

If we cannot get that peace out of this war, what hope is there that it will ever come to humanity? Was there ever such a chance offered to the world before? Was there ever a time when the peoples of all nations looked towards America as they are looking today, because of our unselfishness in our dealings with them during the war?

We have not always been unselfish, but we have been in this war. Because of this they are looking to us, with hope. There were never such devastated countries as there are now over there where great nations were destroyed. The war is over as far as the fighting is concerned, but it is only begun as far as the life of the people is concerned. They have got to come back, to build up a new life and a new hope and a new home.

What would there be of inspiration to these people to come back to their ruined homes and build up again their cities, if, within a few years, the same thing could be repeated and homes destroyed and cities devastated, the people outraged and made slaves as they have been? What hope would there be to these people? Why, men and women, they are looking to us as the hope of the world. And whenever I look on our flag, whenever I look on those stars on their field of blue and those stripes of red and white I say to myself, "I do not wonder that when that flag went over the trenches and surmounted the barriers, the people of the world took heart of hope."

SECURITY FOR THE FUTURE

It was then that they began to feel they could unite with us in some sort of security for the future. And that flag means so much to me. I never look on its stars but that I see in every star the hope that must stir the peoples of the old world when they think of us and the power we have of helping to lead them up to a place where they may hope for their children and their children's children the things that have not come to them.

It is because we stand in such a position before the world that we cannot afford to quibble. We cannot even for political advantage, we cannot afford because of personal hatred, to take from them one hour of hope, one ray of light. And yet, a few weeks ago I was in the Capitol at Washington, talking to one of the Senators.   I tried to talk to him upon another subject; he could not talk upon that subject, he was so full of having been slighted, so full of not having been consulted, so full of not having been recognized as a great and important and dignified member of that dignified body.   When Senators have to tell how dignified they are in order for people to find it out, it is about time they rested upon something else because that is a very shaky kind of dignity.   This Senator's attack was not upon the League of Nations at all.   It was all because something was not done which he thought ought to have been done.   There is no doubt that a great many things have not been done which all of us think ought to have been done.   There is not one of us who does not think he can do things better than anybody else.   Most of us would like to have been set upon a pedestal and had Mr. Wilson sit down in front of us and ask our opinion.

But still, notwithstanding that, we are perfectly willing to accept what has been evolved by those men who have all the facts before them, as the best thing which can be done now.

I do not think the League of Nations is perfect.   I say that because everybody else says it.   I really do not know why it is not perfect.   And it is not because I have not read it, for I have read it and reread it and reread it.   A particular friend of mine, after we had been reading it aloud together, said to me, "Now what could you put into it that is not there?"   And I said, "The thing that bothers me is how they found so many things to put into it that ARE there."

TREATY--A MARVELOUS DOCUMENT

The Treaty of Peace which has been submitted to the Germans I think is the most marvelous document in the world, and I have been wondering how many hundred men it took to think up all the demands they put into that peace pact. Congress says the League Covenant has delayed peace.   Congress has been feeling fearfully because of that.   The Senators have been blaming Mr. Wilson because he delayed peace because of the League of Nations, and all the time that the Peace Conference has been working up this marvelous peace pact on this League of Nations and investigating the conditions of all Europe in order to make it a pact that is fair and just, Congress was not able to pass an appropriation bill, so we have been running into debt because we have no money to pay bills.   If Congress had been attending to its job, Mr. Wilson would not have been fretted quite so much in Paris and perhaps his job would have been ended long ago.

This is the thing we are facing in this country.   It is a sort of quibble among a group of men, for what?

One, however, is honest enough in his dishonesty--Mr. Reed, who does not know what honor is and never did--he has been honest enough at least to say that he does not want any League of Nations at all. There are a lot of other people who want this nation to go alone in this world. But the time has gone by when any country can stand alone. The time has gone by when a country no more than an individual can live to itself or die to itself.(2)

HEAVEN OR HELL--WHICH?

We have come to the place now where we can fly in a day from this country to any other country on the earth, almost, and we have become so closely interallied that national interests merge the one with the other, in such a manner that we cannot go alone. We must look facts in the face. All humanity is one. The world is one. And no nation can suffer unless all nations suffer. No nation can prosper without all nations prospering. We have got to take facts as they are and we have got to find out the best thing we can have. The best thing that has been given us and the only thing we have before us is this League of Nations. We have no other League of Nations. We have only this one. We must take this one or no one can tell what will come. We have no midway point. We have no purgatory. We have to choose either Heaven or Hell. We must take it or we must reject it.

Suppose the Senate of the United States amends that League of Nations, so as to make it radically different. What will happen? What is happening to us all over the country today? You and I have felt the slump that has come into our national life since the armistice. We have felt it in business; we have felt it in the morale of the people; it is everywhere apparent. We are simply waiting. Waiting for what? Waiting for that peace which will give to us a basis upon which we can start out new life, and we will not be able to recover unless we do have something of that sort to bring us back again to the high plane upon which we stood during the war. To stand where we stood before the war will not do. We must have an incentive before us, an incentive for the intellectual and moral and industrial advancement of the people; the incentive must be universal in its application and we are waiting for it--waiting until this League of Nations Treaty of Peace has been signed.

IF THE SENATE AMENDS

Suppose the Senate rejects the League in its present form and makes amendments, as it says it has a right to do, but as some distinguished lawyers think it has not--suppose they do that. What will happen? The thing that will happen is that they will have to take it back again and deliver it to thirty-one different nations to see if they will ratify these amendments which our Senate has made. It will have to go to Germany as well as the other nations to see whether Germany will accept it. And it may not be accepted. And then some other nation, seeing that we have distinguished ourselves by making amendments and changes, will want to make changes and amendments and it will have to come back, and then we will make some more, and then it will go back and forth and Heaven alone knows when Peace will come or anything else to give us a start in the upward way.

Suppose we do not sign the Peace Treaty as it is. Suppose the Senate of the United States refuses to sign it with the League of Nations Government in it as it is now, but amends the League of Nations provision so that it is of no value whatever, what will happen? We are told by the press that there is one clause in that Treaty which declares that if any three nations sign the Treaty with Germany as it stands, then they may enter into international relations with Germany. They may open up trade and start to do business with Germany just the same as if all the other nations had signed it.

Suppose Japan and France and Great Britain and Italy should sign that pact and we should refuse to do it; what would happen? They would be at peace, and we would be at war with Germany. That is what would happen. We have not signed the Peace Treaty and we are still at war. They would be in a state of peace while we, isolated, would be standing alone.

ANOTHER BIG JOB FOR WOMEN

Women, what have you been doing the last few weeks? You have been going from house to house raising the Victory Loan. I think one of the greatest jobs that women have done for the country has been the Liberty Loan. The country came to you in the beginning to send your boys across the seas; what was the cry! Send them provisions! Send them munitions! That was the cry. What have you been doing the last three or four weeks? You have been going out from house to house in the same old way, as women always do. Men do not. They think it is easy work. I have been in a great many political campaigns for reform, reform mayors and other people, and when the reform group get together and decide what they want to do they always say that the women are too feeble to vote for the reform mayor but they are not too feeble to do the work which is assigned to them, which is to go from house to house and do the canvassing and raise the funds. That is all they ask us to do.

Now it is the habit of men to lay that kind of house to house canvassing on women. In the Liberty Loan campaigns they told us, "You must not touch these big sums; we will stand behind our counter or desk and when a man wants ten thousand dollars or a hundred thousand or a million dollars worth of bonds we will take the subscription, because they are so big you could not understand it. You may go from house to house; you may set your booths on the corner; you may take a fifty dollar subscription or a hundred dollar subscription." And the women have done it in every Liberty Loan drive.

I was in a city where, in the last campaign, in that kind of hard drudgery women raised fifty percent of the entire quota, just the women, going from house to house, and in all our cities and states they have done their full share and have done it splendidly.

What was the cry this time? Was it, "Send the men across the sea," as it was in the beginning? Quite different. One sign I saw all over New York, all over Pennsylvania, all over Boston--"If you could sell bonds to send the boys across, can't you sell more bonds to bring the boys home?" That was the cry--TO BRING THE BOYS HOME. How the boys would be cheered when they knew the men and women of the country were raising money to bring them home.

But if all the other nations except ours sign the Treaty of Peace and accept the League of Nations, and we still remain at war with Germany, are we going to bring the boys home with this money or are we going to keep them over there and provide for them while they are still holding the forts along the Rhine?

BUGABOO WORDS

But our Senate is talking, talking! We women and men are so afraid of words. If they are unfamiliar enough they scare us to death. To call a woman strong-minded in my girlhood days was enough to throw her into a spasm, because it meant in that day that she was a little bit inhuman or unhuman; and then women began to discover that there were only two kinds of minds, strong minds and feeble minds, and they all wanted strong minds, they were not frightened by that word.

Then came the word "suffragist," which used to fill them with terror. By and by they came to understand that the suffrage of the people was the method of registering the will of the people, and then we were not at all afraid of that word because it dignified us.

Then they used the word--"feminist," and a lot of women got frightened for fear they would be called feminists. And when I speak upon the subject in which I am so much interested, the democracy of the country, which includes women, they always hurl at me the word "feminist," and what does that mean? It is woman aspiring to be human, which is not a bad thing at all.

We are so afraid of words, and the Congress of the United States, knowing our fear of words, invented the word "super-sovereignty." That is a wonderful word--"super-sovereignty."

There is only one thing they have produced that is new in their arguments against this League of Nations, that has not been used against the enfranchisement of women for the last forty years; and that is the Monroe Doctrine--that I believe has never been used against women's political freedom. When they couldn't do anything else they have always gone back to the fathers. You have heard about the fathers and what the fathers did. Why, the Chinese never worshipped their ancestors so much as Congress worships the fathers, when they haven't any reason to give for their attitude upon any subject.

Then when they have exhausted the fathers they bring out the Constitution and they say, "it is unconstitutional." Everything is unconstitutional.

THE MEANING OF A LEAGUE

President Lowell, of Harvard, has clearly explained every single idea there is in the League and every purpose of it--simply that we may be able to have some sort of an organized body by which we may have international cooperation in keeping peace, international cooperation in helping to protect weaker peoples, international cooperation in providing a certain uniformity of law in the protection of the laboring people of the world, international cooperation to prevent the spread of disease and other evils. There is little for me to say on that last proposition. When influenza was sweeping over the country didn't we wish that we had some kind of an international health bureau by which we could have kept that disease out? And that is only the beginning of many diseases which will sweep the world as a result of the war, of the impoverished condition of Europe, and the unhealthful conditions of living forced upon the soldiers in the trenches.(3)

And from those evils come back to us the lesson we must learn, that the "sins of the fathers are visited upon the children even to the third and fourth generations." When I read that Peace Pact and I thought how hard it is, how difficult it is, there appeared before me just as if it were written in words of light, "The sins of the fathers shall be visited upon the children unto the third and fourth generation." So Germany's children will bear the burden to the third and fourth generation of the crimes against them and the children of the world will bear the burdens of the obligations which they are compelled to assume because of the sins of the peoples of the world.(4)

We women, the mothers of the race, have given everything, have suffered everything, have sacrificed everything, and we come to you now and say, "The time has come when we will no longer sit quietly by and bear and rear sons to die at the will of a few men. We will not endure it. We demand either that you shall do something to prevent war or that we shall be permitted to try to do something ourselves."

Could there be any cowardice, could there be any injustice, could there be any wrong greater than to refuse to hear the voice of a woman expressing the will of women at the peace table of the world and then for men not to provide a way by which the women of the future shall not be robbed of their sons as the women of the past have been?

TO YOU MEN WE LOOK FOR SUPPORT. WE LOOK FOR YOUR SUPPORT BACK OF YOUR SENATORS AND FROM THIS DAY UNTIL THE DAY WHEN THE LEAGUE OF NATIONS IS ACCEPTED AND RATIFIED BY THE SENATE OF THE U.S. IT SHOULD BE THE DUTY OF EVERY MAN AND EVERY WOMAN TO SEE TO IT THAT THE SENATORS FROM THEIR STATE KNOW THE WILL OF THE PEOPLE; THAT THEY KNOW THAT THE PEOPLE WILL THAT SOMETHING SHALL BE DONE, EVEN THOUGH NOT PERFECT: THAT THERE SHALL BE A BEGINNING, FROM WHICH WE SHALL CONSTRUCT SOMETHING MORE PERFECT BY AND BY; THAT THE WILL OF THE PEOPLE IS THAT THIS LEAGUE SHALL BE ACCEPTED, AND THAT IF, IN THE SENATE OF THE U.S., THERE ARE MEN SO BLINDED BY PARTISAN DESIRE FOR PRESENT ADVANTAGE, SO BLINDED BY PERSONAL PIQUE AND NARROWNESS OF VISION, THAT THEY CANNOT SEE THE LARGE PROBLEMS WHICH INVOLVE THE NATIONS OF THE WORLD: THEN THE PEOPLE OF THE STATES MUST SEE TO IT THAT OTHER MEN SIT IN THE SEATS OF THE HIGHEST.

Notes

Part I

INTRODUCTION

1. Carrie Chapman Catt and Nettie Rogers Shuler, *Woman Suffrage and Politics* (New York: Charles Scribner's Sons, 1926), p. 268.

2. Quotation from the New York *Sun* cited by *The Literary Digest*, August 16, 1919, 62:54-56; Mary Earhart Dillon to Lucy E. Anthony, December 28, 1942, Shaw papers, box 18, folder 409; *Wisconsin State Journal*, March 7, 1917; *The Woman Citizen*, July 12, 1919.

3. Anna Howard Shaw (AHS), with the collaboration of Elizabeth Jordan, *The Story of a Pioneer* (New York: Harper and Bros., 1915), p. 42.

4. Ibid., pp. 39-40.

5. Ray Strachey, *The Common Cause*, July 11, 1919; Shaw, *Pioneer*, p. 42.

6. Shaw, *Pioneer*, pp. 44-45.

7. Ibid., p. 44.

8. Unidentified newspaper clipping, Shaw papers, box 20, folder 42.

9. Ida Husted Harper, unpublished biography of Anna Howard Shaw, Shaw papers, box 19, folder 441, p. 13.

10. Letter from Women's Christian Temperance Union (W.C.T.U.) to AHS, n.d., Shaw papers, box 20, folder 471; Shaw, *Pioneer*, p. 175.

11. *In Memory of Anna Howard Shaw* (New York: National Woman Suffrage Publishing Company, n.d.), p. 9. The increase in membership was largely the result of new membership plans; at the same time, Shaw's rhetorical effectiveness was instrumental in winning many new members; Shaw, *Pioneer*, p. 335.

12. *The Omaha Bee*, May 25, 1919.

13. Unidentified newspaper clipping, Shaw papers, box 20, folder 455.

14. *Current Opinion*, December 1915, 59:398-399, quoting Shaw.

15. *Wichita Daily Eagle*, June 22, 1894; *The Arizona Republican*, October 16, 1912.

16. Shaw papers, box 22, folder 481; Harper, unpublished biography, p. 179; Shaw papers, box 19, folder 441.

17. *The Arizona Republican*, October 16, 1912; *The Leavenworth Weekly Times*, May 20, 1894.

18. Shaw, *Pioneer*, p. 196. Lucy Stone stated that Shaw never used notes; *The Kansas City Star*, February 9, 1892, reports that Shaw spoke completely without notes.

19. AHS to Lucy Anthony, Daytona, Florida, March 1905; Harper, unpublished biography, p. 68; Unidentified clipping, Shaw papers, box 20.

20. Harper, unpublished biography, p. 94.

21. Shaw, *Pioneer*, pp. 167-168.

22. *The North American*, Philadelphia, July 3, 1919; Maud Wood Park, "Campaigning State by State," in *Victory How Women Won It* (New York: H. W. Wilson, 1940), vol. 4. p. 76; *The Washington Post*, quoted by *The History of Woman Suffrage*, (Indianapolis: The Hollenbeck Press, 1902), p. 361; *Fort Worth Star-Telegram*, April 1, 1915; *Kansas City Star*, February 9, 1892; Unidentified newspaper clipping, Shaw papers, box 20.

23. Harper, unpublished biography, p. 178; Shaw, *Pioneer*, p. 33; Letter from Harriet E. Grim to one of the authors, November 30, 1959. Grim was an active suffragist during the latter stage of the movement and heard Shaw speak on a number of occasions.

24. Anna Howard Shaw, "Fundamental Principle of a Republic," see below, p. 146.

25. Anna Howard Shaw, "Other Half of Humanity," see below, pp. 174-175.

26. Ibid., pp. 174-175.

27. Anna Howard Shaw, "Farewell Presidential Address, Washington, D.C., December 14-19, 1915, found in Wilmer Albert Linkugel, *The Speeches of Anna Howard Shaw*, unpublished dissertation, University of Wisconsin, 1960, vol. 2, p. 635; or see Shaw papers, box 23, folder 541.

28. Shaw, "Other Half of Humanity," p. 172; *Topeka Daily State Journal*, October 2, 1912; from the *Buffalo Express* as cited by *The History of Woman Suffrage*, 5, p. 216.

29. AHS to Lucy Anthony, as reported by Harper, unpublished biography, p. 107.

30. Lucy E. Anthony to Mary E. Dillon, July 27, 1943.

31. Anna Howard Shaw, "The Fundamental Principle of a Republic," see below, p. 149.

32. Anna Howard Shaw, "All Absorbing Love," eulogy given in Rochester, N.Y., March 15, 1906, Shaw papers, box 22, folder 508, p.

33. Anna Howard Shaw, "Heavenly Vision," see below, pp. 116-117.

34. Shaw, "Other Half of Humanity," see below, p. 165.

CHAPTER 1

1. Elizabeth Anthony Dexter, *Women in Organized Religion, 1860-1900*, Shaw papers; Anna Howard Shaw (AHS) with the collaboration of Elizabeth Jordan, *The Story of a Pioneer* (New York: Harper and Bros., 1915), p. 65; Shaw, *Pioneer*, pp. 123-124.

2. Interview with AHS, *The Kansas City Star*, February 9, 1892.

3. The record of the Congress does not contain a full text of the sermon, but lists it as "Die Frau als Predigerin," and gives an extensive summary. This summary reflects the material contained in the extant undated draft in the Shaw papers, box 22, folder 498. See *Der International Frauen-Kongress in Berlin 1904*, (Berlin SW., Wilhelmstrasse 33: Verlag von Carl Kabel), pp. 276-277. "Women in the Ministry" in Wilmer Albert Linkugel, *The Speeches of Anna Howard Shaw*, unpublished dissertation, University of Wisconsin, 1960, vol. 2, p. 414.

4. Anna Howard Shaw, "Woman's Right to Suffrage," Linkugel, vol. 2, p. 96.

5. Ida Husted Harper, unpublished biography of Anna Howard Shaw, Shaw papers, box 19, folder 441.

6. Shaw, *Pioneer*, p. 44. Ibid., p. 56. Ibid., p. 62. A footnote to this passage indicates that the brother-in-law erred in reporting Shaw's age; she was twenty-three at the time.

7. The source of the text is a small booklet in the Shaw papers, box 22, folder 497. Marginal notes indicated she also delivered the sermon in Hingham, Massachusetts, September 30, 1877, and East Dennis and West Dennis, January 21, 1883, during her pastorate there.

8. See, for example, Shaw, *Pioneer*, p. 279.

9. *Report of the International Council of Women*, (Washington, D.C.: Rufus H. Darby, 1888), pp. 24-29.

10. *Bible Knowledge Commentary*, edited by John F. Walvoord and Roy B. Zuck (Wheaton, Ill.: Victor Books, 1985), p. 842.

11. *Holy Bible*, Revised Version, (Cambridge, Mass.: University Press, 1885), vol. 3, 152.

12. This may be a reference to Bankin Chunder Chatterjee (1838-1894), who was a prominent Bengali writer and reformer particularly concerned with the plight of young widows in India.

13. Aileen S. Kraditor, *The Ideas of the Woman Suffrage Movement: 1890-1920* (New York: W.W. Norton and Co., 1981), pp. 43-74.

14. Hugh Dalziel Duncan, *Communication and Social Order* (New York: The Bedminister Press, 1962).

15. Kraditor, p. 17.

CHAPTER 2

1. Anna Howard Shaw (AHS), with the collaboration of Elizabeth Jordan, *The Story of a Pioneer* (New York: Harper and Bros., 1915), p. 152; Shaw, *Pioneer*, p. 157.

2. Mary A. Livermore to AHS, September 1-5, 1885.

3. AHS to Lucy E. Anthony (LEA), enroute to Rochester, N.Y., March 7, 1906; Shaw, *Pioneer*, p. 148, 195.

4. Shaw's Diary, 1898; AHS to LEA, Kansas, 1892; AHS to LEA, Erie, Penn., January, 1895; AHS to LEA, Madison, Wis., July 22, 1900.

5. AHS to LEA, enroute, Toledo, Ohio, October 15, 1892; AHS to LEA, Brittan, S.D., October 14, 1890; AHS to LEA, Buffalo Gap, S.D., October 14, 1890; AHS to LEA, enroute, Toledo, Ohio, October 15, 1892.

6. AHS to LEA, Wichita, Kan., March 3, 1892.

7. AHS to LEA, Yosemite Valley, Calif., January 4, 1895; AHS to LEA, Santa Rosa, Calif., October 28, 1895.

8. Thomas Shaw to AHS, February 12, 1893; Unidentified newspaper clipping, Shaw papers, box 20, folder 450.

9. AHS to LEA, September 19, 1912; Shaw, *Pioneer*, pp. 161-162, 164-165, 302; AHS to LEA, Kosiusko, Miss., December 2, 1903; AHS to LEA, Pittsburg, Kan., March 22, 1890.

10. *The History of Woman Suffrage*, vol. 6 (Indianapolis: The Hollenbeck Press, 1902), p. 135; AHS to LEA, near Pittsburgh enroute from Erie, Penn., December 17, 1895; AHS to LEA, Troy, Ohio, February 2, 1892.

11. Shaw, *Pioneer*, pp. 95-97, 155, 158.

12. Ida Husted Harper, unpublished biography of Anna Howard Shaw, Shaw papers, box 19, folder 441, pp. 45-48. Shaw, *Pioneer*, p. 159.

13. Letter from Women's Christian Temperance Union (W.C.T.U.) to AHS, n.d.

14. Shaw, *Pioneer*, p. 72; *The History of Woman Suffrage*, vol. 4, p. 215; Frances Willard to AHS, 1889.

15. Shaw papers, box 22, folder 490; *Women in Social Life, The International Conference on Women 1899*, edited by the Countess of Aberdeen (London: T. Fisher Unwin, 1900), pp. 160-163.

16. Wilmer Albert Linkugel, *The Speeches of Anna Howard Shaw*, unpublished dissertation, University of Wisconsin, 1960, vol. 2, p. 849.

17. Ibid., pp. 839, 942, 843.

18. Ibid., pp. 965-970. A version of this lecture can be found in the Shaw papers, box 22, folder 491; AHS to LEA, December 19, 1899.

19. *National Council of Women of the United States, 1891,* Rachel Foster Avery, ed. (Philadelphia: J.B. Lippincott Co., 1891), pp. 242-249. See also Linkugel, p. 2; AHS to Clara Osburn, March 7, 1891.

20. Aileen S. Kraditor, *The Ideas of the Woman Suffrage Movement: 1880-1920* (New York: W.W. Norton and Co., 1981), pp. 78-86.

CHAPTER 3

1. Ida Husted Harper, *The Life and Work of Susan B. Anthony* (Indianapolis: The Bowen-Merrill Co., 1899), vol. 2, p. 537; Mary Earhart, *Frances Willard: From Prayers to Politics* (Chicago: University of Chicago Press, 1944), p. 197.

2. Earhart, p. 152.

3. See Carrie Chapman Catt and Nettie Rogers Shuler, *Woman Suffrage and Politics: The Inner Story of the Suffrage Movement* (New York: Charles Scribner's Sons, 1926); Reprint University of Washington Press, 1969, esp. Chapter 10, pp. 132-159, "The Invisible Enemy."

4. Abigail Scott Duniway, *Path Breaking* (Portland, Ore.: Abbott Co., 1914), pp. 183-188, 197, 221.

5. Quoted in Ida Husted Harper, unpublished biography of Anna Howard Shaw, Shaw papers, box 19, folder 441, p. 65; Anna Howard Shaw (AHS) to Mrs. Chambers, 1904;*The Woman's Journal,* October 15, 1904; AHS to Lucy E. Anthony (LEA), Columbus, Ohio, 1912; AHS to LEA, 1889.

6. Quoted in Harper, unpublished biography, p. 65.

7. AHS to Mrs. Chambers, 1904. *The Woman's Journal,* October 15, 1904; AHS to LEA, Columbus, Ohio 1912. AHS to Mrs. W. A. Johnston, April 12, 1912, Kansas Historical Society Archives; Anna Howard Shaw, with the collaboration of Elizabeth Jordan, *The Story of a Pioneer* (New York: Harper and Bros., 1915), pp. 207-208.

8. Alma Lutz, *Susan B. Anthony: Rebel, Crusader, Humanitarian.* (Boston: Beacon Press, 1959), p. 248; Shaw, *Pioneer,* p. 189.

9. Shaw, *Pioneer,* pp. 189, 195; AHS to LEA, San Francisco, Calif., May 28, 1895; AHS to LEA, Cincinnati, Ohio, January 28, 1900.

10. Shaw, *Pioneer,* p. 191.

11. Ibid., pp. 234-235.

12. Thomas Shaw to AHS, Big Rapids, Mich., February 9, 1894, and May 13, 1895.

13. The *Washington Post* for January 22, 1889, reports her having given a lecture with this title. Interestingly, that report quotes the passage below alluding to Jefferson Davis and his disfranchisement after the Civil War, which does not appear in the best copy of the speech we have. This fact, however, does

show how Shaw adapted even standard texts for special occasions and reveals her characteristic wit and sarcasm: "When Jeff Davis was captured all the great men of this country were at a loss what to do with him. They discussed hanging him, and they discussed banishing him, but concluded these punishments would not do. Then a sudden light broke upon them, and they shouted, 'Let's disfranchise him and then he will be no better than a woman,' and now he is a living monument of these great men's appreciation of us." *The Congress of Women. World's Columbian Exposition,* Chicago, Ill., Mary Kavannaugh Oldham Eagle, Chairman of the Committee on Congresses, ed. (Kansas City, Mo.: E. H. Gregg and Co., 1894), pp. 152-156.

14. Carol Gilligan, *In a Different Voice: Psychological Theory and Women's Development* (Cambridge, Mass.: Harvard University Press, 1982).

15. The source of this text is Shaw papers, box 22, folder 540.

16. The source of this text is *The Ogdenburg Advance and St. Lawrence Weekly Democrat,* July 1, 1915. The clipping from this newspaper is in the Shaw papers, box 20.

CHAPTER 4

1. Katherine Anthony, *Susan B. Anthony: Her Personal History and Her Era* (New York: Doubleday, 1954), p. 453; Anna Howard Shaw (AHS), with the collaboration of Elizabeth Jordan, *The Story of a Pioneer,* (New York: Harper and Bros., 1915), p. 285; Katherine Anthony, p. 453.

2. Katherine Anthony, p. 453; Alma Lutz, *Susan B. Anthony: Rebel, Crusader, Humanitarian* (Boston: Beacon Hill Press, 1959), p. 290. Lutz, p. 290; Shaw, *Pioneer,* pp. 284-285; Shaw, *Pioneer,* p. 284; Katherine Anthony, p. 453.

3. Lutz, p. 197. Shaw, *Pioneer,* p. 286.

4. Shaw, *Pioneer,* p. 246; Eleanor Flexner, *A Century of Struggle: The Woman's Rights Movement in the United States* (Cambridge, Mass.: Harvard University Press, 1959), p. 175, 262; *In Memory of Anna Howard Shaw* (New York: National Suffrage Publishing Co., n.d.), p. 91; Flexner, pp. 251-252; Quoted in Flexner, p. 250, from Harriet Stanton Blatch and Alma Lutz, *Challenging Years: The Memoirs of Harriet Stanton Blatch* (New York: G.P. Putnam, 1940), p. 92.

5. AHS to Official Board, August 15, 1910, Clay papers.

6. Paul E. Fuller, *Laura Clay and the Woman's Rights Movement* (Lexington: Univ. of Kentucky Press, 1975), p. 114; Ibid., p. 114; AHS to Official Board, September 22, 1911, Clay papers.

7. Fuller, pp. 105-112, 122-125.

8. Blatch and Lutz, pp. 92-94, quoted in Flexner. AHS to state president in Virginia, 1914. Quoted in Ida Husted Harper,

unpublished biography of Anna Howard Shaw, Shaw papers, box 19, folder 441, p. 257.

9. Flexner, pp. 267-268; Christine A. Lunardinei, *From Equal Suffrage to Equal Rights: Alice Paul and the National Woman's Party, 1910-1928* (New York: University Press, 1986), pp. 56-60; AHS to McCulloch, August 17, 1914, McCulloch papers; *The Woman's Journal*, November 21, 1914.

10. Quoted in Harper, unpublished biography, p. 116; Shaw, *Pioneer*, pp. 295-297. Quoted in Harper, p. 146.

11. Wilmer Albert Linkugel, *The Speeches of Anna Howard Shaw*, unpublished dissertation, University of Wisconsin, 1960, vol. 2, pp. 684, 712-838; Ibid., p. 757.

12. Ibid., 703-711. This speech was published in the report of the Select Committee on Woman Suffrage, U.S. Senate, 1902, on the Joint Resolution proposing an amendment to the Constitution of the United States extending the right of suffrage to women.

13. Ibid., pp. 825, 826. From the published report of the Committee on the Judiciary, House of Representatives, 64th Congress, 1st session, December 16, 1915.

14. June 30, 1905. Quoted in Linkugel, vol. 2, p. 433; *The History of Woman Suffrage*, vol. 5 (Indianapolis: The Hollenbeck Press, 1902), p. 156; Quoted in Linkugel, vol. 2, p. 475.

15. Linkugel, vol. 2, p. 437; From *The Woman's Journal*, July 15, 1905; Linkugel, vol. 2, p. 518.

16. Linkugel, p. 565; From *The History of Woman Suffrage*, vol. 5, p. 317; Linkugel, vol. 2, pp. 651-652.

17. Linkugel, vol. 2, p. 477; Ibid., p. 480.

18. Ibid., pp. 469-470; Ibid., p. 660-661. A pamphlet containing this address is in the Shaw papers, box 22, folder 541.

19. Ibid., pp. 445, 426, 449.

20. Ibid., pp. 454-455.

21. Ibid., p. 492.

22. Jacqueline Van Voris, *Carrie Chapman Catt: A Public Life* (New York: Feminist Press at the City University of New York, 1987), p. 50.

23. Flexner, p. 249.

24. *In Memory of Anna Howard Shaw* (New York: National Woman Suffrage Publishing Co., n.d.), p. 9. Although the increase in membership reflected largely new plans of membership, Shaw was instrumental in winning a large number of new members. Shaw, *Pioneer*, p. 335.

25. Correspondence between AHS and Oswald Garrison Villard, Houghton Library, Harvard University.

CHAPTER 5

1. Anna Howard Shaw (AHS), with the collaboration of Elizabeth Jordan, *The Story of a Pioneer* (New York: Harper and Bros., 1915), p. 268. The building of the house was significant enough to her that she devoted an entire chapter of her autobiography to the topic; Ibid., p. 269.

2. Eleanor Flexner, *Century of Struggle* (Cambridge, Mass.: Harvard University Press, 1959), p. 274; Quoted in Flexner, p. 274; AHS to LEA, June 1916.

3. Elizabeth Jordan, "Anna Howard Shaw: An Intimate Study," *Chicago Tribune*, July 27, 1919.

4. Shaw, *Pioneer*, p. 336.

5. Ibid., pp. 337-338.

6. Wilmer A. Linkugel, *The Speeches of Anna Howard Shaw*, unpublished dissertation, University of Wisconsin, 1960, vol. 2, p. 857.

7. American Library Association, *Booklist*, December 1915, vol. 12, p. 135; *New York Times Book Review*, September 26, 1915, vol. 5, p. 346.

8. AHS to Caroline Bartlett Crane, box 20, folder 462; Constance Drexel, "Dr. Shaw Begins Task of Directing Women's War Work," *Philadelphia Ledger*, May 27, 1917.

9. *The History of Woman Suffrage*, vol. 5 (Indianapolis: The Hollenbeck Press, 1902), p. 489; Flexner, p. 279, quotes a much softer response by Shaw without clear attribution: "We have waited so long, Mr. President, for the vote--we had hoped it might come in your administration."

10. *The History of Woman Suffrage*, vol. 5, pp. 720-725.

11. The members of this committee were the secretaries of war, navy, interior, agriculture, labor and commerce; Ida Husted Harper, unpublished biography of Anna Howard Shaw, Shaw papers, box 19, folder 441, p. 16; *Philadelphia Ledger*, May 27, 1917.

12. AHS to Woodrow Wilson, March 26, 1917; AHS to Lucy Stone, 1917.

13. Speech at Temple University, 1917; Linkugel, p. 861; Anna Howard Shaw, "Women in Industries," 1917, pp. 863-876; Linkugel, vol. 2, p. 864; Ibid., p. 865.

14. Linkugel, vol. 2, p. 866; *History of Woman Suffrage*, vol. 5, pp. 737-738.

15. Anna Howard Shaw, "Select Your Principles of Life," 1917, pp. 850-862; Linkugel, vol. 2, p. 861; Shaw, "Women in Industries," Linkugel, vol. 2, p. 873; AHS to Woodrow Wilson, November 22, 1918. Constance Drexel, "Dr. Shaw Begins Task of Directing Women's War Work," *Philadelphia Ledger*, May 27, 1917; AHS to State Chairmen, November 19, 1917. This appeal may have been published in newspapers through the Creel Bureau.

16. AHS to Caroline Bartlett Crane, August 18, 1917; AHS to Luch E. Anthony (LEA), August 1917.

17. Shaw, "Women in Industries," 1917, Linkugel, vol. 2, p. 887.

18. Anna Howard Shaw, "Women's War Service," Linkugel, vol. 2, p. 888, 892; Shaw, "Women in Industries," 1917, Linkugel, vol. 2, p. 868; *Wisconsin State Journal*, March 7, 1919.

19. Linkugel, vol. 2, p. 867; *Wisconsin State Journal*, March 7, 1919.

20. Linkugel, vol. 2, p. 867.

21. Ibid., p. 867. Ibid., p. 872. Shaw, "Women's War Service," 1917, Linkugel, vol. 2, p. 900.

22. Anna Howard Shaw, "Select Your Principle of Life," see below, p. 187.

23. AHS to LEA, October 18, 1917. Only one article appeared there signed by Shaw: "Two New Cabinet Members," April 1919, p. 47. Report by Shaw on her southern tour, April 15, 1918, Shaw papers, box 22, folder 495; enclosure in AHS to Ida Husted Harper, October 3, 1917, Harper papers.

24. News release, quoting Shaw's authorized statement, Harper papers.

25. *History of Woman Suffrage*, vol. 5, p. 758.

26. Library of Congress, United States Government Printing Office, 1918. For a complete picture of accomplishments see Emily Newell Blair's compilation, *Report of the Woman's Committee, U.S. Council of National Defense, An Interpretative Report, 1919/1920.*

27. Report by Shaw on southern tour, April 15, 1918, Shaw papers, box 22, folder 495.

28. Wil A. Linkugel and Kim Giffin, "The Distinguished War Service of Dr. Anna Howard Shaw," *Pennsylvania History Quarterly Journal* (October 1961): 378; Linkugel and Giffin, p. 383.

29. Harper, unpublished biography, ch. 16, Shaw papers, box 19, folder 439; AHS to LEA, March 5, 1919.

30. *History of Woman Suffrage*, vol. 5, p. 758.

31. Ida Husted Harper, *The Passing of Anna Howard Shaw*, Shaw papers, box 19, folder 443; Elizabeth Green to AHS, October 4, 1918.

CHAPTER 6

1. Anna Howard Shaw, with the collaboration of Elizabeth Jordan, *The Story of a Pioneer* (New York: Harper and Bros., 1915), pp. 323-334.

2. *The New York Times*, January 21, 1918. For a complete history of this group see Ruhl J. Bartlett, *The League to Enforce Peace* (Chapel Hill: University of North Carolina Press, 1944).

3. Wilmer A. Linkugel, *The Speeches of Anna Howard Shaw,* unpublished dissertation, University of Wisconsin, 1960, part 2, pp. 907-917.

4. Bartlett, p. 127.

5. Anna Howard Shaw, "What the War Meant to Women," see below, p.

6. *The History of Woman Suffrage,* vol. 5 (Indianapolis: The Hollenbeck Press, 1902), p. 760.

7. Ibid., pp. 760-761.

8. *The Woman Citizen,* July 12, 1919.

CONCLUSION

1. Letter from Carrie Chapman Catt to Anna Howard Shaw (AHS), February 14, 1897.

2. *The History of Woman Suffrage,* vol. 4 (Indianapolis: The Hollenbeck Press, 1902), p. 149; Carrie Chapman Catt and Nettie Rogers Shuler, *Woman Suffrage and Politics* (New York: Charles Scribner's Sons, 1926), p. 268; Letter from Catt to AHS, January 2, 1916; Abigail Scott Duniway, *Path Breaking* (Portland, Oreg.: James, Kerns and Abbot Company, 1914), p. 221.

3. *The Leavenworth Weekly Times,* May 10, 1894; *Nebraska State Journal,* October 3, 1906; *Boston Post,* November 26, 1940; *The Arizona Republican,* October 16, 1912. *The North American,* July 3, 1919; *The Burlington Independent,* May 25, 1894.

4. Lecture advertisement, Shaw papers; *The History of Woman Suffrage,* vol. 4, p. 760; Ibid., p. 760.

5. *The Rhetoric of Aristotle,* Lane Cooper, trans. (New York: D. Appleton-Century Co., 1932), p. 163; Wilmer Albert Linkugel, *The Speeches of Anna Howard Shaw,* unpublished dissertation, University of Wisconsin, 1960, vol. 2, p. 789.

6. Linkugel, vol 2, pp. 302-304. Ibid., p. 208. Ibid., p. 209.

7. Ibid., p. 397.

8. Ibid., p. 304; Ibid., p. 228.

9. Ibid., pp. 249-251.

10. Ibid., p. 167.

11. Ibid., pp. 390-391; Ibid., pp. 393-394.

12. Ibid., p. 147; Ibid., p. 103.

13. Ibid., pp. 228-229.

14. Ibid., p. 170; Ibid., p. 250.

15. Ibid., p. 207; Ibid., pp. 258-259.

16. Ibid., p. 104.

17. Ibid., p. 245; Ibid., p. 245.

18. Ibid., p. 158.

19. Unidentified typed manuscript. Shaw papers.

20. Linkugel, vol. 2, p. 281.

21. Ibid., p. 274.

22. Ibid., p. 282; Eleanor Flexner, *Century of Struggle*, (Cambridge, Mass.: Harvard University Press, 1959), p. 216.

23. Anna Howard Shaw, with the collaboration of Elizabeth Jordan, *The Story of a Pioneer* (New York: Harper and Bros., 1915), p. 667.

24. Ibid., pp. 261-268.

25. Linkugel, vol. 2, p. 267.

26. Herbert Simons, "Requirements, Problems, and Strategies: A Theory of Persuasion for Social Movements," *Quarterly Journal of Speech*, February 1970, pp. 1-11.

27. Typewritten manuscript, Shaw papers;*The New York Times*, November 23, 1915.

28. Shaw, *Pioneer*, p. iii.

Part II

THE HEAVENLY VISION

1. This is a quotation from the American Revised Version of the Bible (1901), Psalms 68:11.

2. This does not appear to be a direct Biblical quotation. It could have foundation in numerous passages. For example, see Romans 1:22-23. These quotations seem to be expressions of general biblical philosophy rather than direct quotations.

3. The account of Saul's conversion is found in Acts 26:1-19. See also Acts 9:1-9 and Acts 22:6-21.

4. Acts 26:16-18 reads: "But rise, and stand upon thy feet; for I have appeared unto thee for this purpose, to make thee a minister and a witness both of these things which thou hast seen, and of those things in which I will appear unto thee: Delivering thee from the people, and from the Gentiles, unto whom now I send thee, To open their eyes, and to turn them from darkness to light, and from the power of Satan unto God, that they may receive forgiveness of sins, and inheritance among them which are sanctified by faith that is in me."

5. See Genesis 28:10-22 for a full account of Jacob's vision.

6. See Luke 22:39-46, Mark 14:32-42, and Matthew 26:36-46 for the story of Jesus in the Garden of Gethsemane.

7. The story of Jesus' trial before Pilate and the crowd's choice of a robber is found in Matthew 27:17-21, Mark 15:11, Luke 23:18, and John 18:40.

8. The story of the widow's mite is found in Mark 12:42 and in Luke 21:2-4. For the story of Christ's journey to Calvary see Luke 23:26-33.

9. This is a reference to the World's Anti-Slavery Convention held in London in 1840. A group of women delegates was barred from taking their seats. Elizabeth Cady Stanton and Lucretia

Mott were two of the delegates. This experience led them to contemplate the first woman's rights convention.

GOD'S WOMEN

1. This is essentially a paraphrase of biblical passages. See all of Judges 4 and 5, and especially 4:7.

2. Miriam was the sister of Moses. References to Miriam are found in Exodus 15:20-21, Numbers 12:1-15, 20:1, 26:59, Deuteronomy 24:9, 1 Chronicles 6:3, Micah 6:4.

3. See Exodus 2:1-9 for the account of Moses being hidden to prevent his death.

4. See the book of Ruth. Rachel was Jacob's second wife, for whom he worked fourteen years. Genesis 29-31, 33, 35, 46, 48 recounts the story of Rachel. ..... see 1 Samuel 10:2, Jeremiah 31:15, and Matthew 2:18 for references to Rachel. For a delineation of the Biblical Marys Shaw refers to in this speech, see notes 5-8.

5. Mary Magdalene. Luke 16:9; 8:2; This reference is not certain. Mary, the sister of Martha and Lazarus, anointed Christ's feet with a pound of ointment and wiped them with her hair. (See John 12:1-8). It is more likely, however, that Shaw is referring to the unnamed woman (Luke 7:36-50) who washed Christ's feet with tears and wiped them with her hair. Since the name of Mary Magdalene appears at the very beginning of the next chapter, many have associated her name with the unnamed woman. Confusion has especially resulted from the fact that the woman who washed Christ's feet was a harlot who received forgiveness, and Mary Magdalene had at one time been possessed by "seven devils." Most biblical scholars now think that they were two different women.

6. Luke 10:38-42 gives the account of Mary and Martha.

7. See Matthew 28 and John 20. There were two Mary's at the open tomb: Mary Magdalene and Mary, the mother of James and John. The reference no doubt is to Mary Magdalene, who plays the leading part in this episode.

8. See especially Matthew 1 and 2; Luke 1 and 2 for the story of the birth of Jesus.

9. See Numbers 13:6, 30; 14:24, 30, 38; 26:65; 32:12, Deut. 1:36, Joshua 14:13; 15:14, 16, Judges 1:15, 1 Sam. 25:3, and 1 Chr. 2:18, 42, 50; 4:15 for information about Caleb. See Esther 1:9-19; 2:1-17 for an account of Vashti.

10. 1 Timothy 2:15 reads, "She shall be saved in child-bearing." In order to gain perspective for this passage see all of 1 Timothy 2.

THE FATE OF REPUBLICS

1. Joseph Maull Carey (1845-1924), territorial delegate, U.S. Senator, and governor.
2. See Judges 4, 5.

THE FUNDAMENTAL PRINCIPLE OF A REPUBLIC

1. Genesis 2:18 reads, "It is not good that man should be alone; I will make him an help meet for him."
2. Literacy legislation for immigration was vetoed by Cleveland in 1897, by Taft in 1913, by Wilson in 1915 and again in 1917; but in the last year, Congress overrode the presidential veto. After a short, disappointing trial, the literacy test gave way to the quota system. Shaw's reference is probably to the Burnett immigration bill, which Wilson vetoed in 1915.
3. We changed "suffragette" to "suffragist." This is true throughout the speech. Since Shaw objected vociferously to the name "suffragette" it is unlikely that she used that word but that the reporter mistakenly used it, a common happening.
4. Rev. Dr. Lyman Abbott of Brooklyn. The spelling Abbot is changed to Abbott in the text.
5. This seems to be based on Matthew 23:8-10, which reads: "But be not ye called Rabbi; for one is your Master, even Christ; and all ye are brethren. And call no man your father upon the earth: for one is your Father, which is in heaven. Neither be ye called masters: for one is your Master, even Christ."
6. This thought stems from Christ's injunction to Peter to put up his sword when he cut off the ear of a servant of the high priest at the time of Judas's betrayal of Christ. See Matthew 26:52.
7. See *Congresso Internazionale Femminile Roma*, May 16-23, 1914, (Torre Pellice, Coisson, 1915).
8. Thomas Nelson Page, appointed ambassador to Italy by President Wilson in 1913.

THE OTHER HALF OF HUMANITY

1. This seems to be based on Matthew 23:8-10, which reads: "But be not ye called Rabbi; for one is your Master, even Christ; and all ye are brethren. And call no man your father upon the earth: for one is your Father, which is in heaven. Neither be ye called masters: for one is your Master, even Christ."
2. This harks back to the early days of the Church in the New Testament. It was a feast or supper which preceded the communion itself and had varying usages in the history of the Christian Church. It has probably nothing to do with a meal in the 20th century but was a very high state of community in which people shared their deepest experiences.

3. See Esther I:9-19; 2:1, 4, 17 referring to Vashti. Numbers 13:6, 30, 38; 14:24, 30; 26:65; 34:19, Deuteronomy 1:36, Joshua 14:13; 15:14, 16, Judges 1:15, I Samuel 25:3, and 1 Chronicles 2:18, 42, 50; 4:15 refer to Caleb.

4. Presumably Queen Elizabeth I (1533-1603); ascended throne in 1558.

5. Emperor William of Germany, June 15, 1888.

6. Genesis 2:18 tells the story of how it came to be that God created woman.

7. Literacy legislation for immigration was vetoed by Cleveland in 1897, by Taft in 1913, by Wilson in 1915 and again in 1917, but in the last year, Congress overrode the presidential veto. After a short, disappointing trial, the literacy test gave way to the quota system. Shaw's reference is probably to the Burnett immigration bill, which Wilson vetoed in 1915.

8. See *Congresso Internazionale Femminile Roma*, May 16-23, 1914, (Torre Pellice, Coisson, 1915).

SELECT YOUR PRINCIPLE OF LIFE

1. Matthew 26:36-46 and Mark 14:32-42 describe the evening Jesus prayed in the Garden of Gethsemane.

2. Big Rapids, Michigan, High School no longer has records dating as far back as the 1870s. Other sources indicate that Shaw probably had closer to two years of high school.

3. Stephen Samuel Wise (1874-1949), rabbi, educator, author.

4. Newton Diehl Baker, secretary of war, 1916-1921.

WHAT THE WAR MEANT TO WOMEN

1. Newton Diehl Baker, secretary of war, 1916-1921.

2. James Alexander Reed (1861-1944), Democratic U.S. Senator from Missouri, 1911-1929.

3. Abbott Lawrence Lowell, President of Harvard University, 1909-1933.

4. This quotation is based on Exodus 20:5; 34:7; Numbers 14:18; and Deuteronomy 5:9.

Bibliography

CHRONOLOGY OF SPEECHES

Because Shaw usually spoke extemporaneously, few complete texts of her speeches remain. Transcriptions of partial speeches can be found in newspapers wherever Shaw spoke nationally; however, we are including only complete, or nearly complete, texts in our chronology. The Shaw papers, the source of a number of texts, are housed at the Schlesinger Library, Racliffe College, Cambridge, Mass., as part of the Dillon collection, A-68. Throughout the chronology we will simply refer to the Shaw papers rather than give a complete citation of location each time. All surviving texts of Shaw's speeches have been collected in Wilmer Albert Linkugel, *The Speeches of Anna Howard Shaw: Collected and Edited with Introduction and Notes*, unpublished dissertation, University of Wisconsin, 1960. (This dissertation is also found at the Schlesinger Library, Radcliffe College, Cambridge, Mass.)

Sermons

Sermon no. 1. Ashton, Michigan, 1871. Shaw papers, box 22, folder 497.

"The Heavenly Vision." Washington, D.C., March 25, 1888; *Women's Tribune*, March 27, 1888, also in *Report of the International Council of Women*. Washington, D. C.: Rufus H. Darby, Printer, 1888, pp. 24-29.

"Lift Your Standards High." Chicago, Illinois, May 21, 1893. In *The World's Congress of Representative Women*, edited by May Wright Sewall. Chicago and New York: Rand, McNally, 1894, pp. 857-869.

"Let No Man Take Thy Crown." Washington, D.C., February 1894. In *The History of Woman Suffrage.* vol. 4. Indianapolis: The Hollenbeck Press, 1902, pp. 229-231. Partial text.

"Strength of Character." Washington, D.C., February 11, 1900. *Washington Post*, February 12, 1900. Partial text.

"The Women Who Publish the Tidings Are a Great Host." 1917 or later. Shaw papers, box 22, folder 492.

Lectures

"God's Women." Washington, D.C., Feb. 1891. *National Council of Women of the United States 1891.* Edited by Rachel Foster Avery. Philadelphia: J.B. Lippincott, 1891, pp. 242-249.

"The Fate of Republics." Chicago, Illinois, 1893. *The Congress of Women, World's Colombian Exposition.* Edited by Mary Kavannaugh Oldham Eagle, chairman of the Committee on Congresses, Kansas City, Mo.: E. H. Gregg & Co., 1894, pp. 152-156. Also Shaw papers, box 22, folder 499.

"The New Man." 1898 (given throughout the decade). Shaw papers, box 22, folder 491. Partial text.

"The White Man's Burden." October 1899. Shaw papers, box 22, folder 502. Partial text.

"The Cowardice of the Mob." New York City, May 5, 1919. Shaw papers, box 23, folder 563.

Temperance Lectures

"Influence Versus Power." 1886-1892. Shaw papers, box 22, folder 490. Excerpts from an address from a Women's Christian Temperance Union leaflet.

"The Temperance Problem." London, England, June 30, 1899. *Women in Social Life, The International Congress of Women, '99*, London: T. Fisher Unwin, 1900, pp. 160-163.

Campaign Speeches

"Woman's Right to Suffrage." Chautauqua, N.Y., August 8, 1892. *Chautauqua Assembly Herald*, August 9, 1892.

"The Law of Justice." Syracuse, N.Y., November 14, 1892. *Syracuse Standard*, November 15, 1892. Partial text.

"Chivalry." San Jose, Calif., October 15, 1895. *San Jose Daily Mercury*, October 16, 1895.

"The Bulwarks of the Commonwealth." New York State, 1908-1910. Shaw papers, box 22, folder 485.

"After Twenty Years." Topeka, Kan., October 26, 1912. *The Topeka Daily Capital*, October 27, 1912. Partial text.

"Enlightened Kansas." Leavenworth, Kan., October 30, 1912. *The Leavenworth Times*, October 12, 1912. Partial text.

"The Great Defect in our Government." Cornell University, Ithaca, N.Y., 1912 or 1913. Shaw papers, box 22, folder 522.

"Working Women and a Living Wage." October or November 1913. Shaw papers, box 22, folder 524.

"Divine Harmony Through Equal Suffrage." Tennessee, 1914. Shaw papers, box 23, folder 521.

"The Declaration of Independence." N.Y. Harbor, Statue of Liberty, 1914. Shaw papers, box 23, folder 532.

"The Other Half of Humanity." Birmingham, Ala., April 16, 1915. Shaw papers, box 23, folder 540.

"Humanity: The Real Basis of Suffrage." Malone, N.Y., June 19, 1915. *Malone Evening Telegram*, June 21, 1915. Partial text.

"The Fundamental Principle of a Republic." Ogdenburg, N.Y., June 21, 1915. *The Ogdenburg Advance* and *St. Lawrence Weekly Democrat*, July 1, 1915.

"A Republican Form of Government." New York State, 1917. Shaw papers, box 23, folder 545.

"Women Have Earned Freedom." Fort Worth, Tex., April 9, 1919. *Fort Worth Record*, April 10, 1919. Partial text.

Convention Addresses

"The Reason Women Seek the Ballot." Presented to Kentucky Equal Rights Association, Louisville, December 8, 1891. *The Courier-Journal*, Louisville, December 9, 1891.

"Open Your Doors." Presented to National Council of Women of the United States, 1891. *National Council of the Women of the United States, 1891.* Edited by Rachel Foster Avery. Philadelphia: J.B. Lippincott. Philadelphia, PA, 1891, pp. 20-21.

"God's Women." Presented to National Council of Women of the United States, February 1891. *National Council of Women of the United States, 1891.* Edited by Rachel Foster Avery. Philadelphia: J.B. Lippincott, 1891, pp. 242-249.

"What is Marriage?" Presented in Chicago, Ill., May 1983. *The World's Congress of Representative Women,* Edited by May Wright Sewall. Chicago and New York: Rand, McNally, 1894, pp. 599-602.

"The Fate of Republics." Presented in Chicago, Ill., 1893. *The Congress of Women, World's Columbian Exposition.* Edited by Mary Kavannaugh Oldham Eagle. Kansas City, Mo.: E.H. Greggs, 1894, pp. 152-156.

"Susan Anthony's Right-Hand Man." Vice-Presidential Report, Washington, D.C., February 1900. *The History of Woman Suffrage.* Vol. 4. Indianapolis: The Hollenbeck Press, 1902, pp. 351-352.

"A Word of Welcome." Presented to First International Woman Suffrage Conference, Washington, D.C. *First International Woman Suffrage Conference,* Boston, Mass.: John Youngjohn, 1902.

"Women in the Ministry." Presented in Berlin, Germany, 1904. See Shaw papers, box 22, folder 498, for original 1879 manuscript. For an extensive summary of "die Frau als Predigerin," delivered in 1904, see *Der Internationale Frauen=Kongress in Berlin 1904,* Verlag von Carl Kabel, Berlin S.W., Wilhelmstrasse 33, pp. 276-277.

"Humanity's Most Potent Weapon." Presidential acceptance speech. Washington, D.C., February 11, 1904. Shaw papers, box 22, folder 503. Partial text in stenographic form.

"Heroic Service in the Cause of Truth.," First annual presidential address. Portland, Oreg., June 29, 1905. Shaw papers, box 22, folder 504. Also, *The Woman's Journal,* July 15, 22, and 29, 1905.

"Others Will Follow." Second annual presidential address, Baltimore, Md., February 7, 1906. Shaw papers, box 22, folder 506. Also, *The Woman's Journal*, February 17 and 24, 1906.

"The Greatest Victory." Third annual presidential address, Chicago, Illinois, February 14, 1907. *The History of Woman's Suffrage*. Vol. 5, Indianapolis: The Hollenbeck Press, 1902, pp. 200-201. Partial text.

"The Rewards of Truth and Justice." Fourth annual presidential address, Buffalo, N.Y., October 15, 1908. Also *The Woman's Journal*, November 21, 1908. Partial text.

"Suffrage and Rights of Citizenship." Presented in Toronto, Canada, June 21, 1909. *International Council of Women, Report of the Fourth Quinquennial Meeting.* Edited by Countess of Aberdeen London: Constable and Co., 1910.

"For the Common Good." Presented at New York convention, (probably at Troy), 1909. Shaw papers, box 22, folder 511.

"Freedom Is Coming." Sixth annual presidential address. Washington, D.C., April 14, 1910. Shaw papers, box 22, folder 514.

"The Rapid Progress of Suffrage." Seventh annual presidential address. Louisville, Ky., July 20, 1911. *The History of Woman Suffrage*. Vol. 5. Indianapolis: The Hollenbeck Press, 1902, p. 317. Partial text.

"Is Democracy a Failure?" Presented at New York convention, March 2, 1911. Shaw papers, box 22, folder 516.

"An Insuperable Barrier to Self-Government." Eighth annual presidential address. Philadelphia, Penn., November 1912. *The History of Woman Suffrage*. Vol. 5. Indianapolis: The Hiollenbeck Press, 1902, p. 338. Partial text.

"The Emotional Sex." Ninth annual presidential address. Washington, D.C., November 30, 1913. *The History of Woman Suffrage*. Vol. 5. Indianapolis: The Hollenbeck Press, 1902, p. 370. Partial text.

"Woman Suffrage Triumphant in the Eternal City." Presented to International Council of Women. Rome, Italy, May 13, 1914. Shaw papers, box 23, folder 536.

"Equal Justice-Not Chivalry." Response to official welcomes from the city of Nashville, Tenn., November 12, 1914. *Handbook of the National American Woman Suffrage Association* and

Proceedings of the 46th Annual Convention held at Nashville, Tennessee, November 12-17, 1914.

"It's Coming." Tenth annual presidential address. Nashville, Ten., 1914. *The Woman's Journal*, November 21, 1914. Partial text.

"Woman Suffrage and the National Constitution." Address given during the National American Woman Suffrage Association Convention at Nashville, Tenn., November 12-17, 1914. Shaw papers, box 23, folder 530. See also box 23, folder 531.

"Farewell." Farewell presidential address, Washington, D.C., December 14-19, 1915. Shaw papers, box 23, folder 541.

"What Is Americanism?" Presented in Atlantic City, N. J., September 1916. *The History of Woman Suffrage*. Vol. 5. Indianapkolis: The Hollenbeck Press, 1902, pp. 511-512. Partial text.

"Feminism." 1918. Shaw papers, box 23, folder 553.

Legislative Addresses

"The True Voice of God." *Report of the Hearing before Committee of Judiciary, House of Representatives*, January 20, 1892. Complete Text.

"The Injustice of Woman's Subjection." *Report of the Hearing before Select Committee on Woman Suffrage, U.S. Senate*, February 18, 1902.

"Justice for Women." *Report of the Hearing before Committee of Judiciary, House of Representatives*, February 13, 1900.

"The Need for an Investigating Committee." *Report of the Hearing before Select Committee on Woman Suffrage, U.S. Senate*, February 18, 1902.

"Government Inheres in the People." *Report of the Hearing before Select Committee on Woman Suffrage, U.S. Senate*, March 1908.

"The Fulfillment of American Ideals." *Report of the Hearing before Committee on Woman Suffrage, U.S. Senate*, April 19, 1910.

"Give Us a Favorable Report." *Report of the Hearing before Joint Committee of the Committee on the Judiciary and the Committee on Woman Suffrage, U.S. Senate,* March 13, 1912.

"The Test of Experience." Hearing before a Pennsylvania commission, Philadelphia, March 22, 1912. Shaw papers, box 22, folder 520.

"The Nature of Democracy." *Report of the Hearing before Committee on Woman Suffrage, U.S. Senate,* April 26, 1913.

"The Need for a Special House Committee." *Report of the Hearing before the Committee on Rules Establishing a Committee on Woman Suffrage, House of Representatives,* December 3, 1913.

"We Demand Equal Voting Qualifications." Hearing before New Jersey Legislature, January 25, 1915. Shaw papers, box 23, folder 539.

"A National Issue." *Report of the Hearing before Committee on the Judiciary, House of Representatives,* December 16, 1915.

"The Forty-Fifth Year." *Report of the Committee on the Judiciary, House of Representatives,* December 16, 1915.

"Suffrage for Hawaiian Women." *Report of the Committee on Woman Suffrage, House of Representatives,* April 29, 1918.

"Democracy-The Fundamental Cause." Hearing before Committee on Woman Suffrage, House of Representatives, January 1918. *The History of Woman Suffrage.* Vol. 5. Indianapolis: The Hollenbeck Press, 1902, pp. 578-580. Partial text.

World War I and League of Nation Speeches

"Select Your Principle of Life." Temple University, Philadelphia, PA, 1917. Shaw papers, box 23, folder 546.

"Women in Industries." Speech at conference regarding work of the Women's Committee of the Council of National Defense, 1917. Shaw papers, box 23, folder 554. Partial text.

"Women's War Service." Delivered at the Women's Section, Maryland Council of Defense. Baltimore, Md., January 4, 1918. Shaw papers, box 23, folder 555.

"The Degradation of Childhood and Womanhood." Presented at Win the War for Permanent Peace Convention, Philadelphia, May 16, 1918. Shaw papers, box 23, folder 557.

"What the War Meant to Women." Speech in support of the League of Nations, 1919. Shaw papers, box 23, folder 560. Pamphlet available in many libraries.

Eulogies

"Two Friends of Reform." Washington, D.C., January 1893. In *The History of Woman Suffrage.* Vol. 4. Indianapolis: The Hollenbeck Press, 1902, pp. 205-207.

"An Ideal Life of Woman." Berkshire, Mass., July 29, 1897. In Ida Husted Harper, *The Life and Work of Susan B. Anthony.* Indianapolis and Kansas City: Bowen-Merfrill, 1898, pp. 945-946. Partial text.

"We Are Coming." Washington, D.C., February 15, 1900. In *The Woman's Tribune*, February 24, 1900. Shaw papers, box 22, folder 508. Partial text.

"Greater than the Discoverer of a Continent." Copenhagen, Denmark, June 1906. Shaw papers, box 22, folder 509.

"Indomitable Courage." Washington, D.C., April 15, 1910. Shaw papers, box 22, folder 496.

"All Absorbing Love." Rochester, N.Y., March 15, 1906. Shaw papers, box 22, folder 508. Also in Ida Husted Harper, *The Life and Work of Susan B. Anthony*, pp. 1440-1443.

SOURCES

Primary Sources

Books
The only book published by Anna Howard Shaw was *The Story of a Pioneer*, New York: Harper and Bros., 1915. The book was based on transcriptions of oral interviews done by Elizabeth Jordan, who also edited the transcripts to remove embarrassing passages and arranged the material chronologically.

Articles

Articles written for *Ladies Home Journal*, 1917-1918. Shaw papers, box 23, folder 552. "The Woman's Committee of the United States Council of National Defense."

"Equal Suffrage--A Problem of Political Justice." *Annals of the American Academy of Political Science* 56(November 1914): 94-96.

"If I Were President." *McCall's*, July 1912. Shaw papers, box 22, folder 519.

"Rights of Women. *American Journal of Politics* 1:309.

"Why I Went into Suffrage." *Harper's Bazaar*, September 1912, vol. 46, p. 440.

"Women and the Law." *National Sunday Magazine*, April 12, 1914.

"Miss Anthony's Birthday." *National Suffrage News*, February 1917, pp. 6-7.

"Women as Office Holders." *Trend*, May 1914. Shaw papers, box 23, folder 534.

Ladies Home Journal, August 1917, p. 3; September 1917, p. 3; November 1917, p. 3; December 1917, p;. 2; "Thank You," Jan. 1918, p. 3; February 1918, p. 28; March 1918, p. 30; April 1918, p. 28; May, 1918, p. 4; June 1918, p. 3.

Letters

Shaw's extensive correspondence has never been collected and edited. The following archives containing substantial numbers of letters from and to Shaw.

Laura Clay papers. Margaret I. King, Library at the University of Kentucky. This collection of about 450 letters from Shaw as president of NAWSA to Laura Clay, who was on the board are very useful in tracing the tensions and problems of the NAWSA during Shaw's tenure as president. Almost all of these letters are official correspondence.

Sarah Brown Ingersoll Cooper papers. Albert R. Mann Library at Cornell Univeristy. This collection contains sixty-three Shaw letters dating from 1895 to 1896.

The Houghton Library of Harvard University has several letters from Shaw to Oswald Villard about the formation of a men's suffrage league.

Library of Congress. The Susan B. Anthony papers, the Ida
     Husted Harper papers, and the Olivia B. Hall papers all
     contain a few letters from Shaw, mostly about personal
     matters or arrangements for meetings.

The Leland Huntington Library, San Marino, California, contains
     eleven letters from Shaw to six different women between
     1890 and 1912. The letters are to Frances Elizabeth
     Willard, Mary E. Holmes, Jessie Anthony, Ida Husted
     Harper, and Alice Locke Park.

Johnston papers. Kansas Historical Society Library in Topeka,
     Kansas. This collection contains about fifty letters written
     by Shaw as president of NAWSA to Mrs. W. B. Johnston, who
     was president of the Kansas Woman Suffrage Association.

Catharine Waugh McCulloch papers. Dillon Collection,
     Schlesinger Library, Radcliffe College.

Michigan Historical Collections at the University of Michigan,
     Ann Arbor, has a copy of Ida Husted Harper's unpublished
     biography of Anna Howard Shaw.

National Headquarters, League of Women Voters in Washington,
     D.C.,has a few letters from Shaw to Helen Gardener.

Shaw papers, box 18, folders 420-428a, which are part of the
     Dillon Collection at the Schlesinger Library, Radcliffe
     College, Cambridge, Mass., contain copies of letters Shaw
     wrote to Lucy Anthony, her secretary, 1888-1919. About six
     thousand letters were originally found by Ida Husted Harper
     when she attempted to write Shaw's biography; however,
     less than a thousand remain, and many of these have been
     excerpted and reproduced in typewritten form.
     Unfortunately, the bulk of the correspondence was
     destroyed. These letters might have constituted an
     extraordinarily detailed diary, because Shaw wrote Lucy
     Anthony almost daily when she was on a speaking tour.

Shaw papers, box 20, folders 456-476, and box 22, folders 477-
     480, contain correspondence with and regarding: Jane
     Addams, 1912; Susan B. Anthony, 1897; Rachel Foster
     Avery, 1892-1898; Clara Barton, 1886; Carrie Chapman Catt,
     1892-1919; Mrs. Crosset, 1908-1914; Julia Ward Howe,
     1882, 1888; Clara Osburn, 1903-1906; Eliza W. Osborne,
     1903-1906; Elizabeth Cady Stanton, n.d.; Lucy Stone, 1884,
     1887; M. Carey Thomas, 1915-1919; Mrs. Coonley Ward,
     1904-1006; Frances E. Willard, 1888-1904, and others of

Women's Christian Temperance Union interest; Letters and petition received on Shaw's announcement not to stand for reelection as president of NAWSA, November and December 1915; re Woman Suffrage, 1916-1919; Council of National Defense, 1917; Letters received on her 70th birthday, 1917; Letters from Caroline Reilly to "Ladee" in Florida, February 2 - March 16, 1918; also November 22, 1915; Council of National Defense, 1918-1919; Women's Committee of Council of National Defense to the Queens and their replies, 1918-1919; League to Enforce Peace, 1919; and Greensboro, N.C., Women's College, 1917, 1921.

Sophia Smith Collection. Smith College Library, contains varied correspondence and other relevant documents..

Wisconsin Historical Society Library is a good source for newspapers reporting on suffrage campaigns.

Newspaper Clippings
Numerous newspaper clippings about Shaw's work, some unfortunately not identified, are found in the Shaw papers, box 20, folders 450-455, and the Susan B. Anthony papers at the Library of Congress. See also box 21, vols. 56-57 of the *Shaw papers* for scrapbook of newspaper clippings re Shaw, 1913-1915.

Diaries and Appointment Books
Box 20A of the Shaw papers contains diaries from 1898 to 1919; however, these "diaries" are little more than appointment listings. The only real diary Shaw kept, as noted earlier, were her letters to Lucy Anthony. Box 21, vols. 34-55, contain Shaw's appointment books, 1889-1911, lacking 1908.

Secondary Sources

Books and Monographs
There are no published critical monographs devoted exclusively to Anna Howard Shaw. The only biography of her remains unpublished: Ida Husted Harper, *Biography of Anna Howard Shaw*. The typescript of this, lacking the final chapter, is available at the Michigan Historical Collection at the University of Michigan, Ann Arbor. A carbon copy of the complete work is found in the Shaw papers, box 19.

Dexter, Elizabeth Anthony. *Women in Organized Religion, 1860-1900* Shaw papers.

Jordan, Elizabeth. *The Speaker.* Shaw papers.

Woman's Committee of the Council of National Defense.

War Work for Women. Library of Congress, Washington, D.C., 1918.

Theses and Dissertations
Eggleston, Jean Marie. *A Study of the Development of Dr. Anna Howard Shaw--Reformer and Orator.* Master's thesis, Northwestern University, 1934.

Giel, Dorothy. *Anna Howard Shaw: A Leadership Study.* Masters thesis, Central Michigan University, Mount Pleasant, 1987.

Linkugel, Wilmer Albert. *The Speeches of Anna Howard Shaw, Collected and Edited with Introduction and Notes.* Unpublished dissertation, University of Wisconsin, 1960.

Critical Essays
Jordan, Elizabeth. "Anna Howard Shaw: An Intimate Study." *Chicago Tribune*, July 27, 1919.

Linkugel, Wil A. and Kim Giffin. "The Distinguished War Service of Dr. Anna Howard Shaw." *Pennsylvania History* 28:4 (October 1961): 372-385.

Linkugel Wil A. "The Speech Style of Anna Howard Shaw." *Central States Speech Journal* 13:3 (Spring 1961): 171-179.

Linkugel, Wil A. "The Woman Suffrage Argument of Anna Howard Shaw." *Quarterly Journal of Speech* 49:2 (April 1963): 165-174.

McGovern, James R. "Anna Howard Shaw: New Approaches to Feminism." *Journal of Social History* (Winter 1969): 135-153.

Portraits
"Brave Woman and Her Work." *Saint Nicholas.* September 1919, vol. 467, p. 1036.

Bulletin of the Pan American Union. January 1921, vol. 52, p. 43.
The Chautauquan. 59 (June 1910): 79.

Current History Magazine, New York Times, October 1920, vol. 13, p. 27a.

Good Housekeeping, December 1913, vol. 57, p. 745.

Good Housekeeping, December 1915, vol. 61, p. 769.

Harper's Bazaar, March 1905, vol. 39, p. 255.

Independent, May 11, 1914, vol. 78, p. 78.

"Inveterate Optimist of the Woman Suffrage Movement." *Current Opinion*, 59: (December 1915), p. 769.

Outlook. 102 (December 28 1912): 932.

"President and the Suffragists." *Literary Digest*. December 20, 1913, vol. 47, pp. 1209-11.

"Three Pioneer Women." *Outlook*. 112: (February 9, 1916), p. 347.

The Woman Citizen, 4:6, (July 12, 1919), pp. 137-139.

"Woman Pioneer of the West." *World Outlook*. 112: (April 1916), p. 10.

"The Women Who Get Together." *Good Housekeeping*. December 1913, vol. 57, p. 745.

World Today. 13 (July 1907): 696; 15 (October 1908): 1007.

Appreciations
Anna Howard Shaw: A Memorial. National American Woman Suffrage Association, 1919.

In Memory of Anna Howard Shaw. National Women Suffrage Publishing Company, New York, n.d.

Methodist Recorder. January 1, 1927, pp. 4-9. Shaw papers, box 23, folder 566.

Michigan Club Bulletin. April 1927, pp. 41-43. Shaw papers, box 23, folder 566.

Nation. July 12, 1919, vol. 109, p. 33.

Outlook. July 16, 1919, vol. 122, p. 420.

Public. July 12, 1919, vol. 22, p. 734.

The Woman Citizen. July 12, 1919, vol. 4, no. 6, pp. 137-139.

Articles on Shaw by Her Contemporaries

"Dr. Shaw's Revolt." *Literary Digest*. January 10, 1914, vol. 48, pp. 50-51.

"At the Mercy of Puritans." *Literary Digest*. March 13, 1915, vol. 50, pp. 566.

"Kansas Courtin'." *Literary Digest*. November 6, 1915, pp. 1048-1049.

"Two New Cabinet Members." *Ladies Home Journal*. April 1919, vol. 36, p. 47.

Other Cited Works: Books

Algeo, Sara MacCormack. *The Story of a Sub-Pioneer*. Providence, R.I.: Snow and Farnham Company, 1925.

Anthony, Katharine. *Susan B. Anthony: Her Personal History and Her Era*. Garden City, N.Y.: Doubleday, 1954.

Bennett, Helen C. *American Women in Civic Work*. 1915.

Blair, Emily N. Report of *The Woman's Committee, U. S. Council of National Defense, An Interpretative Report, 1919/1920*.

Buechler, Steven M. *The Transformation of the Woman Suffrage Movement: The Case of Illinois, 1850-1920*. Brunswick, N.J.: Rutgers University Press, 1986.

Catt, Carrie Chapman and Nettie Rogers Shuler. *Woman Suffrage and Politics*. New York: Charles Scribner's Sons, New York, 1923.

Flexner, Eleanor. *Century of Struggle*. Cambridge, Mass.: Harvard University Press, 1959.

Kraditor, Aileen S. *The Ideas of the Woman Suffrage Movement, 1890-1920*. New York and London: Columbia University Press, 1965.

Lutz, Alma. *Susan B. Anthony: Rebel, Crusader, Humanitarian*. Boston: Beacon Hill Press, 1959.

Morgan, David. *Suffragists and Democrats: The Politics of Woman Suffrage in America*. Lansing: Michigan State University Press, 1972.

O'Neill, William L. *Everyone Was Brave: The Rise and Fall of Feminism in America.* Chicago: Quadrangle Books, 1969.

Scott, Anne F. and Andrew M. Scott. *One Half the People: The Fight for Woman Suffrage.* The American Alternatives Series. Edited by Harold M. Hyman. Philadelphia: J. B. Lippincott, 1975.

Van Morris, Jacqueline. *Carrie Chapman Catt: A Public Life.* Feminist Press of the City University of New York, New York, 1987.

Index

Adams, Samuel, 99
Address, "Farewell," 71-72,
   107
Albion College, 6
Allusions, 19, 20
Amendment, Shafroth-
   Palmer, 64
American Woman Suffrage
   Association, 8, 39, 52
Analogy, 20, 55
Anecdotes, 102, 104, 105
Anna, 25
Anthony Amendment, 10, 67
Anthony, Lucy, 14, 37, 51,
   52, 78, 96
Anthony, Susan B., 3, 4, 8, 9,
   19, 21, 39, 49, 51-53, 60-
   62, 97, 103
Anthony and Shaw, 52
Anti-Suffrage Association, 67
Appeals, value, 106
Appearance, 11, 109
Argument, 99-102; from
   circumstances, 99; from
   consequences, 99, 102;
   from definition, 99, 101,
   102; from expediency,
   101; "If then," 103-104;
   natural rights, 59
Aristocracy of sex, 152
Ashton, 6
Audience response, 38-39
Autobiography, 10, 78-81,
   111

Baker, Secretary of War, 89
Bain, George W., 98
Barrett, Mrs., 7
Big Rapids, Michigan, 5, 6
Blackwell, Antionette Brown,
   24
Blatch, Harriet Stanton, 63,
   64
Board, National, 9
Boston, 6
Boston University Medical
   School, 8
Brent, Margaret, 70
Brown, Olympia, 24
Burns, Lucy, 64
Burleigh, Celia, 24

Cape Cod, 7
Catt, Carrie Chapman, 3, 9,
   61-63, 65, 78, 80, 81, 97,
   98, 110
Chapin, Augusta, 24
Colby, Clara Bewick, 56
Commonplaces, 54
Conclusions, 104
Congressional Committee, 64
Council of National Defense,
   10
Crane, Caroline Bartlett, 80

Dansforth, Clarissa H., 23
Death, 11, 95-96; of Susan B.
   Anthony,, 53
Debate, 6, 52
Deborah, 25, 45, 56
Delivery, 13

Democracy, 99-100
Dillon, Mary Earhart, 3
Distinguished Service Medal, 10, 90
"Doldrums," 62
Dress, 12
Duniway, Abigail Scott, 98

East Dennis, 7
Education, 5
Effectiveness, 107-111
Entrance exams, 6
Ethos, 47, 56
Evidence, 56
Examples, 105
Executive Board, 63
Expediency argument, 59
Extemporaneous delivery, 13, 14, 17, 19

Farewell Address, 71-72, 109
"Fate of Republics," 10, 55
Figures of speech, 19
Flexner, Eleanor, 108
Food, 37-38
Foot, Lucy, 5
Franklin, Benjamin, 99
"Fundamental Principles of a Republic," 58

Gifford, W.D., 8
Goddard, Mary Catharine, 70
"God's Women," 44
Grand Rapids, Michigan, 4
Grammatical slips, 17
Graves, Mary, 24
Greensboro, North Carolina, 9
Grim, Harriet, 15

Hair, 12
Harper, Ida Husted, 12, 97
Harrison, Mary St. Leger Kinglsey, 73
Hathaway Agency, 36
Health, 7, 37
"Heavenly Vision," 29-34
Hoover, Herbert, 87

"Home protection" theme, 40, 50
Humor, 17, 26, 46, 57, 104-105, 109
Hutchinson, Anne, 23

Illustrations, 102
Images, 19
Inconsistencies, 57
Ingalls, Senator John J., 52
International Council of Women, 40, 72, 101
International Suffrage Alliance, 10, 92
Introductions, 102
Jordan, Elizabeth, 10, 78, 79

Kansas, 8

Ladies Home Journal, 87
Lapel pin, 16
Lawrence, Massachusetts, 4
Leadership styles, 7
League to Enforce Peace, 10, 92, 93
Lectures, 4, 6; price of, 53; schedule, 36-37
Lee, Anne, 23
Legislative addresses, 67-69
Licensed preacher, 7
Livermore, Mary, 8, 21, 36, 39, 52
Lowell, Abbot Lawrence, 90, 93

Malet, Louis, 73
Manuscript speaking, 70
Marshall, Vice President Thomas R., 96
Mary, 45, 46
Massachusetts Woman Suffrage Association, 35, 98
Mecosta County, 5; Council for the Arts, 96
Medical Training, 8
Medical Woman's National Association, 89

Men's League for Woman
    Suffrage, 76
Methodist Episcopal
    Conference, 7
Methodist Protestant
    Church, 8
Miriam, 25
"Missing Link," 14
Mott, Lucretia, 23

National American Woman
    Suffrage Association, 8,
    10, 36, 54, 62, 63, 78
National Board, 9
National headquarters, 63
National Lecturer, 8
Natural rights argument, 59
Nestor, Agnes, 81
Newcastle-on-Tyne, 4
"New Man" lectures, 41
"New Woman," 42-43, 47,
    107
Notes, 13
Oligarchy of sex, 59
Otis, James, 100
"Oracle of Baltimore," 74
Ordination, 7, 8
Organization of speeches, 54,
    102-104
Osburn, Clara, 44
"Other Half of Humanity," 56

Pacificism, 59-60
Parades, suffrage, 9
Parental reconciliation, 53
Pastor, 7
Patterson, Hannah J., 81
Paul, Alice, 64, 76, 80, 110
Paul, Apostle, 115, 116, 121-
    122
Peace Movement, 92
Peck, Dr., 6, 26
Persona, rhetorical, 15, 46
Pleurisy, 11
Presidency, 9; assessment,
    75; candidate, 61-62;
    oratory, 65-67; problems,
    62-65; rhetoric, 69-75

Quakers, 23
Queen of the Suffrage
    Platform, 97

Rachel, 45
Rebellion against father, 5
Redpath Lecture Bureau, 8,
    11, 36, 98
Refutation, 57, 105-107, 109
Representation, virtual, 100
Rhetorical effectiveness,
    107-111
Rhetorical persona, 15, 46
Ridicule, 106
Roosevelt, Theodore, 72
Ruth, 45

Sacajawea, 70
Safford, Mary, 24
Sarcasm, 95, 105
Schoolteacher, 5
Seneca Falls, 71
Sermons, 27-34; first, 6, 26-
    27
Sexton, Lydia, 23
Shafroth-Palmer
    Amendment, 65
Shaw, and Anthony, 52
Shaw, Henry, 4
Shaw, James, 4, 8
Shaw, Mary, 5
Shaw, Nicolas, 4
Shaw, Thomas, 3, 4, 53
Simons, Herbert, 110
Slaton Bureau, 36
Society of Friends, 23
"Solitude of Self," 32
Speeches, as Chair of
    Woman's Committee of
    Council of National
    Defense, 84-87; Farewell,
    107; League of Nations,
    93; Suffrage, 54;   Temple
    University, 86
Spunk, 12
Stanton, Elizabeth Cady, 32,
    45, 52, 108
Stenographers, 18

Story of a Pioneer, 78-81,
   111
Strategies, persuasive, 104-
   107
S.S. Anna Howard Shaw, 96
Stone, Lucy, 82
Stoutness, 12
Style, 17
"Suffragists, New," 110
Superintendent of Franchise
   in W.C.T.U., 51

Taft, William Howard, 10, 93,
   98
Temperance, 6, 8, 39-41;
      pay, 40; lectures, 40-41;
      and suffrage, 49-52
Theological school, 6
Thompson, Marianna, 26
Tone, 15
Training as a preacher, 26-
   27

Uncle Tom's Cabin, 4
Unitarian community, 4
Upton, Harriet Taylor, 63

Value, appeals, 106, 110
Vashti, 45
Vice-President-at-Large, 9
Virtual representation, 100
Vision, 116; to David, 114
Vitality, 12
Voice, 15
Vote, restrictions on right to,
   100

Wallace, Ziralda, 39
Willard, Frances, 8, 12, 39,
   50, 52
Wilson, Woodrow, 89, 98
Wit, 17
Woman's Bible, 45, 108
Woman's Committee of the
   Council of National
   Defense, 81-83, 109
Womanhood, 45
Woman, new, 42-43, 47,
   107, 117

Women's Christian
   Temperance Union, 8, 50,
   51
Woodhull, Victoria, 108
Women as homemakers, 74
Women in industry, 72
Women in the ministry, 23-
   24
Women's Political Union, 63-
   64

About the Authors

WIL A. LINKUGEL is Chairman of the Department of Communication Studies at the University of Kansas. He has written *Contemporary American Speeches; Speech: A First Course;* and *Responsible Public Speaking.*

MARTHA SOLOMON is Professor of Speech Communication at the University of Maryland. She is editor of the *Quarterly Journal of Speech,* author of *Emma Goldman: A Critical Biography,* and has written numerous articles.

Great American Orators

Defender of the Union: The Oratory of Daniel Webster
Craig R. Smith

Harry Emerson Fosdick: Persuasive Preacher
Halford R. Ryan

Eugene Talmadge: Rhetoric and Response
Calvin McLeod Logue

The Search of Self-Sovereignty: The Oratory of Elizabeth Cady Stanton
Beth M. Waggenspack

Richard Nixon: Rhetorical Strategist
Hal W. Bochin

Henry Ward Beecher: Peripatetic Preacher
Halford R. Ryan

Edward Everett: Unionist Orator
Ronald F. Reid

Theodore Roosevelt and the Rhetoric of Militant Decency
Robert V. Friedenberg

Partick Henry, The Orator
David A. McCants